D1598791

LIBRARY
OF
ADVENTIST THEOLOGY

The Judgment and Assurance

Series Editors:

George R. Knight
Woodrow W. Whidden II

Other books in the Library of Adventist Theology series:

BOOK 1: *The Cross of Christ* (George R. Knight)
BOOK 2: *Sin and Salvation* (George R. Knight)
BOOK 3: *The Body of Christ* (Reinder Bruinsma)

Other books by Woodrow W. Whidden II include:

E. J. Waggoner
The Trinity

To order, call **1-800-765-6955**.

THE
JUDGMENT
AND ASSURANCE

*The Dynamics
of Personal Salvation*

WOODROW W. WHIDDEN II

REVIEW AND HERALD® PUBLISHING ASSOCIATION
Since 1861 | www.reviewandherald.com

Published by Review and Herald® Publishing Association, Hagerstown, MD 21741-1119

Review and Herald® titles may be purchased in bulk for educational, business, fund-raising, or sales promotional use. For information, e-mail SpecialMarkets@reviewand herald.com.

The Review and Herald® Publishing Association publishes biblically based materials for spiritual, physical, and mental growth and Christian discipleship.

The author assumes full responsibility for the accuracy of all facts and quotations as cited in this book.

This book was
Edited by Gerald Wheeler
Copyedited by Daun Redfield
Designed by Trent Truman
Cover art by © ernestking/istockphoto.com
Typeset: Bembo 11/13

PRINTED IN U.S.A.

16   15   14   13   12   5   4   3   2   1

Library of Congress Cataloging-in-Publication Data
Whidden, Woodrow W. (Woodrow Wilson), 1944-   .
   The judgment and assurance: the dynamics of personal salvation / Woodrow W. Whidden II.
      p. cm.
1. Assurance (Theology) 2. Seventh-Day Adventists—Doctrines. I. Title.
BT785.W45 2011
234—dc22
                                      2010041815

ISBN 978-0-8280-2565-2

Dedicated to

My faithful and loyal wife, Peggy Gibbs Whidden

Contents

A Word to the Reader

Assurance and judgment. The latter topic has seen a great deal of discussion by Seventh-day Adventist authors, while they have almost totally neglected the former. In this important contribution to the Library of Adventist Theology, Woodrow Whidden treats both topics and the complex relationship between them. An understanding of their intertwined connection is absolutely crucial, since some have argued that a future judgment, including an investigative judgment, conflicts with the idea that Christians can have any present assurance of their salvation. And then, of course, there is the Ellen White statement that people should never say that they are saved.

The past three decades have seen these and other topics related to judgment and assurance at the center of much heated Adventist theological discussion. In his usual vigorous style Whidden enables his readers to understand better this controversial but important field. He not only presents the relevant biblical evidence and the historical background undergirding the debate, but also includes a chapter on Ellen White's seemingly conflicting statements on the topic of assurance. A major contribution for Adventist readers is the treatment of assurance in the context of end-time events.

The Judgment and Assurance: The Dynamics of Personal Salvation is the fourth volume in the Library of Adventist Theology. The first three were *The Cross of Christ: God's Work for Us* (G. R. Knight, 2008), *Sin and Salvation: God's Work for and in Us* (G. R. Knight, 2008), and *The Body of Christ: A Biblical Understanding of the Church* (R. Bruinsma, 2009).

After Whidden's contribution the series will make a major shift on two levels. First, while the first four volumes in the Library have treated theological beliefs that Adventists share with other Christians (albeit from an Adventist perspective), volumes 5 through 8 will focus on doctrinal issues that make Adventism distinct as a religious movement, such as the theology of the Sabbath, principles of prophetic interpretation, spiritual gifts, and the sanctuary. Those topics stand at the very heart of Seventh-day Adventism's reason for existing as a separate religious body.

The second change of direction between volumes 4 and 5 will be a transfer of editorship. In the first four volumes and in the general planning of the series, Whidden and I worked closely together as coeditors of the Library of Adventist Theology. But with the publication of volume 4, as previously agreed upon, I am resigning because of an ongoing work overload. Darius Jankiewicz, a professor of theology in the Seventh-day Adventist Theological Seminary at Andrews University, will take my place with Whidden. Under their guidance the series will continue to provide its readers with important treatments of those theological topics that stand at the center of the Seventh-day Adventist belief system.

George R. Knight
Series Editor

Introduction

Christian Assurance: Who Needs It?

Old Testament scholar Roy Gane tells a story of a vacation expedition to Minnesota when he was 13 years old. The family brought along their little dog, Tippy, for the holiday. The pet insisted on being included in all the activities, including paddleboating. During an outing on the lake the boat entered a garden of large lily pads. Believing that green equaled grass and safe terra firma, Tippy decided to go exploring. Of course, to his utter doggy dismay, the lily pads turned out to be neither grass nor solid ground. Only his frantic dog-paddling skills and the frenetic efforts of the Gane family saved the animal.[1]

Many Christians are like Tippy—afflicted with a misinformed grasp of either the seriousness of sin or the expensiveness of God's loving grace, both of which form the very foundations of any genuine experience of the assurance of salvation. In my pastoral and teaching work, I have found at least four basic types of "Tippy" Christians.

The first type is represented by professed believers who lead lives of license in the tradition of the infamous goddess of sex Diana of the Ephesians, and of Balaam, the Old Testament prophet who, in the name of religion, worshipped money and exploited immoral indulgence. Such a "Christian" Diana liked to talk a lot about grace, forgiveness, and the so-called unconditional love of God. She enjoyed the emotive, or feeling, side of religion, and could relate riveting testimonies about her freedom in Christ and its devotional raptures. But illicit love affairs, substance abuse, and gross financial irresponsibility filled her life. Thus she is emblematic of many "cheap grace" Christians.

The members of this presumptuous tribe of professed Christians can have no real assurance until they have had a deep repentance that leads to the "expensive grace" of God. Without a humble response of sobering penitence, the professed saints in the tradition of Diana and Balaam simply will not be able to fully appreciate the costliness of God's grace. Genuine assurance will prove to be very elusive, and they will continue to crucify Christ anew and put Him to open shame. Thus, while none of us deserve the grace of God, its effectiveness can be truly real only for those who un-

11

derstand that He gives assurance not to comfort sinners in their sins but to save them from sin as they steadily grow in grace.

(1) Then there are the Martha types, believers symbolized by the faithful, hardworking sister of Mary and Lazarus, the intimate friends of Jesus. Such individuals also bear a close affinity to the stay-at-home brother of the parable of the prodigal son. They are the obsessive-compulsive conscientious types who pay close attention to diet and dress and who speak much of Christian duty, both practical and moral. Often they spearhead movements for personal reform and social justice. Yet they are all too often without peace and are the ones most inclined to fall into the pit of practical or doctrinal legalism (the opposite of the religious presumption of Diana and Balaam).

I do not want to be seen as belittling the Martha variety of Christians in any way. They are normally utterly sincere and deserve our respect for their practical, ethical zeal. While they seem vulnerable to the lure of legalism, the main thing necessary for their growth in grace and assurance is for them to get a clearer perspective on the radical nature of sin (it is worse than they could ever imagine) and to gain a greater sense of what their proper spiritual priorities should be. As Jesus told the busy, conscientious Martha, "Mary has chosen that good part" (Luke 10:42). And this is probably the greatest need of the Martha types: to learn to spend more time with Jesus. If they could grasp these two key factors, they would find peace and renewing power in their pursuit of faithful moral and practical Christian duty.

(2) The third group consists of believers whose conscientious attention to duty has led them to the point of despair. Normally this despair results from the lack of any clear understanding of the rich blessings that the gospel offers, both the gift of justification by faith alone and the blessings of sanctification. In other words, these sincere believers do not understand the delicate relationship (in either theology or actual experience) that exists between forgiving and transforming grace. And people who do not clearly grasp the gospel are open to discouragement, especially when confronted by their most persistent weaknesses. But this group has the infinitely good news that Jesus can fully deliver the true believer from both the guilt and the power of besetting sins.

This sizable third category of believers also includes a fairly large number of good, loyal church members who have a basically sound grasp of the theological and spiritual issues related to both sin and salvation. But they find themselves constantly struggling with the challenges of life. They faithfully pursue responsibility in their marriages and family privileges (raising kids, looking after needy loved ones, or grieving over the lack of a family) and professional goals, and they attempt to support their loved ones financially and emotionally.

Furthermore, they are loyal and uphold their church family, serving in areas most appropriate to their skills and spiritual gifts. But their major challenge is that they just simply are having a hard time making meaningful spiritual contact with God. In the hustle and bustle of their stressful lives they simply want to be closer to God in order to experience the deeper reality of His presence and leading, and they want more power to overcome the temptations that regularly play on their inherited and cultivated tendencies to selfishness and sin. They are the stalwarts in our families and churches: the good steady Joes (shall we say Joseph, the son of Jacob?) and Beths (Elizabeth, the mother of John the Baptist?) who daily cinch it up and make their world go round.

The final group includes Christian leaders and evangelists, both lay and professional. Such individuals are those who stand out on the front lines in their daily lives and intentional ministries. They certainly have, to one degree or another, many of the same personal challenges of those in the previously mentioned categories two and three, but they are also looking for greater theological clarity on the main issues that this book addresses. As a result, they not only seek this for their own spiritual and theological growth, but also want to have a better grasp of the historical, practical, and biblical factors that will help them to reach out more effectively to those with whom they are sharing their faith in the course of their varied ministries.

Furthermore, this final category especially desires to minister more successfully to those struggling with a lack of assurance or to those who are sincerely espousing false, presumptuous versions of the judgment and the Christian's assurance of salvation. Such individuals are the Andrew Christians who are constantly bringing people to Jesus. They search for better methods, ideas, theology, and just plain wisdom so that they can successfully witness for Jesus and the wonderful blessings that He has in store for all who hunger for a more authentic Christian experience.

The Theological Context of Adventism and Assurance

Three key, closely related factors set the historical and theological context for this book's treatment of the judgment and Christian assurance. The most foundational factor involves Seventh-day Adventism's strong affirmations of what has been called Protestant Arminianism. This larger segment of Protestant Christianity is especially indebted to the thought of both James Arminius (a late-sixteenth- and early-seventeenth-century Dutch Calvinist) and John Wesley (the founder of English Methodism, who ministered from the late 1730s until early 1791).

Scholars refer to this branch of Christianity as Wesleyan/Arminian. As the core of its distinctive theological perspective it has taken seriously the concept characterized as a "grace-induced 'freed will.'" In other words, Wesleyan/Arminian Christians view God as taking the initiative in reaching out to all sinners by imparting to them a grace-created "free will" that can cooperatively and responsively receive the saving benefits of Christ. Such a theological perspective especially stands out when contrasted with the views of those Christians who identify with the Augustinian/Calvinistic tradition (also referred to as the Reformed Tradition—believers such as the Baptists, Presbyterians, conservative Congregationalists, and many in both the German and Dutch Reformed denominations).

Reformed/Calvinistic Christians stress the doctrines of irresistible election or unconditional predestination that John Calvin and his successors in Switzerland, France, Germany, Holland, and Great Britain so forcefully taught from the sixteenth century onward. Furthermore, the disciples of Calvin have placed great emphasis on the doctrine that has been called irresistible perseverance, or as more popularly described, "once saved, always saved" (or "once in grace, always in grace").

They have seen their version of assurance as the logical work of God who, they claim, has irresistibly predestined some to salvation and the rest to damnation. *Thus it seems inevitable to them that if God has predestined such individuals to a salvation that they can't refuse, He must impart to them a grace that they cannot lose!* In other words, they will be kept continually saved, whether they want it or not. And such a rationale has become known as the popular doctrine of eternal security (but normally expressed as "once saved, always saved").

Not surprisingly, Reformed Christians claim great comfort in such a teaching, especially when it unfolds in their loudly proclaimed challenges to Arminians that the Reformed/Calvinistic version of assurance cannot be lost or frittered away. Thus among the key themes that this book addresses are the persistent objections of our "once saved always saved" brothers and sisters in Christ. Must we admit that their perspective imparts to them any real advantages when it comes to genuine Christian assurance? We think not! And in fact, we offer the following preliminary analysis as a theological and practical appetizer for what will follow later in our study of this issue.

We humbly submit that Reformed Christians have a major difficulty in their own individual experiences of the grace of God: like Arminians, they also come up with evidences or signs of their own individual election and perseverance. But that is a delicate consideration that we must put off to a subsequent chapter in our treatment of genuine, biblical assurance.

Yet despite these shared challenges, many Arminians have found the doctrine of assurance, as taught by the Reformed Calvinists, quite alluring. Needless to say, most Christians tempted by such a doctrine tend to ignore the irresistible election (predestination) side of Reformed Calvinism. But they certainly find themselves drawn to a version of irresistible perseverance that we could characterize as an Arminianized view of election and perseverance: while a true believer will not be forced to be saved, onced saved, that salvation cannot be lost.

The second major theological perspective of this book derives from a major implication of the Wesleyan/Arminian teaching of free grace. Simple logic suggests that if any believer has been given a "freed will," then that individual becomes at least partly coresponsible for the moral and spiritual choices that they make as followers of Christ. And this idea has quite naturally led to a more conscious appreciation of the biblical doctrine of the investigative judgment. Let's try to make the rationale of this simple, even straightforward idea as clear as possible.

If God gives people the graced option to choose or reject His offer of salvation, there must be something like an investigative judgment whereby He can reveal the sum total of the spiritual and moral decisions that all humans have made in response to His saving initiatives. And once more, not surprisingly, John Wesley and Seventh-day Adventists have discovered such a scriptural doctrine. Called the doctrine of the pre-Advent investigative judgment, it concludes that the records of the words, attitudes, and actions of all professed believers in Christ will come up for a judicial review.[2]

Unfortunately, the doctrine of the investigative judgment has led many sincere Christians to claim that such a concept has undercut their assurance of salvation. Therefore, especially in the Adventist context of Arminian teaching, we must address at least two questions: (1) Is the doctrine of the pre-Advent investigative judgment biblical? and (2) If it is biblical, how can individual believers have a confident assurance of salvation when their names come up for review?

Finally, one other key theological factor further defines the context for our study. And that factor has to do with another concept related to

15

the practical concepts normally associated with the rationale of "responsible grace." It involves the emphasis placed on the doctrine and experience of sanctification in the larger Wesleyan/Arminian tradition of Protestantism.

Stated another way, if one is truly responding to God's saving grace, that grace must have the power to engender a sanctified life. And in this vital spiritual arena, Adventism has clearly stressed the theme of sanctifying grace and its fruit of obedience to the law of God. Observant, faithful Seventh-day Adventist Christians can readily testify to the many sermons, articles, and books that their church has collectively devoted to the issues of sanctification and perfection. Furthermore, much of this emphasis has had its source in the writings of Ellen White, which are replete with the optimistic theme of transforming grace.

Now, just as many Seventh-day Adventist Christians have testified that the pre-Advent investigative judgment doctrine has compromised their sense of assurance, so have many felt that the strong accent on sanctification and obedience has also contributed to a perceptible sense that unless a believer is perfectly obedient, there can be no genuine assurance of ultimate salvation. Such claims (or challenges) thus raise an urgent question: Are such claims based on sincere but wrongheaded misunderstandings (thus unbiblical), or are they the true, biblically based Adventist versions of the Wesleyan/Arminian concepts of responsible grace, judgment according to works, and sanctification?

It is my sincere conviction that while many experience a lack of genuine Christian assurance because of theological and practical misunderstandings, it is not true that the bona fide, biblically based Seventh-day Adventist teachings on grace, judgment, and sanctification are inherently injurious to any experience of the genuine Christian's assurance of salvation. Therefore, as subsequent chapters unfold, we will seek to make the following case: far from being injurious to Christian assurance, the biblical, historical, theological, and practical teachings inherent in the Adventist doctrines of grace, law, salvation, judgment, and final events are, in fact, filled with valuable resources and perspectives that will inspire a deeply satisfying sense of the assurance of salvation!

An Overview of the Following Sections and Chapters

Five distinctive sections, or sets of chapters, will present a comprehensive treatment of all of the relevant issues appropriate to the believer's personal sense of God's gracious gift of assurance. I will seek to demonstrate

God's faithfulness to His commitment to save all who will freely respond to His generous offer of salvation.

The first section includes two chapters that directly address the question of whether the Bible actually teaches the doctrine of a cosmic, pre-Advent investigative judgment according to faith and works. And when we have clearly established that the Bible does present a pre-Advent judgment that will draw upon a faithful record of the believer's works, we will then proceed to highlight the resources available to believers so that they can stand in that solemn, sobering day.[3]

The second major section (chapters 3 through 6) will then treat those resources of grace. As the four chapters explore the varied facets of the dynamics of personal salvation, they will provide a relatively brief overview of the divine provisions that God has established to enable believers to approach Christ and will show how each contributes to the personal assurance of salvation.[4]

The third section contains just one chapter, entitled "The Spirit Witnesses to Our Spirit and With the Witness of Our Spirit—Can There Be Perceptible Assurance?" Though the section consists of only one chapter, the subject it addresses is pivotal for all Protestant Christians to understand because it reflects on how any believer can actually know that he or she is truly and personally saved. It is one thing to believe that Jesus made provision to save the "world" (John 3:16). But the key question of this chapter is how we (or any Spirit-led Christian) can know that the "world" includes you and me.[5] And it is this issue that puts all professed believers in essentially the same boat of personal experience, whether they be Calvinist or Arminian. Thus, as we turn to the issues of the actual personal experience of salvation, we will begin to wrestle with the issues in salvation experience that are more peculiarly Arminian and Adventist.

The fourth major section confronts special Adventist challenges in the area of assurance. As Seventh-day Adventists advance in their experience of salvation and begin to reach out to other Christians, sooner or later they will find themselves confronted by some Reformed Evangelical who will enquire, "Are you saved?" And, as previously noted, what normally undergirds such a question is the assumption that once any believer says yes to Jesus, that individual is sealed and saved for time and eternity. Thus chapter 8 will wrestle with the question of Do the "once saved, always saved" Calvinists have an assurance advantage? Are Arminians, especially the Adventist adherents to this branch of Christianity, especially prone to severe disadvantages from which Reformed believers are exempt?

Chapters 9, 10, and 11 are even more Arminian– and Adventist-specific. Thus chapter 9 addresses the themes associated with the latter rain, the close of probation, and the time of trouble. Such concepts have traditionally been a veritable happy hunting ground for many who have made a specialty of developing various versions of sinless perfection. But what we will demonstrate is that these aspects of the final crisis of earth's history inevitably point to the primacy of justification by faith alone in the righteousness of Christ. Furthermore, a deeper experience of justification provides the key to the vital assurance that will be the privilege of God's people during those fearful, crisis-ridden events.

Chapter 10 will then follow up with a more focused treatment of the final generation perfectionist explanation of the time of trouble. In this chapter we will provide the most sustained treatment of the issues that have swirled around the Adventist discussions of Christian perfection. While probably no words have struck more fear in the hearts of Adventists than "time of trouble" and "perfection," it is our conviction that a closer study of the issues will demonstrate that in Christ we have no reason to fear either of these terms or the genuine experience that God envisions for His last-day believers.

The fourth section concludes with chapter 11 and seeks to survey the contributions of Ellen White to the subject of assurance. This important chapter explores whether her writings are a help or create a stumbling block, and has been primarily composed by my colleague and collaborator, Jerry Moon. Be prepared for some pleasant surprises, especially as you discover how comforting the counsels of Ellen White have been for those who have struggled with not only spiritual discouragement but even sadness that one could justly describe as either spiritual or emotional depression (or a combination of the two). I found myself not only with new insights but also simply being wonderfully blessed by the comforting and encouraging messages of the Adventist prophet.

The fifth and final section of the book focuses on the highly practical theme of life in the Spirit. Chapter 12 explores the challenges of spiritual growth in the life of the assured Christian. We have especially designed the chapter to convey helpful counsel on how to enjoy a lively devotional experience, both in the private and public spheres of life in the "body of Christ," the visible, organized church.

Chapter 13, entitled "What to Do With Failure, Backsliding, and Fear of the Judgment—Can Sin Arise a Second Time?" not only concludes this final section, but effectively serves as the summary epilogue for the entire book. The good news is that in Christ we can retain the assurance that throughout all of the rest of eternity sin will never again be enabled to rear its death-dealing head.

It is our prayer that your experience of salvation will deepen and your sense of assurance will greatly increase through your study and practical application of the truths that this book seeks to communicate. If your readings of and reflections on the contents prove to be as rewarding to you as the writing of it has been for us, I know that you will reap many blessed benefits. May the God of abundant "free grace" be with you as you begin this challenging theological and spiritual journey.

---

[1] Roy Gane, *Altar Call* (Berrien Springs, Mich.: Diadem, 1999), p. 140.

[2] While Wesley did not teach a *pre-Advent* judgment of investigation, he did recognize that at the time of the Second Coming, God will conduct a detailed investigative judgment of believers. We will explain this in greater detail in chapters 1 and 2.

[3] In fact, we will argue that the Bible teaching on "free grace" inevitably leads to a doctrine of an "investigative judgment" that has to take place sometime, somewhere during the unfolding of the great salvation plan.

[4] Traditional Christian discourse on the assurance of salvation refers to these doctrines or teachings that God is a loving and merciful being who desires the salvation of all and has thus, in Christ, made full provision to save sinners as the a priori factors of assurance. Thus they provide the very loving nature of God Himself as the objective basis or foundation for any believer's experience of the assurance of salvation.

[5] Once more, we must remind ourselves that Christian discourse on assurance regards such experiential considerations as the a posteriori factors that can engender a reasonably legitimate conviction of assurance. They include such ideas as the (a) experience of, or the exercise of, faith itself (my sense of the exercise of faith thus provides evidence that I am trusting God to save me from both the guilt and power of sin), (b) the "witness of the Spirit" directly to my soul that I am a child of God, (c) the fact that I am battling with sin assures me that I am on the right track to be saved (rather than just passively being blown about by temptations and character weaknesses), and finally (d) the conscious awareness that my most self-evident concerns and preoccupations are with Christ and His will (both moral and practical) and love for not only God, but also other human beings (both the saved and the lost). When we consciously review these different facets of personal experience (a posteriori means reflecting on the facts after the facts have been demonstrated in experience), one can have a reasonable assurance that God is assuredly working to personally save any responsive, trusting believer.

Does the Bible Teach a Cosmic, Pre-Advent Investigative Judgment According to Works?

Chapter 1

The Evidence
From the Book of Daniel

Introduction

My Adventist background in prophetic interpretation has greatly shaped my spiritual journey. It certainly came in handy during my teen years when I experienced a real struggle with questions about God's existence and a strong challenge to belief in scriptural inspiration and authority. Thankfully, the remarkable fulfillments of Bible prophecy (especially the outline prophecies of the books Daniel and Revelation) greatly helped in rebuilding my faith in God and in the Bible as His authoritative and inspired Word.

Such affirmations received additional reinforcement as I studied the basic outlines of Adventist prophetic interpretation in college and seminary religion classes. Furthermore, I preached them faithfully during my early ministry. I simply did not have any serious problems with understanding or believing the great prophecies after my teenage bout with doubt and unbelief in scriptural authority.

Though I clearly understood and believed the prophecies, I was, as a Seventh-day Adventist evangelist, somewhat challenged by how to communicate the complex interrelationships between the key concepts involved—something especially evident as I sought to explain the prophecies of Daniel. And the biggest challenge was the doctrine of the sanctuary, including the key components of its earthly types and heavenly antitypes, the 2300 days, the 70 weeks, and the pre-Advent investigative judgment. Yet the more I taught it and preached it, the clearer it became to me.

But all of this early, positive experience as a doubting-recovering teen, maturing student, and pastor/evangelist suddenly changed when I went through what became one of the defining moments of my more mature theological pilgrimage: the Desmond Ford/Walter Rea crisis of the late 1970s and the balance of the 1980s. For those unfamiliar with this troubling passage in late-twentieth-century Seventh-day Adventist history, a little background will set the context for our study of the judgment and genuine Christian assurance.

While Desmond Ford[1] and Walter Rea focused on somewhat differing burdens, an undergirding relationship existed between their core concerns. For Rea the issue was the question of the inspiration, reliability, and authority of the Adventist prophet, Ellen G. White.

Rea had earlier distinguished himself as an avid student of Ellen White and compiler of numerous topical compendiums of her statements on a variety of prophetic, biographic, and spiritual themes. His compilations, though privately published, were widely available at many Adventist Book Centers across North America, and Rea enjoyed a solid reputation as a reliable Ellen White believer.

But what began to trouble Pastor Rea was the unsettling discovery of significant literary dependence in her writings. It provoked the once-avid student and promoter of Ellen White to level serious charges of plagiarism against the writer whom he had once revered as a genuine prophetic messenger sent from God.

By Rea's time, however, the charges of literary plagiarism had already been around for at least 100 years. Thus the issue was nothing new. But it was the shock of the realization of the greater extent of Ellen White's literary dependency that incited his strong and critical reaction. He embodied his chagrinned response in the explosive title of his book on the issue, *The White Lie.*[2] Thus his criticism called into question the very credibility of Ellen White's prophetic authority. Inevitably this led to a quite severe and negative effect on the faith of many Seventh-day Adventists who had been firm believers in Ellen White's role as a formative interpreter of the Bible and a key shaper in the development of Adventist doctrine.

Though somewhat troubled, I was not nearly as disturbed by Rea's charges as I was by the challenges initiated by Desmond Ford. Thankfully, I had been blessed with balanced and honest teachers who had helped me to develop a more realistic view of the way the genuine biblical doctrine of revelation and inspiration works. This was especially evident when compared to the assumptions of inerrancy that seemed to have originally undergirded the concepts of Walter Rea and many of his sympathizers.

The long and the short of the prophetic inspiration issue boils down to this: literary originality is not a legitimate biblical test to determine if a given document is inspired or not. Space does not permit us to conduct an in-depth inquiry into this subject.[3] But suffice it to say, Rea's attacks, coming in the historical context of Ford's challenges, made the latter seem all the more traumatic. It was an unsettling time to be a more traditional Adventist believer! Some major concepts, which had been quite central to Adventist identity, appeared to be under serious threat. But what about the more specific challenges of Desmond Ford?

His burden was to call into question a whole range of Seventh-day Adventist interpretive assumptions (including an effectual denial of the doctrinal authority for Ellen White, though he did not fully reject her claims to prophetic guidance). His most disturbing challenges, however, centered on such key doctrines as the sanctuary and the pre-Advent investigative judgment. Ford was no stranger to the issues of prophetic interpretation and their implications for the ongoing discussion of righteousness by faith issues.

As a person and writer he had many attractive features, and I began to be drawn to him when he published a helpful and readable commentary on the book of Daniel in 1978.[4] I greatly profited from reading it. In fact, as a pastor in the New Jersey Conference at the time, I was asked to give a brief review of Ford's Daniel commentary for the purposes of promoting it at a traditional camp meeting book sale (held at most North American Seventh-day Adventist summer camp meetings). And I gladly made the pitch with genuine enthusiasm, having earlier benefited from reading numerous articles published by him in *Ministry* and other Adventist journals.

Furthermore, when Ford transferred in the mid-1970s from his long-time teaching position at Avondale College in Australia to Pacific Union College (in northern California), I found myself even more exposed to his thinking. His arrival in North America greatly increased his influence on Adventist theological discussions and made his message much more accessible to those interested in the long-simmering debates over salvation and prophetic interpretation. Thus there ensued a period of about three to four years during which Ford's writings were never very far from my eyes and his forceful and eloquent words (via cassette tapes) were never far removed from my ears. It was a time of great excitement and discovery for me on so many fronts, including the study of the pre-Advent investigative judgment.

But the disturbing realization that Ford's views were more radical than I had first suspected eventually sobered my enthusiasm. On a late October Sabbath afternoon in 1979, at an Association of Adventist Forums[5] meeting held on the campus of Pacific Union College, Angwin, California, Ford shocked the Adventist world by forthrightly renouncing many of the key aspects of the Adventist sanctuary doctrine, including its traditional understanding of the 2300-day prophecy and the alleged commencement of the pre-Advent investigative judgment on October 22, 1844.

At this juncture of our study, we need not go into all of the exegetical, interpretive, and theological challenges raised by Ford in this debate. But suffice it to say, at the heart of his initiative was a desire to restore the assurance of salvation to many allegedly fearful, guilt-ridden Adventists. Somehow he fervently felt that the traditional Adventist doctrine of the sanctuary and its investigative judgment not only was biblically suspect on numerous counts but injured the believer's assurance of salvation.

As already noted, Ford had also been deeply involved in the righteousness by faith debates so intensely discussed during this period of denominational history.[6] They largely centered on the closely related issues of how justification, sanctification, and perfection all intersected with the atonement, the humanity of Christ, the closing events of human history, and the vindication of God in the pre-Advent investigative judgment. But ultimately Ford seemed to reserve his heaviest burdens on the side of a strong doctrine of justification by faith that he felt would carry fearful Adventists through the period of the investigative judgment during the last days. As became more and more apparent, his salvation views meshed with his beliefs on prophetic interpretation, especially when it came to perfection, justification, and the pre-Advent investigative judgment.

While Ford did admit that the Bible taught a brief investigative review/judgment of the records of all professing Christians before the Second Coming, he clearly denied that it began in 1844. Furthermore, he claimed that any judgment of investigation had little or nothing to do with any unique events going on in any literal Most Holy Place of the heavenly sanctuary since 1844.

The key impression left by his entire challenge lay on the side of promoting Christian assurance through a powerful emphasis on justification by faith alone and a softening of the demands for the character perfection of the last-day remnant by the sovereign Judge of the universe. Needless to say, I was deeply intrigued by Ford's claims and felt the need to get to the bottom of these issues and make a serious attempt to come to terms with the challenges he had so forcefully raised.

We will deal in subsequent chapters with the salvation aspects (justification, sanctification, and perfection) that Ford and others debated. Those questions still cry out for a balanced exposition and are directly relevant to our issue of the Christian's assurance of salvation. Ford was correct in at least one point: Christian assurance has an intimate relationship to the way any Bible-believing student comes to terms with the issues of any divine judgment based on works in the context of personal salvation.

But for now what we want to do is to explore what the Bible teaches about the pre-Advent investigative judgment. What follows is not an attempt to vindicate the entirety of the chronology of the 2300 days of Daniel 7-9 or the issues of the sanctuary imagery (in both Old and New Testaments) and the high-priestly ministry of Christ.[7] The only aspects of the doctrine of the pre-Advent investigative judgment that we will seek to clarify here are (1) whether a biblical judgment does take place before the Second Coming; (2) whether the saints will have to answer for the record of their deeds done in the flesh; and (3) the purpose such a judgment plays in the triune God's great salvation plan. What saith the Word of God?

Is the Pre-Advent Judgment Biblical?

Probably the strongest evidence for a pre-Advent judgment, one involving a searching review of any celestial records of human works (good and bad), appears in the Old Testament book of Daniel, especially in the great prophecy of chapter 7. Thus what follows is a relatively brief exposition of the chapter's major teachings on the location and timing of the judgment.

The most immediate and obviously striking features of the entire chapter are the repeated judgment sequences described by Daniel. In fact, we find three of them. The first occurs in verses 3 through 14.

The First Judgment Sequence of Daniel 7

These verses unfold in a way that strongly parallels the earlier vision of the great image in Daniel 2, one that has long been a staple of Adventist prophetic interpretation and teaching. What Daniel had seen in the visions of both chapters 2 and 7 involved a series of four great empires. After their introduction, there followed the rise of 10 nations (symbolized by the toes of the feet of the image [of chapter 2] and 10 horns of the fourth beast [of chapter 7]). In chapter 7 the 10 horns symbolically arose out of the fourth empire, the head of the terrible fourth beast. Henceforth, our primary concern is with Daniel 7, not Daniel 2. The image of Daniel 2 simply reveals the foundational, historical sequence of Daniel's prophecies, with a global judgment taking place on the earth. A great stone destroys the image, and out of it emerges the everlasting kingdom of God (an obvious anticipation of the second coming of Jesus).

In Daniel 7 the procession of four great beasts rising up out of the sea represents a steady march of nations across time and continents, a remarkable parade kicked off by a great lion that aptly symbolized the Chaldean or neo-Babylonian Empire then holding Daniel captive. Next emerges a bear with three ribs in its mouth, a vivid symbol foretelling the rise of the Medo-Persian Empire. Then there arises a four-headed leopard standing for the Hellenistic Empire of Alexander the Great of Macedonia. The four heads of the leopard aptly represent the four major divisions that Alexander's empire promptly split into after his untimely death.

But the last beast was really frightful, the attention-grabber of this vivid prophetic menagerie. A great "nondescript" beast, it featured the aforementioned 10 horns coming out of its head, menacing and devouring iron teeth, and stamping feet with toenails of brass.

One may wonder why Scripture refers to the fourth beast as nondescript. The answer is really quite simple. It was unlike any other known beast of prey—such as the preceding lion, bear, and leopard. But it was certainly "descript" enough to catch one's attention—whether you were the prophet in vision or the latest reader of Daniel 7.

Very clearly, this fourth beast presents a stunning symbol of imperial Rome and its enveloping might that would overwhelm the Mediterranean basin (including northern Africa, western and southeastern Europe, and the Near East). And it is here that the parallels with the great symbols of Daniel 2 clearly began to diverge.

What we now have is the beginning of a succession of vivid visions. And one of the keys to their proper interpretation is the principle of "repetition for the purposes of further elaboration." In other words, a gradual filling out of the larger, progressively fuller prophetic picture with more detail as each prophetic series unfolds.

Thus, what we have in Daniel 7 is newer and more vivid symbolism than that given in chapter 2 (terrible, rapacious beasts, in contrast to an awesome statue of varied materials). One image especially offers the most marked elaboration, or amplification, found in Daniel 7: the introduction of the "little horn" symbol. It arises from among the 10 horns of the terrible and rapacious fourth beast. And it would dominate the rest of the vision and the subsequent explanations of all the imagery in Daniel 7. Nothing in Daniel 2 anticipated the image of the little horn of Daniel 7 and its stunningly evil work.

With the introduction of the little horn there follows, in quick succession, an instructive sequence of events described in verses 8 through 14.

The following images and scenes are the most important for our purposes.

The little horn promptly uproots three of the first 10 horns sprouting from the head of the fourth beast, and it manifests the "eyes of a man" and a loud "mouth speaking pompous words" (verse 8). Now, what is truly striking about its emergence is that Daniel's description of the arrogant horn suddenly breaks off and the vision promptly pivots in its focus. It turns away from the frightening earthly little horn to a great heavenly vision of the "Ancient of Days" who is seated on a fiery throne of celestial judgment. A vision of heavenly glory and deliverance abruptly supersedes the earthly horror.

When our prophetic gaze finally refocuses, things really become interesting. Suddenly there comes forth "One like the Son of Man," who advances into the presence of the "Ancient of Days" (verse 13) and promptly embarks on a great work of judgment before the throne of the everlasting God of the universe. Furthermore, the scene becomes even more riveting when the vision depicts the "Son of Man," as being attended by "a thousand thousands" and "ten thousand times ten thousand" who stood with Him before the celestial throne. But the most instructive and compelling words used in describing this vast scene are the following: "The court was seated ["the judgment was set," KJV], and the books were opened" (verse 10).

Most obviously it was the terrible appearance and words of the little horn that had provoked the great divine judgment scene introduced in verses 9 and 10. But this was only a prelude. The grand finale described in verses 13 and 14 pictures the coming of "the Son of Man" before the "Ancient of Days" to receive "dominion, and glory, and a kingdom, that all peoples, nations, and languages, should serve Him" (the "Son of Man"), and "His dominion" is to be "everlasting," never to "pass away," and thus "His kingdom" will never "be destroyed" (verses 13 and 14).[8]

Let's take a brief time-out to catch our collective, interpretive breath and ponder the larger picture that has just unfolded before our wondering eyes. The sequence is one of judgment, and it begins with the parade of four great beasts (parallel to the four major sections of the statue of Daniel 2). The procession of beasts climaxes with the description of the 10-horned fourth beast. But then there comes up among the 10 horns a frightening little horn that stares with "eyes like the eyes of a man" and speaks "pompous words" ("great things," KJV) with his obviously provocative, even blasphemous "mouth" (verse 8). Thus what we have here is the first great symbolic representation of the fearsome "antichrist" of apocalyptic biblical prophecy.

While we could say much more at this stage of our exposition, the most instructive aspect of the revelation of the little horn antichrist is that it provokes a totally new direction in the flow of the vision of Daniel 7. Quickly the vision pivots in its focus from the description of the earthly little horn and swings heavenward in order to behold a glorious vision of the "Ancient of Days" and "One like the Son of Man." Quite obviously these two celestial beings are engaged in a great scene in which "the court ["judgment," KJV] was seated, and the books were opened" (verse 10). Thus all of this was most evidently provoked by "pompous words which the [little] horn was speaking" (verse 11). The ultimate result of this great supernal judgment, in which "the books were opened," will be the destruction of the fourth beast and its little horn (verse 11) and the arrival of an "everlasting dominion" (verse 14). The latter is a glorious "kingdom" inhabited by citizens from "all people, nations, and languages" who had learned to serve "the Ancient of Days," not the beastly powers and horned kingdoms of this world.

From this striking judgment scene there will come a heavenly verdict of deliverance for the saints, a proclamation that will originate from the great fiery throne of judgment presided over by the "Ancient of Days." But the truly good news is that the "One" who is "like the Son of Man" will be the being that carries out this awesome deliverance. And when does this happen? When He appears before the great God of the universe! The grand finale of this judgment scene will be the giving of the everlasting kingdom to the people of God, through the work of the "Son of Man."

But the prophet was not through with his explanations of the judgment sequence. Daniel 7 will present the pattern two more times. And they will not only repeat the basic sequence of verses 3 to 14 but also continue to further amplify and expand it to make one central emphatic point: the key to the deliverance of the people of God from the terrible scourges of the little horn will be the work of the judgment, a great assize that most obviously takes place in heaven before the coming of the "kingdom," God's "everlasting dominion" (verse 14). A few more comments on the latter part of the chapter, which contains the two final judgment sequences of the chapter, are thus in order.

The Second and Third Judgment Sequences of Daniel 7

The second series, recorded in Daniel 7:19-22, begins with Daniel's expressed desire for a clearer understanding of the vision he has just beheld. And why such a deep longing to grasp the vision? The vision had made a profoundly troubling impression on the prophet. In his consternation he turns to a certain celestial being involved with the giving of the vision and asks him the meaning of the unfolding scenes.

After receiving the briefest of explanations in verses 17 and 18, Daniel responds with a telling question: what he really wanted to know was not the meaning of the first three beasts and the fact that ultimate victory for the saints was assured. What most deeply troubled him was the terrible fourth beast, the work of its 10 horns, and especially the subsequent little-horn power. Thus Daniel replied to the celestial interpreter with pressing questions that steadily focused on the fourth beast, the 10 horns, and then the little horn.

They were the symbols that were most obviously the central focus of Daniel's interpretive concern. The first three powers had momentarily fallen off of his prophetic screen. As we say in rural America, "when the big male deer arrives at the salt lick, all the other pretenders to dominance must yield the stage of action to the big buck." The little horn was most certainly the frightful "big buck of the lick" in the drama of Daniel 7!

Obviously the evil little horn caught Daniel's attention. As the prophet pours out interpretive questions to his heavenly guide, we must again note the sequences and the way Daniel's questions further clarify the issues that will climax with the judging work of the Ancient of Days. And most significantly, the divine verdicts will be against the little horn and in behalf of the long-suffering people of God championed by the Son of Man.

Moreover, the supernatural guide's explanations of the meaning of the vision (the further filling out of the details of the vision in verses 19-22) do not center on the first three beasts, but upon the latter figures and events of the vision. Most obviously, they include the fourth beast, the 10 horns, the little horn (and its blasphemy and warfare), God's judgment in favor of the saints, and then the ultimate climax of the entire sequence: "the time" for "the saints to possess the kingdom" (verse 22).

Once more, we must carefully note the panoramic sequence: it is the same as has earlier unfolded before Daniel's startled and fearful gaze. Only now the focus is on the fourth beast and the little horn. But the repetition does not end with those terrible earthly powers. Thankfully, the sequence then continues with the grand news that following the persecutions and warfare of the little horn there will arise the great day of the "judgment" deliverance through the work of the Son of Man. And it is through this glorious deliverance of the "saints of the Most High" that they are enabled to possess God's everlasting kingdom.

In summary, what we have in Daniel 7 are the key events in their clearly chronological sequence: the "fourth beast," the "ten horns," the "little horn" and its blasphemies and warfare, the "judgment" presided over by the "Ancient of Days," its victory in behalf of "the saints of the most High" (through the work of the "Son of Man"), and the saints' possession of the kingdom. And all of this will flow directly out of the great pre-Advent heavenly judgment.

Yet Daniel was not content with merely posing his urgent interpretive questions (as recorded in verses 19-22). His persistence culminated in one of the great teaching moments in all of the history of prophetic revelation and interpretation. In verses 23-27 Daniel's heavenly instructor elaborates the now familiar visionary sequence one more time. But the heavenly being, like Daniel, was also not really interested in the first three beasts. He too takes up his explanations with the fourth beast (verse 23) and the horns, with special focus on the terrible words and deeds of the little horn.

And just as we have seen in the first two judgment sequences (verses 3-14 and verses 16-22), this last sequence climaxes with God's solution to the evil and blasphemous activity of the little horn (verse 25): a judgment will take away the "dominion" of this great antichrist, and it is this action that directly leads to the setting up of "the kingdom and dominion, and the greatness of the kingdoms under the whole heaven" (verse 27). This kingdom "shall be given to the people, the saints of the Most High. His kingdom is an everlasting kingdom, and all dominions shall serve and obey" the "Ancient of Days" through the triumphant work of the delivering "Son of Man" (verse 27).

In the face of the repetition of the great judgment sequence, is it not logical to conclude that there will indeed be a great judgment in heaven? And furthermore, will this celestial judgment, in which "One like the Son of Man" comes before the "Ancient of Days," be a judgment that, when "seated" ("set," KJV), involves an active tribunal that includes the opening of "books" (verse 10)?

I would simply suggest that the most obvious answer to these questions is a simple and emphatic yes. Furthermore, will this judgment clearly take place in heaven and then be followed by the setting up of the everlasting kingdom? And once more, the most obvious answer is yes. Thus the undeniable conclusion is that there must be a pre-Advent judgment.

Now, when we come back to the question of whether such a pre-Advent judgment will be an investigative one, we need to recall that Daniel 7 strongly suggests that it will involve the deciding of individual cases. Clearly those verdicts will come down before God grants victory to the saints of the Most High by giving them the everlasting kingdom. And furthermore the opening of "the books" as described in Daniel 7:10 implies some form of investigative hearing or process.

That such an investigation is quite individual and decisive for the eternal destiny of those being judged is also strongly implied and augmented with further details by a later elaborating vision in the book of Daniel that employs language strikingly similar to that of Daniel 7:10. Daniel 12:1 describes Michael's deliverance of the "sons" of Daniel's "people" in the "time of trouble, such as never was since there was a nation, even to that time."

And who is it that shall be "delivered" during "that time"? Once more, Daniel is quite emphatic: "Every one who is found written in the book" (Dan. 12:1). The reference to the previously mentioned judgment of Daniel 7:10 is unmistakable, and the compelling implication is that deliverance in the judgment comes, at least in part, through the vindicating evidence contained in celestial record books.

We deal with this issue of the investigative aspect of the pre-Advent judgment at this juncture only because of the fact that Daniel 7 has already mentioned an "open book." Later we will present other Bible evidence for an investigative phase of a pre-Advent judgment. But for now, the previous considerations and conclusions lead to the following question: Do we have additional Bible evidence for a judgment that is both pre-Advent and conducted on the basis of carefully recorded human deeds? Once more, the answer is an emphatic yes! Moreover, it mainly unfolds in the New Testament. And it is to this evidence that we turn in the following chapter.

---

[1] Milton Hook has sympathetically chronicled the life and thought of *Desmond Ford in Desmond Ford: Reformist Theologian, Gospel Revivalist* (Riverside, Calif.: Adventist Today Foundation, 2008).

[2] Walter T. Rea, *The White Lie* (Turlock, Calif.: M & R Publications, 1982).

[3] Revelation, inspiration, illumination, and prophetic authority will be the central concern of a subsequent volume in the Library of Adventist Theology series.

[4] This volume was a substantial paperback featuring the embossed profile of a lion on its black cover and simply entitled *Daniel* (written in misspelled Hebrew) (Nashville: Southern Pub. Assn., 1978). Ford's doctoral mentor at England's University of Manchester, the renowned evangelical New Testament scholar Professor F. F. Bruce, wrote the foreword to the commentary.

[5] The Association of Adventist Forums, originating during the late 1960s, has chapters in a number of cities and communities, mainly in North America. But the most notable

work of the Adventist Forums has been the publication of *Spectrum*, a quarterly journal of opinion addressing a wide variety of issues germane to Adventism. Furthermore, many forum chapters hold monthly meetings that often feature guest speakers who speak on controversial topics of interest to Seventh-day Adventists.

[6] In fact, the issue of righteousness by faith had become so intense that the newly elected president of the General Conference, N. C. Wilson, called for a moratorium on all confrontational debate over the issue until a special panel could be activated. The group had as its mandate to investigate the issue and make a consensus report to the church through the pages of the *Adventist Review*. While the panel did later render a report in the summer of 1980, the glare of publicity that engulfed the church following Ford's late October 1979 Adventist Forum presentation on the investigative judgment doctrine at Pacific Union College led many to ignore almost completely their findings and conclusions.

[7] For those interested in a deeper study of the relationship of the 2300-day prophecy of Daniel 8:14 to the rest of the book of Daniel and the larger sanctuary doctrine, we suggest the following works: for beginners, the study of Clifford Goldstein's *1844 Made Simple* (Nampa, Idaho: Pacific Press Pub. Assn., 1988) will prove helpful. For a more in-depth study on the issues of the interpretation of the book of Daniel and the 2300 days, see the work of William H. Shea, especially his very readable two-volume commentary in the Abundant Life Bible Amplifier Series, edited by George Knight," *Daniel 1-7* (Nampa, Idaho: Pacific Press Press Pub. Assn., 1996) and *Daniel 7-12* (Nampa, Idaho: Pacific Press Pub. Assn., 1996). For further in-depth study of the book of Daniel, see Jacques B. Doukhan, *Daniel: The Vision of the End*, rev. ed. (Berrien Springs, Mich.: Andrews University Press, 1987), and the two volumes in the Daniel and Revelation Committee Series entitled *Symposium on Daniel*, edited by Frank B. Holbrook (Washington, D.C.: Biblical Research Institute, General Conference of Seventh-day Adventists, 1986).

[8] George Knight has pointed out an interesting nuance of this judgment sequence in Daniel 7 (comments shared in personal exchanges): this first sequence clearly tells us that Christ, "the Son of Man," receives dominion before the Second Advent (verse 14), while in the two following judgment sequences, the "saints" (verse 22), or "the people of the saints of the Most High" (verse 27, RSV), receive dominion at the Second Advent. Thus the first sequence has a pre-Advent climax, while the last two reveal an Advent consummation for the "saints." But all are certainly tied to the end-time events and thereby support a pre-Advent judgment.

Chapter 2

Further Evidence From Both the Old and New Testaments

The New Testament Evidence for a Pre-Advent Judgment

One of the most memorable aspects of the whole debate that took place during the earlier Desmond Ford crisis of the late 1970s and the 1980s was his acknowledgment that there would be a pre-Advent judgment. And one of his prime pieces of evidence was Revelation 22:11 and 12. These two verses, so well known to prophecy-loving Seventh-day Adventists, are most straightforward. Once again they refer to an obvious sequence of unfolding events. Moreover, the series is consistent with the logic of God's judging actions, especially as to when He examines every human being who has ever lived on the earth.

According to John the revelator, a day will arrive when every case will be settled for either eternal life or eternal death. God, if He is in any sense just, must reach a time when all things will inevitably be brought to a judging conclusion. But He will do so only when everyone who has ever lived has finally and definitively settled whose side they will be on: either God's or Satan's. When one ponders the alternatives of eternity, it just doesn't get much more basic and elemental than this! And these arresting verses speak to the issue with sobering force and finality.

Most certainly there will finally come a day when those who are "unjust" and "filthy" will finally find themselves left as "still" in the same unholy condition. And those who are "righteous" and "holy" will remain in the same irreversibly righteous condition (verse 11). When does such a state of eternal "still" begin? We find the inevitable answer to this question strongly implied in the next verse. As the days of probation finally end, the voice of Jesus cries out in an obvious response to the settled nature of things on the earth: "And, behold, I am coming quickly; and My reward is with Me, to give to every one according to [his or her] work" (verse 12).

Taken according to their most evident and logical intent, such passages clearly point to a time that every case will be eternally settled for weal or woe. And when will that day be? It will obviously occur just before the second coming of Christ, when every person on earth will have his or her eternal reward decided. That final decision will be made on the basis of clear evidence provided by their "works" recorded in celestial records.

Thus there will arrive a time for settled conviction, both on the part of every human being and upon the part of the Great Judge in a cosmic hearing that is most obviously pre-Advent. The cases are decided, and the "rewards" will have been determined according to the recorded evidence of human "works." And then the Judge of all the earth, the great "Alpha and Omega," will arrive to give out the "rewards" at His glorious second coming—that is, when He comes "quickly."

I once more ask the reader a simple question: Is or is not the above interpretation the most simple and straightforward reading of the text? The more I ponder it, the more it seems that the only truly biblical answer is an emphatic *yes, it is!* In fact, I would suggest that on this point Desmond Ford got it quite right. Most evidently there will be a great pre-Advent judgment in which Jesus, basing His verdicts on the records of the decisions and actions of all who have ever lived on the earth, will reveal the reasons that each and every person will receive either everlasting life or death.

Now, already Daniel 12:1 and Revelation 22:12 have strongly suggested that this great decisive judgment will be not only pre-Advent but also one in which the evidence of recorded deeds, preserved in celestial "books," will be admitted as evidence. And it is such evidence that vindicates what the appropriate decisions should be for every person, whether it will be eternal life or death as their just reward. But do we find in Scripture additional support that the great pre-Advent judgment will turn on the evidence of "works" gleaned from the life-records of those who will have to stand before God's judgment bar?

Further Bible Indication of a Judgment According to Works

Once more, we will not try to be exhaustive in presenting scriptural evidence for a judgment according to works. But we will try to offer the most obviously straightforward biblical witness. Again we ask, What does the Word of God say?

Probably the clearest indication comes from one of the wisest of all human beings as he reflected on the meaning of a life that had not lived up to its early promise. And as he begins to consider what it means finally to face up to the meaning of one's life record, King Solomon reaches the following, sobering conclusion: "Fear God, and keep his commandments: for this is the whole duty of man" (Eccl. 12:13, KJV).

Now, that is a pretty amazing conclusion for one who had, by all accounts, acted in a way that almost totally ignored the virtue expected of any wise and righteous person. But Solomon simply lays it out in unmistakably simple terms: you can live however you want to, but there is coming a day when you will have to face the music of a very sobering, symphonic chorale. And the text of the score goes like this: "For God shall bring every work into judgment, with every secret thing, whether it be good, or whether it be evil" (verse 14, KJV).

Could words be more plain and the evident conclusion more emphatic and straightforward? Thus, according to the wisest human who ever lived (aside from Christ), we should keep God's commandments, and there will come a day when the Judge of all the earth will check up on how we all did in the obedience department. Will there be a judgment based on the evidence of our obedience and disobedience? Solomon was convinced that there will be.

A similar line of evidence for a judgment according to works appears in the writings of the apostle Paul. In Romans 14:10-12 the great evangelist, in a context of human evaluation of one another, reminds the Roman believers that "we shall all stand before the judgment seat of Christ" (verse 10). Paul does not indicate here whether the event will be pre-Advent, co-Advent, or post-Advent. But the no-nonsense apostle does make it clear that eventually all shall "stand before the judgment seat of Christ" and that every person "shall give [an] account of himself to God" (verse 12). Surely the giving of an "account" involves explaining the record of our thoughts and actions. To conclude anything else is to ignore the plainest meaning of the word "account" in a judgment setting.

Second Corinthians 5:10 echoes Romans 14:10-12: "For we must all appear before the judgment seat of Christ, that each one may receive the things done in the body, according to what he has done, whether good or bad." Once more we find that in a context of judgment God will assess every believer by the "things done in the body," "whether good or bad." This surely sounds very much like a judgment based on the evidence of works that heaven has accurately recorded and that reflect the actual historical actions of each human being who will stand before Christ's judgment seat in some future day of reckoning.

The Judgment and Assurance

We must remind ourselves that though Paul is the great teacher of justification by grace through faith alone ("not of works, lest anyone should boast" [Eph. 2:9]), he still confounds his cheap-grace interpreters with such statements as we find in Romans 14 and 2 Corinthians 5. But these are not the only passages that undermine any cheap-grace position. Clearly the Lord has ordained the legitimacy of acts of obedience that are the fruit of a genuine faith that actually works.

Romans 2:13 declares, "For not the hearers of the law are just in the sight of God, but the doers of the law will be justified." The context of the apostle's sobering statement is a discussion that claims that both Jews (those who have "sinned in the law") and Gentiles (those who "have sinned without law") shall "perish" and that both will ultimately "be judged by the law" (verse 12).

Quite obviously Paul is not suggesting that Jews and Gentiles will be justified by works, a position that would make of none effect God's free grace. But what he clearly indicates is that there is coming a day when those who have been justified by faith will be called upon to answer for the deeds done in the flesh. And all of this is for the purpose of giving public evidence that their faith was a living and obedient response, one empowered by grace. We will have more to say on this issue in the next few chapters when we take up the connection of faith and works (in other words, how justification by faith alone relates to the transforming experience of Christians so that they will be working, obedient believers, not false professors of the faith). But for now, we just want to make the point clear that a living (loving) faith produces unmistakable public evidence of gracious virtue.

Our final piece of evidence emerges from the sobering counsels of the book of James. James is one of the truly homiletical writers of the Bible. He was first and foremost a preacher of righteousness. His letter has the ring of no-nonsense, down-to-earth practicality and morality about it. And he very much wants to confront the issue of the true nature of what saving faith consists of. In fact, his teaching has been so hard-hitting that some have surmised that he opposed Paul's position of justification by faith alone, without works of the law. But the two authors do not contradict each other when we really get down to the bottom line of what both mean by the nature of saving faith.

In a highly practical setting, one having to do with class discrimination and caring for the poor, James plainly rebukes anyone who does not relieve the suffering of those destitute of daily food and clothing. His conclusion is that such good works are just as important as obeying the plainest requirements of the Ten Commandments (James 2:10, 11). If one does not engage in genuine acts of charity, fairness, and obedience to the Ten Commandments, any claim to faith in Christ proves to be bogus: "But do you want to know, O foolish man, that faith without works is dead?" (verse 20). To be downright blunt about the matter, one can thus see how "that a man is justified by works, and not by faith only" (verse 24). A faith that does not produce acts of charity, equity, and commandment-keeping obedience is a dead faith. And in the Bible, when anything is dead, it has ceased to exist. So *it is that we are saved in the judgment, not by faith plus works, but by a very real and practical faith that works!*

As already promised, we will return to this issue in subsequent chapters, when we will more directly confront the issue as to how faith and works play out in a balanced understanding of a genuine experience of righteousness by faith. But for now James makes it clear that if your faith does not work, you will not be vindicated in the great judgment day. His truly clinching statement on the issue of judgment according to works thus occurs in the heart of his discussion of a genuine working faith.

After laying out the duty of obedience to the plainest requirements of God's commandments (avoiding adultery and murder), James commands, "So speak and so do as those who will be judged by the law of liberty. For judgment is without mercy to the one who has shown no mercy. Mercy triumphs over judgment" (verses 12, 13). Thus we see that James most emphatically agreed with the apostle Paul that there will be a judgment as to how all professed believers obeyed the law of the Ten Commandments, the glorious "law of liberty" (verse 12).

One final line of evidence that there will be judgment according to works emerges in the "great white throne" judgment scene of the wicked at the end of the millennium. Revelation 20:11-13 paints a rather awesome picture: "And I saw a great white throne, and him that sat on it, from whose face the earth and the heaven fled away; and there was found no place for them. And I saw the dead, small and great, stand before God; and the books were opened: and another book was opened, which is the book of life, and the dead were judged out of those things which were written in the books, according to their works. And the sea gave up the dead which were in it; and death and hell delivered up the dead which were in them: and they were judged every man according to their works" (KJV).

Is it going to far too say simply that if the unrighteous are judged "according to their works" before receiving their final rewards, why would it be any less just for God to judge the righteous before they receive their final rewards?

This whole issue seems to turn on the question of why God will convene a judgment that is at least, in part, based on everyone's life records preserved in heaven. We will return to this question momentarily, but before we do so we must examine a text often cited as evidence that the righteous will not have to face judgment at all.

What About John 5:24: Believers "Shall Not Come Into Judgment"?

One of the truly classic pieces of Seventh-day Adventist commentary on John 5:24 appears in the controversial 1957 Adventist classic, *Seventh-day Adventists Answer Questions on Doctrine* (usually referred to as *Questions on Doctrine*, or simply *QOD*). I urge the reader to carefully reflect on the following observations:

"Christ having taken our guilt and borne the punishment of our iniquities, sin has no more dominion over us—provided we remain 'in him.' He is our security. And as long as this attitude of submission is maintained, there is no power on earth that can detach the soul from Christ. No man can pluck the believer out of the Savior's hands (John 10:28).

"But does this mean that the Christian will not come into judgment at all? Some believe this, and they base their concept on John 5:24. In this text—'Verily, verily, I say unto you, He that heareth my word, and believeth on him that sent me, hath everlasting life, and shall not come into condemnation; but is passed from death unto life'—the Greek word for 'condemnation' is *krisis,* and is usually rendered 'judgment.' It is therefore felt by many Christian scholars that the proper understanding of this verse is '. . . shall not come into judgment.'

"It is true that the Greek [word] *krisis* is more often rendered in the Bible by the word 'judgment' than by any other expression. . . . However, this is not absolute, for *krisis* does have other shades of meaning. For instance, it is rendered 'accusation' (Jude 9; 2 Peter 2:11) and 'damnation' (Matt. 23:33; Mark 3:29; John 5:29). It is also rendered 'condemnation' in John 5:24, also in John 3:19, and James 5:12. So while 'judgment' is the prevailing idea, there is the concept of 'accusation' made at such a judgment session, and hence of the individual's being under 'condemnation' because of the sentence of the judgment; and still further, of 'damnation,' the punishment meted out to the offender.

"It is consequently our understanding that the thought in John 5:24 is best rendered by the word 'condemnation' in the sense in which the same Greek word *krisis* is rendered in John 3:19: 'And this is the *condemnation, that* light is come'; and in James 5:12: '. . . lest ye fall into *condemnation.*' Even the R.S.V., which renders *krisis* as 'judgment' in several of the texts cited, renders it 'condemnation' in James 5:12. The Christian believer, being in Christ, is not under the condemnation either of the law or of sin, for if he is fully surrendered to God, the righteousness of our blessed Lord covers whatever lack there might be in his life. The child of God, with his title clear to heaven, need entertain no fear of any judgment day. Abiding in Christ, with Jesus as his Advocate, and utterly given over and dedicated to his Lord, he knows there is 'no condemnation [Greek, *katakrima*] to them which are in Christ Jesus' (Rom. 8:1)."[1]

Now if we accept that all human beings, including the faithful redeemed, will have to somehow stand before God's judgment bar to give an account of the deeds done in the flesh, we still have to explain why God requires it.

Why Does God Have a Judgment Based on Human Deeds?

First of all, we must make it clear that God does not convene a hearing to refresh or jog His memory. The Lord is not ignorant of our works, ways, and thoughts. Troubled by neither short-term nor long-term memory loss, He clearly and exhaustively knows it all. Long ago our Lord could have settled up all of the accounts since all is known to Him in full detail, including the hidden motives that drive the actions of all who have ever lived in the universe. But in another important sense, we can persuasively argue that God does need a judgment according to works.

The great triune Creator and Redeemer is not just our Savior. He is also the great moral governor of the universe that He has created in which He seeks to redeem sinners from the terrible ravages of sin and all of its evil effects. And in His role as redeemer and moral governor, He wants to be seen as true, just, and merciful in all of His dealings not only toward hopelessly lost sinners but also with all who have professed His name.

Furthermore, judgments are not just the concern of those of this world. He also desires that all of the loyal beings who inhabit heaven and the unfallen worlds will clearly see the justice of His judgments. In other words, the entire host of intelligent beings in the universe will review the sum total of the good and bad deeds of all professed believers and compare them against God's decisions regarding their destiny.

Seventh-day Adventists are not alone on this issue of the exposure of the deeds of the redeemed (even their bad acts) in a great judgment day. John Wesley has left us some sage observations in an attempt to vindicate a divine judgment according to the works of the saved.

"Will their evil deeds . . . be remembered in that day, and mentioned in the great congregation? Many believe they will not, and ask . . . How can this be reconciled with God's declaration by the Prophet, 'If the wicked will turn from all his sins that he hath committed, and keep all my statutes, and do that which is lawful and right,' 'all his transgressions that he hath committed, they shall not be once mentioned unto him' (Eze. 18:21, 22)? How is it consistent with the promise which God has made to all who accept of the gospel covenant, 'I will forgive their iniquity, and . . . remember their sin no more'? (Jer. 31:34) . . . .?

"It may be answered, it is apparently and absolutely necessary, for the full display of the glory of God, for the clear and perfect manifestation of his wisdom, justice, power, and mercy toward the heirs of salvation, that all the circumstances of their life should be placed in open view, together with all their tempers, and all the desires, thoughts, and intents of their hearts. Otherwise how would it appear out of what a depth of sin and misery the grace of God had delivered them? And, indeed, if the whole lives of all the children of men were not manifestly discovered, the whole amazing contexture of divine providence could not be manifested; nor should we yet be able in a thousand instances to 'justify the ways of God to man'. . . .

"And in the discovery of the divine perfections the righteous will rejoice with joy unspeakable; far from feeling any painful sorrow or shame for any of those past transgressions which were long since blotted out as a cloud, washed away by the blood of the Lamb. It will be abundantly sufficient for them that 'all the transgressions which they had committed shall not be once mentioned unto them' to their disadvantage; that 'their sins and transgressions and iniquities shall be remembered no more' to their condemnation."[2] Wesley's comments aptly represent one of the finest rhetorical moments in the discussion of the vindication of God's ways of judgment in the history of Christian thought.

If Seventh-day Adventists and John Wesley are correct in the basic outlines of their shared understanding of the judgment, it is thus incumbent upon God to provide public evidence in support of the ultimate decisions that He will render in the great day when the cases of every human being will be finally settled for eternal life or eternal death. This is, of course, the heart of the great controversy (or cosmic controversy) theme that is so central to the larger metanarrative of the entirety of the scriptural canon as well as the very Wesleyan conditioned thought and writings of Ellen G. White. The theme of God's redemptive love, playing itself out in the rough and tumble of the terrible experience of sin (and its ghoulish stepchild, death), involves the vindication of God's love through a perfectly balanced revelation of the equitable administration of His justice and mercy.

If the universe should perceive God as indulging sin (even if in the name of mercy), it would call His justice into question. On the other end of the celestial balancing scale, if God appears to indulge his justice too hurriedly or zealously, then it raises doubts about His mercy. Thus God has taken the long-haul approach to the challenge of sin and its evil results, rather than some quick fix. The loving heavenly Father very much wants to be viewed as a cosmic moral governor who reflects patience, balance, and considered wisdom as He seeks to solve the terrible dilemmas that sin has inflicted on His good creation. He longs for His creatures, made in His moral, physical, and spiritual image, to serve Him through freely chosen responses, not out of fear that if we do not quickly do the right thing, He will give us the back of His judgmental hand.

Most certainly God could have quickly wreaked justice on Lucifer and all of his angelic dupes. But the sum total of such a move would have led to the obedience of craven fear, rather than a response engendered by His divine long-suffering love. And to do this, the Redeemer God has patiently allowed situations to ripen so that when the key issues become clearer, the alternatives will also become appealingly apparent.

I do not know about you, the reader, but as I have pondered the alternatives in the great debate about God's nature of love and the ways in which the Bible and Ellen White portray the divine responses in meeting the twin challenges of sin and evil, I have not come up with a better answer than that which inheres in the overarching theme that we call the great controversy. And the grand finale of this outworking of patient, redeeming grace will be fully revealed to all in the succession of judgments that have begun with the pre-Advent investigative judgment and will conclude with the millennial judgment during the final "Great White Throne" session at the very end of the millennium. And even in this final "White Throne" phase of judgment, Scripture pictures God as using "books" to provide public evidence to demonstrate, even to the hopelessly lost rejecters of His grace, that His decisions have been and will continue to be eminently fair in every aspect of their truth, justice, and righteousness.

But may I here suggest an even more eminently and immediately practical reason, directly related to our current needs, as to why Scripture speaks of a pre-Advent investigative judgment. Such an event will not only display public evidence about the decisions made regarding the professed believers in Christ (demonstrating the delicate balance of His just and merciful love), but also serve as a "consciousness raising" experience for His professed people who are living during the time when such an investigation is in actual process.

Think of it in this way. God is not simply trying to scare us into obedience and goodness with warnings of curses and judgments. While it does involve an element of sober warning, yet at a more profound level the loving God of judgment is mostly seeking to alert all believers as to His deep desire to shower His gracious mercies on those who are, though undeserving, nevertheless the objects of His life-giving beneficence. And this, above all else, is what the judgment is about—it overflows with the good news of God's desire to vindicate us with His merciful love so that He can exonerate Himself in His decision to save us.

Furthermore, this great theme of vindication arises out of the growing, deepening realization that not only is God merciful but His mercy can also be better appreciated by those who have come to share His attitude toward sin. And this attitude has to be one of revulsion to sin, not a presumptuous embrace of it. The only ones who will fully be able to accept God's loving mercy are those who have been transformed by both justifying and sanctifying grace. In other words, the only ones who will by faith be able to buy into God's mercy are those who have given up habitual attitudes and acts of sinning.[3]

Maybe we could put it a bit more simply: God alerts us to the fact that a great investigative judgment of our works and deeds is in session so that we will have a balanced desire to experience all that is involved in His saving grace—not only the great blessings of His justifying, or forgiving grace, but also those of transforming or sanctifying grace. The former provides merciful new standing and status while the latter offers a new set of attitudes and righteous character traits that redound in blessing to others and glory to God. And there is nothing like the realization that the day of final judgment is moving forward to raise human awareness regarding the efficacy of God's grace, both the urgency of imputation (forgiving, or justifying grace) and the transformative efficacy of impartation (the changed attitudes and actions that reflect the practicalities of God's regenerative, sanctifying love).

In our final chapter we will once more return to some of these themes and thoughts in defense of a pre-Advent judgment of human works. We will there briefly review them in the context of an overarching summation.

But we will do so in a way that will seek to meet the often repeated charge that the investigative judgment produces an unhealthy atmosphere of fear that inevitably ruins any sense of Christian assurance of salvation.

For now, however, we simply want to emphasize the point that the teaching of the pre-Advent investigative judgment raises a profound consciousness about the need for a balanced understanding of the manner in which Christ both imputes and imparts His righteousness to His professed and responsive followers.

Therefore, we strongly suggest that the most basic issues of Christian assurance, unfolding in the face of any divine investigative judgment, has to include an informed, balanced understanding of the dynamics of personal salvation. And it is to these wonderful and challenging subjects that we now turn our attention in the next few chapters.

---

[1] *Seventh-day Adventists Answer Questions on Doctrine* (Washington, D.C.: Review and Herald Pub. Assn., 1957), pp. 418-420, and in the newer *Seventh-day Adventists Answer Questions on Doctrine: Annotated Edition,* Adventist Classic Library Series, Notes With Historical and Theological Introduction by George Knight (Berrien Springs, Mich.: Andrews University Press, 2003), pp. 333, 334.

[2] These paragraphs are drawn from John Wesley's key sermon on eschatology entitled "The Great Assize," and is cited from Albert C. Outler, ed., *Sermons, The Works of John Wesley,* bicentennial edition (Nashville: Abingdon Press, 1984), vol. 1, pp. 364, 365. In an interesting little footnote to the author's own search for a clearer understanding of the issues of the investigative judgment, Desmond Ford's privately published manuscript, entitled *Daniel 8:14, The Judgment and The Kingdom of God: A Rebuttal of Criticisms of the Adventist Sanctuary Doctrine* (probably published at Pacific Union College, Angwin, California, sometime during the mid- to late 1970s), pp. 38 and 39, pointed me to this fine discussion by Wesley in vindication of a full revelation of the deeds of all who come into a cosmic public judgment according to works. It is thus no accident that we must consider the theology of John Wesley as an integral part of the larger background of the Adventist development of the biblical doctrine of the investigative judgment. Furthermore, Wesley will also make a number of helpful contributions to the later treatments of the issue of the Christian's assurance of salvation in this present volume.

[3] George Knight offers a sage caveat on the issue of judgment as vindication, not condemnation: "Many mid-twentieth century Adventists appear to have been fixated on judgment as condemnation. But the past fifty years have seen a growing perspective on judgment as the vindication of the saints. In actuality, biblical judgment has two edges— condemnation for those who reject God's grace, and vindication for those who accept it . . . Christians will have a pre-Advent judgment, but the good news is that the Judge is not against them or even neutral. The Judge is on our side. He is seeking to get into heaven as many as possible. Thus even the judgment needs to be viewed as good news (gospel). When the pre-Advent judgment is seen from that perspective, there is no reason why any Christian should want to reject the idea" (*Seventh-day Adventists Answer Questions on Doctrine: Annotated Edition,* p. 334).

Section Two

The Dynamics
of Personal Salvation

Chapter 3
Atonement: The Provisions for
Salvation and Personal Assurance

Chapter 4
Convicting, Converting, and Forgiving Grace

Chapter 5
Regeneration, Justification, Sanctification,
Perfection, and Personal Assurance

Chapter 6
Perfection and Assurance—
The Reassuring Implications

Atonement: The Provisions for Salvation and Personal Assurance

Introduction

As we explore what the genuine article of personal Christian assurance of salvation consists of, we must always keep in mind a fundamental principle: the fact is that the most important sources for personal assurance will directly arise out of the revealed provisions that God, in Christ, has made for our salvation. Moreover, closely related to these central means of grace is the wonderful way that Christ works to communicate, or make effective, those saving blessings to lost, sinful humanity.

In essence, if anything will generate a sense of genuine assurance for believers, we will find it in what we have traditionally referred to as the "benefits" of all that Christ has done, is doing, and will do to reconcile sinners to Himself—a process commonly referred to by theologians as the "communication of Christ's saving benefits." Furthermore, the manner in which it unfolds is known as the "way of salvation" (*via salutis* or the *ordo salustis*—the way or order of salvation). Maybe we could call it the "highway to heaven."

All of these benefits lovingly emerge out of Christ's incarnation, sinless life, sacrificial death, resurrection, ascension to heaven, priestly intercession, and second coming. In some manner, all such aspects or benefits of His salvation must be offered and effectively communicated to sinners. And their communication actually makes His grace a saving fact in their lives. Moreover, key among them are the conviction of sin (or our great need) and of God's merciful love for sinners. When the divine salvational benefits have done their work, the desired result will be the experience of regeneration, which then successively leads to repentance (sorrow for sin), conversion (the new birth), justification, sanctification, perfection, and finally glorification (the receiving of a new perfect body) at the Second Coming.

What we aim to do in this chapter and the next few chapters is to follow the "way" or "order" of salvation. We will do so in order to clarify (1) how the saving benefits of Christ's atoning (reconciling) work are communicated to responsive, repentant sinners and (2) how each gift contributes to the dynamics of Christian assurance.

But first we will consider some key aspects of God's love for the human race, humanity's desperate condition in sin, and what the atoning provisions, or saving benefits of Christ, actually provide and accomplish. And then we will more fully examine each key aspect of Christ's salvation.

Once more, our primary goal is not so much a detailed treatment of each benefit but a concise review of the most important ones and their implications for the believer's personal assurance of salvation. They are what we have earlier referred to as the a priori factors of God's redemptive love that make such a strong, foundational contribution to personal Christian confidence.

God's Loving Grace

The most basic issue that undergirds any developing sense of Christian assurance is the simple fact that God does love every person born into our sinful world. The very heart of God's merciful attitude is what we normally refer to as *grace*. "For God so loved the world that He gave His only begotten Son, that whoever believes in Him should not perish but have everlasting life. For God did not send His Son into the world to condemn the world, but that the world through Him might be saved" (John 3:16, 17). Christians justifiably treasure this most famous of all Bible passages for the simple reason that it so concisely expresses the undergirding foundation of God's plan of redemption—that He is a being of loving, merciful, and saving purposes who has been, and still is relentlessly intent on saving every sinner who has ever existed.

Thus when the Holy Spirit inspired John to write "whoever," His intention was not limited to some predetermined small group arbitrarily elected by the supposedly "secret will" of the inscrutably and irresistibly predestinating work of the Godhead. Absolutely not! Most obviously, it is not God's intention for any person to be left to languish in sin and the prospect of eternal death. Peter is clear on the issue: God is "not willing that any should perish but that all should come to repentance" (2 Peter 3:9). So the most basic principle of this book is that God, out of the benefits of His love, has had as His goal salvation for all who are willing to respond to His gracious offer.

point of this book

50

The next thing that we need to realize is that the God who loves us is so serious and relentless in His saving intentions that He has not left the provisions of His loving grace to be in any way dependent on the slender threads of the works or initiatives of sinful human beings. All of the provisions or benefits of salvation that God has made are solely the doing, dying, and advocacy of Christ and the persistent work of the Holy Spirit. The way that God saves the lost is through the fruit of His loving grace, from beginning to end!

Christ is literally the alpha and the omega of all the provisions and communications of His redeeming grace. In fact, when one really begins to reflect carefully and prayerfully on the whole issue, we find not one single thing that any sinful human could ever do either to initiate or to merit salvation.[1] Thus we simply conclude that any human "glory" is laid "in the dust" and all the glory of salvation belongs to God.[2]

Yet we do need to address one objection briefly. If salvation is all of God and nothing of sinful humans, what about the issue that human choice may then give a pretext for humanity to claim some credit for their salvation? Most certainly, God does respect the decisions that are an integral part of His loving will to save. Yet even on this issue we find no room for human boasting.

When we really get to the bottom of the issue of human choice, it will become abundantly evident that there is no such thing as a natural free will in any created, sinful being, at least when it comes to the dynamics of salvation and reconciliation with God. But more on that issue a little later when we turn our attention to the basic dynamics of calling, convincing (that is, convicting), regenerating grace.

Now, if what we have said in the previous paragraphs is true, can there be any reason any human should doubt the sufficiency of Christ to save from sin? From the perspective of the reconciling work of Christ, the answer is an emphatic no!

Before, however, we reflect any further on the benefits that Christ has generated for our personal salvation, we need to address the issue of human inability to contribute anything to it. This vital factor cries out for some further explanation. And here the key issue involves just what it is that sinful humanity needs to be saved from.

Therefore, as we explore the "way of salvation," the first stop is at the wayside that we will call God's "Love Inn." What we find here is a welcoming, even winsomely beckoning atmosphere. But before we will be able to appreciate the delights of God's "Love Inn," we must make a preliminary, exploratory stop at heaven's "Sin Clinic." Such a rather painful stop is necessary so that we can more intelligently receive an accurate diagnosis of our condition that will help us know where to turn next to find appropriate healing for our desperately sinful state. It is therefore a most reassuring thought that such a visit is all under the watchful, reassuring eye of Jesus, the Great Physician of the soul.

Human Sinfulness

What will Christ uncover as He probes into the spiritual and moral condition of humanity? He will fully expose the extent of our deadly spiritual and moral afflictions. And what Christ reveals we find soberly described in Scripture. The Bible presents a radical analysis of the tragic dimensions of the human condition. Thus it is that before we can really value the good news of salvation, we must first recognize just how bad the news is concerning our plight.

Ephesians 2 and Romans 7

If any student of the Bible should look for verses to affirm humanity's essential goodness, these are certainly not the passages to turn to! In fact, both chapters paint a rather unflattering portrait of human corruption, depravity, and pressing need. Humans are collectively described in Ephesians 2 as "dead in trespasses and sins" (verse 1) and profoundly under the control of "the prince of the power of the air, the spirit who now works in the sons of disobedience" (verse 2). Such a dreadful status includes "the lusts of our flesh, fulfilling the desires of the flesh and of the mind" and being "by nature children of wrath" (verse 3). And Romans 7 also doesn't provide much relief in its confirmations of the bluntly realistic revelations of Ephesians 2.

In this challenging chapter Paul says that while the "law is spiritual," we are "carnal," even "sold under sin" (Rom. 7:14). He observes that any good things we might choose to do are the very ones we don't do and the very things we hate are what we just so easily and naturally seem to do (verse 15). Paul then remorselessly proceeds to sum it up with the fact that sin "dwells" in all of us (verse 17), even to the extent that we become absolutely convinced that while we seek to choose the good, we not only do not do it, but the evil we despise is what we actually do (verses 18-23). This "law," or principle of sin, wars with the "law of our mind," creating a cycle of frustration that wells up into one of the most plaintive cries of despair in all of Holy Writ—"O wretched man that I am! Who will deliver me from this body of death?" (verse 24).

But thankfully, not all is diagnostic doom (and we could have adduced much more depressing news). The story does not end with the sad tidings of depravity, failure, frustration, and death. The very good news is that "through Jesus Christ our Lord" we have hope for deliverance (verse 25) and that despite all that we are it has not stopped God from loving us.

Ivan Blazen has noted that some of the best news in the Bible unfolds through many of its graciously grammatical adversatives—the good news "buts."[3] One of the best examples appears in Ephesians 2, immediately following the bad news of verses 1-3:

"*But God*, who is rich in mercy, because of His great love with which He loved us, even when we were dead in trespasses, made us alive together with Christ (by grace you have been saved), and raised us up together, and made us sit together in the heavenly places in Christ Jesus, that in the ages to come He might show the exceeding riches of His grace in His kindness toward us in Christ Jesus" (verses 4-7). And then comes that other memorable, grace-laced memory verse: "For by grace you have been saved through faith, and that not of yourselves; it is the gift of God, not of works, lest anyone should boast" (verses 8, 9). It is thus no small wonder that Isaac Watts felt inspired to pen the somewhat unflattering yet realistically honest words that grace was sufficient to save "such a worm as I"!

Human Depravity and Redeeming Love

When we consider the wages of sin and to what depths it has debased humanity, it is only in this light that we can begin to grasp the costliness of God's redeeming love. If we are as bad off as the Bible suggests, is this not powerful evidence of the relentlessly persisting love *with* which God has been assuredly pursuing us and the surpassing worth that such a salvation invests *in* the entirety of the sinful human race? And if God can love the messed-up race that we are, how then can anyone doubt His loving ability to sustain and steadily retain us as His children?

As we examine God's reconciling, or atoning, work, we will discover further evidences of His loving, assuring grace!

Atoning Reconciliation and Assurance

Since "atonement" is one of the most theologically loaded words in all of religious terminology, it is prudent for us to seek a clear definition as to what it seeks to communicate. From the perspective of traditional Christian theological discourse, the word has been almost exclusively associated with the redemptive significance of the death of Christ. In other

atonement - death of Christ

words, it has sought to answer the following question: "Why did Christ have to die?" or "What is the meaning of Christ's death?"

Most certainly Seventh-day Adventists have fervently affirmed the Calvary phase of atonement and have collectively engaged in many a lively discussion in our search for answers to the persistent questions about the saving significance of Christ's death. Furthermore, all agree on two major points: (1) the word "atonement" refers to what God has done to generate the *provisions* or redemptive "benefits" for lost humanity; and (2) it is important to distinguish the provisory aspects of atonement from the manner in which God has sought to *communicate* them to responsive sinners.

But while these two facets of God's redeeming work (*provisions* and their *communication*) are to be *distinguished*, they are never to be *separated* or placed in opposition to one another. Both aspects of God's redemption plan are the fruit of His loving grace.

Perhaps we can best clarify the links between the various blessings of God's atoning work in the following three ways:

(1) Atonement as *provision* refers to all that God has done, is doing, and will continue to do to generate the *benefits* that are essential to reconcile sinful humans from their state of alienation into a renewed status of "union with God." Furthermore, all such benefits emerge more specifically out of the earthly life and death of Christ.

(2) By way of some contrast, the atonement as *communication* refers to the manner in which God seeks to impute and impart the *benefits* of Christ so that sinful humans are actually reconciled. And when this process of communication becomes effective, it readies the redeemed to be granted immortality at the Second Coming. It is only then that believers will be enabled to spend eternity with God (and one another).

(3) Furthermore, as suggested in a previous chapter, this *communication* aspect of the atoning work of Christ will also include God's efforts to *demonstrate* that He has done the right thing in the settlement of the cases of every person who has ever lived—both human and angelic. And when that process will have been definitively concluded, then the final aspect of atonement will be the merciful and just *annihilation* of those who reject God's infinitely costly, loving, and beneficial provisions and the establishment of His everlasting heavenly kingdom.

Thus from the Seventh-day Adventist perspective, atonement has a rich breadth and depth of meaning. Yet we need to say still more about the benefits of atoning grace. And in the next few sections of this chapter we will seek to define the *benefits* of Christ in the light of His life and death.

54

The Beneficial Provisions of Christ's Life and Death

The work of Christ is best understood in relationship to the other two members of the Godhead. The gist of it goes like this: the Godhead (Trinity), in a mysterious meeting called the council of peace, lovingly and self-sacrificially determined to take different *roles* or *offices* in order to meet any possible eventuality that sin would invade God's peaceful universe. In fact, it almost seems inevitable that there would have been such a council on the part of the Holy Trinity. And the reasons for it appear to be twofold.

First of all, the Bible plainly tells us that God is omniscient—that is, He knows everything. Thus the emergence of sin could not have caught Him by surprise. Of course, this issue raises all sorts of other questions regarding God's foreknowledge in the face of sin. For instance, why did He go ahead and make beings that would have the ability to inflict such a grievous blot on Him and an unsuspecting universe? Quite obviously, we admit that it is a disturbing and uncomfortable thought. And while any fully definitive answer to the question is beyond the focus of this study, a few preliminary comments are in order.[4]

We find the key to any possibly satisfying response, from the Arminian/Seventh-day Adventist perspective, in the concept of God as a being of loving grace. In other words, God's love must allow for some sort of genuine free choice as a part of the mental and spiritual makeup of any being whom He has created in His image (this includes angels, any unfallen beings on other worlds, and the human race). If God had made them in any other way, such beings simply could not function in any other manner except as preprogrammed robots. Therefore, when God gave such individuals real free will, He did so fully aware that they could choose not to do His loving will. The only other alternative was simply not to create freewill beings in the first place.

So what was God to do? He could have just decided to create entities such as our friends the animals. While the lives of many of these creatures have relational aspects, they all only ultimately function by instinct, and their relationships and actions are devoid of any truly moral character. For instance, when we say to our pet dog, "You are a bad dog," we are not saying that the animal is guilty of any sin that will send it to a canine hell.

What we really mean is that the dog has done something by instinct and that we have tried to curb such drives by "rote training" in doggy obedience schools. But when we make such a reference to a fellow human being, we simply expect more from them—that is, unless they have been subjected to developmental deficits that lead us to simply expect nothing truly responsible from them (such as little children still maturing and those struggling with special needs).

It is a terrible situation if, for example, my friends have given up on me because they have reluctantly concluded that I am incapable of relating to others in a responsible manner. We can, however, be abundantly grateful that God has not chosen to take such an attitude toward those who have misused His gift of free will!

Thus God has chosen the chancy but loving route and granted (at creation) to human beings the power to choose moral alternatives, with all of their possibilities for sin and death. And that is exactly what the doctrine of the atonement was designed to deal with.

Therefore, the most basic narrative theme of the Bible is that God has not blithely and vindictively abandoned sinful humans to either despair or damnation. He has neither chosen to indulge us nor written us off with an easy wave of His divine sword of justice. Driven by a love that is both just and merciful, the Holy Trinitarian God has mounted a monumental effort to heal our sinful condition and to restore sinful humanity back to its originally intended state of living in a freely chosen, responsive love relationship with Him (and others).

Therefore, the very first atoning act of love divine that the Trinity engaged in was to make a plan to redeem the lost human race. Moreover, in this gracious council of peace the Father decided to *give up* the Person of the Godhead whom we call the Son so that He could come to our world and make provisions for our reconciliation.

Furthermore, They also mutually determined that the Holy Spirit would almost totally *give up* His personal identity so that all attention would be drawn to the person and work of the Son. And in this abounding attitude of self-giving the Holy Spirit was destined to glorify the Father, who has been willing to sacrifice His Son for the salvation of the alienated race.

In other words, the Father sacrificed by giving over His Son to make the actual provisions of the atonement. The Son sacrificed by becoming truly human in a sin-marred world, endured the stench of human sin as an incarnate being, and died a death of horrible separation from His beloved Father. And finally, the Holy Spirit chose to suffer the loss of personal identity so that the Son and His sacrifice might be exalted for the salvation of humanity and the reconciling vindication of the Father. And the sum total of this effort is that it will ultimately generate the complete satisfaction of every intelligent being in the universe that God has done all that was possible within the principled constraints of His love to solve the challenge of sin and its spawn of death.

Could there have been a more costly and comprehensive redemption plan? If you can come up with such a thing, let me know about it immediately! Therefore, I urge the reader to ponder the following two pressing questions:

1. If the Father was willing to *give up* His most intimate relationship with His Son to allow the Son to endure Satan's most subtle temptations and to ultimately die a wretched death in which Christ could not "see through the portals of the tomb": and that the Holy Spirit was willing to *give up* His personal identity to minister to and sustain the Son through all of His atoning work—could there be found any greater, more reassuring love in the history of the universe?

2. Furthermore, if all that we have said about the love of the Holy Trinity is true, could there be any greater investment of love and value in the human race?

Therefore, if your answer is a responsive and loving no, then I think you would be able to begin to sense that God's love for you is fully assured! But thankfully, the Godhead actually carried it out as a loving, actual accomplishment that They have made available to the lost, sinful race as the fully effective benefits provided for their salvation. Could any thought be more reassuring?

This brings us to the question of exactly what comprised the work of Christ, the incarnate Son and designated agent of atonement. In other words, the issue here includes all that His incarnate activity involved.

Christ's Incarnate Work

The mission of Jesus Christ on earth as the incarnate Son of God revolved mainly around His life of obedience to the Father. It featured two major facets whose central importance cannot be too strongly emphasized. Furthermore, we must constantly keep in mind that those two aspects of redemption unfold in a deeply controversial context. So what are they?

In the beginning of what Seventh-day Adventists call the great controversy, Satan had charged that obedience to the will of God (His law) was impossible for freewill, relational beings. So Christ took on humanity "in the likeness of sinful flesh" (Rom. 8:3), faced the most severe temptations possible, and emerged as victor over Satan. It is what we normally refer to as Christ's *active* obedience.

In doing this, our Lord exposed Satan as a liar and a deceiver in his diabolical claim that obedience to the law was impossible. Furthermore, Christ's *active* obedience qualified Him to be (1) our example to follow in faithful, grace-empowered obedience and (2) our sinless sacrificial substitute at Calvary. In other words, only a sinlessly perfect being could be a perfect example and an atoning sacrifice. The work of being a sacrificial victim thus leads to the next aspect.

The second facet of Christ's life on earth was what we normally refer to as His *passive obedience*. This is the phase of His atoning ministry usually associated with our Lord's passion, that is, His suffering and death.

Furthermore, His intense suffering for sin commenced in what we could refer to as the decisive phase of His atoning work. These critical moments encompassed the sorrowing Savior's entrance into Gethsemane and were consummated when He proceeded onward to His death at Calvary. Thus for Christians, it is the cross of Christ that has been the focus of most of the discussions on the atonement.[5] And it is out of this that there have emerged a number of theories or models that seek to explain the reasons Christ had to die.

The Models or Theories of the Atonement

Space and focus on the issues of Christian assurance do not allow for an extended treatment of the various models of the atonement. But by way of introduction to their relevance for personal Christian assurance, the reader should know what the major classic types have been. The most influential are (a) ransom, (b) "Christus Victor," (c) penalty/substitution/satisfaction, (d) moral influence, (e) exemplarist, and (f) governmental (or rectoral). What follows will be a brief discussion of the key ideas embedded in their broader reach.[6]

First, we need to make two general observations about the various models. The first is that they all affirm the absolute necessity of the death of Christ for the salvation of sinners, even though they do differ in their emphases as to why this death was essential for human salvation. And the second observation reveals that the reasons given for the requirement of Christ's death fall into two broad categories, normally referred to as either subjective or objective.

The term *subjective* points to the effects that the death of Christ have been intended to make on the attitudes of those that God is seeking to save through His death. In other words, Christ is seeking to demonstrate His love through the sacrificial death of His Son so that we sinners will realize the horror of sin and be drawn to embrace the costly benefits of His love for us.

On the other hand, though not necessarily in conflict with the subjective goals, the *objective* terminology has reference to the way or manner in which the death of Christ reveals the varied aspects of God's character of love and how the demands of His holy love have been satisfied. In other words, the objective models or theories seek to reveal how God's attitudes, especially those arising from His holy nature, are satisfied as He goes about His work of saving sinners, while the subjective models are more concerned with demonstrating how God's redeeming acts change the attitudes and characters of the sinners being redeemed (hence sinners are the "subjects" of salvation, thus the term *subjective*).

We therefore suggest that since the two facets are absolutely necessary if God is to win the allegiance of alienated sinners, they are not ultimately in conflict with one another. But there is one possible exception to the harmony that normally exists between the respective thinkers who have advocated for one or the other of the two categories. And such disharmony rears up its ugly head when the advocates for any given model(s) deny the positive claims that the other models seek to make for the saving significance (or meaning) of Christ's death.

The reader, of course, needs to realize that we have reached a most important juncture in any discussion of the atonement. What has normally unfolded in the history of theological debate about the meaning of the death of Christ is that the subjective advocates have consciously chosen to stir the issue by strongly denying key aspects that the major objective model teaches. Thus we have effectively arrived at the essential core of the issue at stake when anybody seeks to define the redemptive significance, or meaning, of the death of Christ.

The advocates for the primary objective model strongly assert that the foundational reason for the death of Christ was so that He would bear the penalty for sin and thereby satisfy effectively the justice of God's holy love. Moreover, when they claim that His death as the sinner's substitute met the requirements of divine justice, it is then, and only then that God can justly be enabled to forgive sinners. At the very heart of this concept is the claim that God's acts of retributive justice reveal His love just as much as do His deeds of mercy. And unless His justice is satisfied, vindicated, or maintained, God will not fully be able to deal with the sin that alienates fallen humans from Him. The denials set forth by the advocates of the various subjective models normally have behind them the persistent claim that such an idea makes God look ruthlessly vengeful, much more intent on carving out His proverbial pound of flesh from sinners than He is in granting merciful pardon.

The defenders of the key objective model, normally designated as the penal/substitutionary/satisfaction theory, pointedly deny such a claim. They therefore suggest that God's satisfaction of His own inherent legal demands is an expression not so much of His wrath or revulsion against sin and sinners as it is the revelation of the costliness of His loving mercy. The death of Christ does not cause God to love sinners, but reveals His terribly expensive grace in such a way that the love of God's justice is not nullified when He offers a justice-conditioned mercy. And it is just such a mercy that properly enables Him to offer the merciful forgiveness of sins to convicted sinners. Once more, we must strongly emphasize that all of the positive reasons that the subjective advocates affirm for the death of Christ, the advocates of the key objective model also embrace.

Obviously the death of Christ reveals the multifaceted goals that God has to accomplish through the work of the sin-bearing Christ on the cross. The death of Christ does demonstrate God's love for sinners in such a way that will hopefully cause them to embrace both His view of sin and His offer of merciful forgiveness. Christ's death vindicates God's moral governance of the universe by demonstrating that His love and mercy will never lead Him to any act of injustice as He manages the affairs of His vast creation. The life and the death of Christ clearly indicate that mercy never nullifies justice, and that mercy never vilifies justice. Both Christ's life and death have shown that He was willing to pay an infinitely costly price to redeem sinners from the penalty for their transgressions of His law of love.

The key point being advocated here fervently affirms that all of the models, both subjective and objective, are absolutely essential to a full understanding of both the life and the death of Christ as uniquely saving events. Furthermore, such affirmations include the model normally associated with the ideas of penalty, substitution, and satisfaction. Now, while the reasons are too numerous to enumerate here, the penalty/substitution/satisfaction model best maintains the inherent balance of the justice and mercy of God's loving nature and character.

Not one Christian that I have ever dialogued with on the issues of the meaning of Christ's death has ever expressed any objection to the fact that God's love is merciful. But many Christians are uneasy with the idea that God's love involves the fulfillment of His justice. Therefore, we simply suggest that if divine justice is just as essential to divine love as is His mercy, both facets of God's nature and character are absolutely vital to a fuller understanding of God's redeeming and assuring love.

The last perspective that we would offer is that only the penal/substitutionary/satisfaction model seems to get at the profound depths of woe involved in the costliness of sin—especially as revealed in Christ's passion. For instance, was Christ just engaging in rhetorical flourishes when He cried out in utter dereliction, "My God, My God, why have You forsaken Me?" (Mark 15:34)? When He died on the cross, was that death, at least in principle, the one that all will suffer in hell if they refuse the offer of mercy generated by our Lord's substitutionary death? The utter horror of the unfolding scenes of Gethsemane and Calvary reveal an infinite love that bore the burden of an inconceivably costly suffering for our redemption. And in the face of such a stunningly expensive mercy, could any believer ever doubt the sustaining, assuring intent of the Godhead to do all that can possibly be done to see that trusting sinners will ultimately be saved in Christ's eternal kingdom?

Once again, we must acknowledge that we could say much more on the issues of the atonement. And for those interested in a more elaborated discussion, I refer you to George Knight's volume in the Library of Adventist Theology series entitled *The Cross of Christ: God's Work for Us* (Hagerstown, Md.: Review and Herald Pub. Assn., 2008).

But for now, please know that the life and death of Christ have provided the key provisions for the great and enduring salvation that Christ seeks to communicate to lost sinners. Moreover, in the light of the love unfolded in His active life and passive death, how can anyone continue to feel that God would willingly waste such an effort on the objects of His redeeming love?

Summation

If God is truly just in all of His demands for perfect obedience, the only way that Christ's death on the cross of Calvary can make sense is that ultimately it must be understood that the sins He died for were those of the whole human race imputed, or reckoned to Him (2 Cor. 5:21). And this imputation, or legal reckoning, of our sins to Christ makes perfect sense once we clearly grasp the fact that God's just demands are just as much an essential constituent of His redeeming love as is His principled, compassionate, loving mercy.

Again we need to emphasize that all of the atonement models are essentially correct in what they *affirm*. But the controversies and problems begin to multiply when the advocates for the subjective models tend to *deny* that the demand of God's justice must be satisfied by Christ's atoning death.

So what can we say about the death of Christ as an atonement for sin? While we acknowledge the vast majority of the positive points made by all the varied classic models or theories, it just seems to make the most sense, in the light of the scriptural revelation (especially the core meaning of the substitution and sacrifice so evident in the Old Testament sacrificial system) and the very forceful testimony of Ellen White,[7] to affirm the following:

While the death of Christ exhibited many things, it was more than just a demonstration. It was also a revelation of saving love, in which at Calvary God actually acted in such a way that He met or satisfied the just demands of His love. Furthermore, He accomplished it in such a profound way and manner that not only enabled Him to offer a merciful forgiveness to penitent sinners, but also prevented the justice of His merciful love from being compromised.

Therefore, when we view the atonement in this light, it reveals both the costliness of sin and the infinity of God's merciful love and thus exalts His saving grace. We can measure the tragedy of Calvary only in the framework of the infinite suffering and self-sacrifice of Christ and the rest of the atonement-making Trinity. Moreover, it raises a most sobering and relevant question: Has a more expensive love ever been demonstrated and carried out in the history of the universe?

I don't know about the reader, but as for myself I must confess that I have searched high and low in all the world of religion and philosophy, and I have yet to find anything that comes even remotely close to the poignantly personal and infinitely powerful intent to save the lost race unfolded at the cross!

But what does all of this suggest about our Christian assurance? In comments on Romans 5:7-11 and 8:38, 39, Adventist New Testament scholar Ivan Blazen has wonderfully portrayed the intimate relationship existing between what God has done to provide the benefits of Christ's *active* and *passive* obedience and our personal assurance of salvation:

God's love is "unlike" that of "human beings, who might be willing to give themselves for a good or righteous person (verse 7)." "Christ died for us while we were morally weak, ungodly sinners and enemies toward God (verses 6-8). The conclusion is that if God was willing to do the hardest thing—give His Son to die to justify or reconcile enemies—how much more will the risen Christ be willing to save His new friends from the ultimate wrath of God (verses 9, 10).

"Thus, believers can rejoice in their reconciliation (verse 11), for it promises glorification to come. As Romans 8 argues, absolutely nothing will be able to separate God's people from His love (verses 38, 39)." Therefore, it is clear that all that God has provided for our reconciliation "involves the reality of complete and lasting assurance."[8]

---

[1] And this includes the exercise of faith. Faith has simply no merit in itself. It has merit only in what it lays hold of: the righteousness of Christ: "Faith is the condition upon which God has seen fit to promise pardon to sinners; not that there is any virtue in faith whereby salvation is merited, but because faith can lay hold of the merits of Christ, the remedy provided for sin. Faith can present Christ's perfect obedience instead of the sinner's transgression and defection. When the sinner believes that Christ is his personal Savior . . . God pardons his sin and justifies him freely" (*Selected Messages* [Washington, D.C.: Review and Herald Pub. Assn., 1958], book 1, pp. 366, 367).

[2] I have drawn the concept of laying human "glory" and pride "in the dust" from the comments of Ellen G. White: "What is justification by faith? It is the work of God in laying the glory of man in the dust, and doing for man that which it is not in his power to do for himself" (originally published in 1897; most readily accessible in *Testimonies to Ministers and Gospel Workers* [Nampa, Idaho: Pacific Press Pub. Assn., 1962], p. 456).

[3] Comments made by Blazen in a camp meeting presentation at Union Springs, New York, during the summer of 1999, in which he claimed that he was developing a sermon entitled "All the 'Buts' of the Bible."

[4] A subsequent volume in the Library of Adventist Theology series will deal with the doctrine of God and the great controversy theme in more biblical detail.

[5] For a good introduction to the issues that swirl around the atonement, let me refer the reader to George Knight's first volume in this Library of Adventist Theology series, *The Cross of Christ: Salvation Provided* (Hagerstown, Md.: Review and Herald Pub. Assn., 2008). See also Woodrow Whidden, John Reeve, and Jerry Moon, *The Trinity* (Hagerstown, Md.: Review and Herald Pub. Assn., 2002), pp. 260-271.

[6] We have listed the various models in the rough chronological order in which they successively appeared in the history of Christian theology.

[7] For an excellent statement of Ellen White on the issues of the atonement, we recommend a careful reading of the chapters entitled "Calvary" and "It Is Finished" in the book *The Desire of Ages* (Mountain View, Calif.: Pacific Press Pub. Assn., 1898). For further samples of her thought on the broader aspects of the life and death of Christ, see Appendix C, entitled "The Atonement," in the book *Questions on Doctrine* (in either the original edition or the more recent "Annotated Edition," edited by George Knight, pp. 549-574, and also reproduced in volume 7A of the *Seventh-day Adventist Bible Commentary* (Washington, D.C.: Review and Herald Pub. Assn., 1970), pp. 457-692.

[8] Ivan Blazen, "Salvation," *Handbook of Seventh-day Adventist Theology*, ed. Raoul Dederen, Seventh-day Adventist Commentary Reference Series (Hagerstown, Md.: Review and Herald Pub. Assn., 2000), vol. 12, p. 289.

Chapter 4

Convicting, Converting, and Forgiving Grace

Introduction

As we resume our pilgrimage on the "Way of Salvation" and depart from sin's diagnostic clinic, we happily return for a renewing visit to God's "Love Inn." And in this beckoning refuge we begin exploring the healing care of Jesus and His loving benefits. Quite happily for us, He proves to be a most willing physician for our sin-sick souls. With deep concern He promptly administers His saving benefits, especially the very important first steps of the conviction of sin, regeneration, conversion, and the healing effects of forgiveness. They lead us to the initial steps absolutely necessary if Christ's healing benefits are to be effectually applied to our desperate cases.

Furthermore, they are essential for any realistic understanding that we can have not only the privilege of healing but the assurance that we will be enabled to stay healed! But first we need to pause for a brief overview of the benefits offered in the context of Christ's renewing work. Following an examination of the saving *provisions* and *benefits* of Christ's *active* and *passive* work, we will then turn our attention to the dynamics of how the Trinity actually *communicates* such *provisions*.

Brief Review of the Unfolding Provisions and Benefits of Christ

After His incarnation and self-sacrificing life and death, Jesus was resurrected or "raised because of our justification" (Rom. 4:25). The resurrection of Christ was the Father's vindicating approval of the completeness and perfection of the atoning benefits generated during the incarnation. Soon after His resurrection there followed the ascension to heaven and His installation as our "Advocate with the Father" (1 John 2:1) in the heavenly sanctuary. As the newly installed king and high priest of the kingdom of grace, Christ made the heavenly sanctuary the central nerve center from

64

reconciling atonement = intercession

which He now communicates His saving *benefits* to earth's lost inhabitants. And it is this phase of reconciling atonement that we refer to as Christ's intercession in heaven.

Moreover, such an understanding has led Seventh-day Adventists to the studied conviction that this vital aspect of Christ's work of atonement is just as essential to the salvation plan as was His earthly obedience. So how then does Christ work to communicate or apply the benefits of His atonement to lost sinners?

The Basic Steps of Atonement and the Communication of Benefits

Christ resolutely begins by seeking to raise the consciousness of each individual sinner as to the utterly serious nature of the results of the bad news uncovered during the sinner's initial visit to heaven's diagnostic clinic. The work of calling, convincing, or convicting grace can commence only if the spiritual patient realizes the gravity of his or her situation. Without the "bad news" of convicting grace there will be no true heart appreciation of the "good news" that Christ has benefits appropriate for the healing prognosis (plan of healing) that He is about to lay before the sin-sick soul.

Theologians refer to the initial phase of healing grace as "prevenient," or "preventing," grace. These two somewhat odd-sounding words[1] derive from the Latin prefix *"pre"* (before) and *"venio"* (to come). In other words, this work includes the grace that comes before sinners even realize how deathly ill they are and what God's love has to offer for the healing of their pitiful, helpless condition.

To express it in more simple terms, "convicting" grace seeks to "convince" sinners of their desperate need of God's undeserved yet sovereign love for them (in spite of the sin-sodden mess that they are). This is primarily the work of the Holy Spirit, as Jesus explained in His great discourse found in John 14-16. We could sum up the gist of the whole redemptive movement with Jesus' words: "And when He has come, He will convict the world of sin, and of righteousness, and of judgment" (John 16:8).

We could say much more about this particular grace of God, but the key point is that the more immediate fruit of "convincing grace" is that it imparts genuine repentance for sin and a deep, heartfelt appreciation of God's undeserved, loving benefits. The very heart of the work of repentance is to instill genuine sorrow for sin: not just for its results, but for the sin itself. Thus with the beginnings of the work of repentance we have arrived at the very heart of the meaning of convincing grace. In actual fact, repentance forms the very core of the regenerating, converting process that leads to the "new birth" (John 3:3, 5-8; cf. Rom. 2:4).

Quite possibly the simplest way to lay out the dynamics of the process is the following: according to Acts 3:19, "repentance" is the very engine of conversion, and it is the converting work of the Holy Spirit that effects the new birth in the hearts of the helpless but now willingly responsive believers. And when any believer consciously chooses (wills) to cast his or her trusting faith on Christ, it is good evidence that the new birth has, in fact, transpired.

As many have noted, sinners are not always fully aware of precisely what it is that has been taking place in them during the "new birthing" process. In some ways it is similar to that of young children who only later become aware that they have been previously begotten and birthed by their earthly parents. So it is in the aftermath of spiritual new-birthing that the children of God will also subsequently become more directly conscious that they have been dealt with in a redemptive manner. And it is then that they reach the critical moment when they are enabled (by grace alone) either to reject the work of God's grace or to cast their helpless selves on Christ for new life and redemption. The Spirit has gifted them with a "freed will" so that they can choose to be "freed" from the guilt and power of sin. While we must not be overly dogmatic about the apparent details of the whole process, it does seem that the best summary description unfolds along the following lines.

Using key New Testament terminology, the word "regeneration" seems to describe all that God does by the Spirit to lead to conversion. As for conversion, it is the change of heart that results when the sinner is convinced of sin and the fact that God loves him or her in spite of that sin. And when conversion has taken place, the new birth can be said to have delivered a new child of God. The new birth effectively brings newly begotten believers to the place at which they are enabled to claim the blessings of initial forgiveness and the first conscious experiences of character change (sanctification). Moreover, all that takes place subsequently continues the process of regeneration, resulting in a fruitful, ongoing "life in the Spirit."

Furthermore, the "regenerative" life in the Spirit includes the process of the ongoing conviction of sin, forgiveness, and the experience of sanctification that manifests dynamic growth in grace. When initial conversion leads to the new birth and forgiveness (all through the witness and power of the Spirit), the newly begotten soul has become fully aware that he or she is truly an adopted child of God. Once again, we must make it clear that this analysis is not meant to be dogmatic in the use of these important terms, but only an attempt to frame or reflect the biblical understanding of how one can make the best sense out of the "Way (or Order) of Salvation."

Furthermore, when believers choose to exercise a conscious faith in Christ, they willingly confess their great need and gratitude by acknowledging both their sinfulness of nature as well as their acts of sin. Such confession of sin and gratitude to God thus emerges as one of the most telling, genuine signs that a real change has not only taken place but is also continually occurring. Genuine, saving repentance always manifests a strong sorrow for sin, the prompt confession of it, and ultimately its forceful renunciation. Such reactions thus become the dominant forces in the new life of faith. And when this initial, powerful work reaches an appropriate stage or maturity, God, for Christ's sake, justifies the believing, trusting individual and declares him or her accepted and forgiven.

The Assurance Implications of Convincing and Converting Grace

One of the first things that emerges from the whole conversion process is that it is so filled with the gentle, yet persistent drawings of the personal Holy Spirit, and a deep individual responsiveness on the part of the newly birthed disciple of Jesus. The new child of God is therefore open to claim by faith all of the graces that God is so abundantly offering. And in the light of such saving influences, we can reach some firm conclusions regarding assurance.

If the Spirit has so personally and persistently led sinners to choose to embark on the "Way of Salvation," then should not every believer also have great confidence that Christ, through the Spirit, will keep faith with them all through the rest of their journey to heaven? If God is for and with us at the very beginning, can we not conclude that He will also be with us all the rest of the way?

Furthermore, the whole process of prevenient grace has a distinctively sovereign quality about it: the Spirit comes seeking us out, whether we want Him to or not. But while this work is sovereign, even persistent, it is never irresistibly deterministic! While Christ, through the Spirit, will repeatedly knock at the heart's door, He will never kick the door in. And we can thus conclude that if the Spirit so unilaterally and persistently pursues us, will He not also do the same to communicate a sense of God's assuring love? This latter is undoubtedly just as much a fruit of the sanctifying work of the Holy Spirit as are calling and conversion. Clearly this is a process of assuring grace, from beginning to end.

We will have more to say in the next chapter about the role of the sanctifying power of the Holy Spirit in the daily life of the converted believer. But before turning to that issue and its relationship to assurance, we need to give additional attention to the blessings of justification and its implications for assurance. Surely when God converts, He also forgives and justifies believers when they accept the benefit. The moment of genuine conversion is also that of a new legal standing with God. The person has moved by faith and God's grace from a state of condemnation to one of no condemnation.

Justification and Assurance

If what we have said about the sovereignty of converting grace is true, we can affirm even more about the sovereign grace that grants justification or divine forgiveness. If it was grace alone that awakened us and drew us to Christ in conversion, it is even more true of the blessings of justification by grace through faith alone. It is one of the most radical of the saving benefits that Christ offers to responsive, trusting believers. Moreover, we must keep in mind that when we employ the word *sovereign* we mean that which solely comes from the redemptive initiatives of God, not through any of the initial efforts and motivations of struggling sinners. All human actions are in response to God's convincing, awakening grace. So what can we conclude about justification and its impact on the Christian believer's personal assurance of salvation?

First of all, we need to remind ourselves that forgiveness is the very first conscious gift that Christ offers to the sin-convicted, awakened, and soon to be converted sinners. Surely we have here one of the most amazing aspects of God's loving grace: that unworthy though sinners are, God still offers to cleanse their sin-marred slates through the forgiveness of their past sins, and in so doing He grants a completely new legal standing before the demands of His justice. Thus, when any penitent sinner is moved to willingly claim (by faith) the justifying, forgiving benefits of Christ, he or she, for Christ's sake, stands fully forgiven and legally declared, or reckoned, to be just, solely for the sake of the doing and dying of Christ. Therefore justifying grace is totally unmerited by any sinful human being and is purely a gift of God that leads to eternal life (Rom. 6:23).

Furthermore, the reason that we describe justification as totally unmerited and received by faith alone is to make the point that nothing involved with human obedience has brought about our new status before God. It is only the doing and dying of Christ "alone" that has been reckoned or accounted to cover the penitent believer's previous life record (Eph. 2:8, 9; Gal. 3:13, 14). Additionally, our new legal standing brings about all of the heart-felt joys that ultimately emerge from such an experience: "Therefore, having been justified by faith, we have peace with God through our Lord Jesus Christ . . . and rejoice in hope of the glory of God" (Rom. 5:1, 2). But there are still other benefits of justifying grace.

Not only are penitent sinners freed from the guilt of the past sins of their pre-Christian life (cast "into the depths of the sea" [Micah 7:19] or "behind" His "back" [Isa. 38:17], even "blotted out, like a thick cloud" [Isa. 44:22; cf. 43:25 and Acts 3:19]), but the new believer is now, moment by moment, being accounted as perfect for Christ's sake. Here is a truth most clearly brought out in 1 John 1:8-2:2, especially the consoling words that "if anyone sins, we have an Advocate with the Father, Jesus Christ the righteous. And He Himself is the propitiation for our sins, and not for ours only but also for the whole world" (1 John 2:1, 2).

Very much in the same reassuring vein are the powerful words of Hebrews 7:25: "Therefore He [Christ] is also able to save to the uttermost those who come to God through Him, since He always lives to make intercession for them." George Knight makes the bold claim that this verse contains "the greatest truth in Hebrews." Because of Christ's "permanent priesthood," "He is able to save fully and completely those coming to God through Him, because He continually lives to intercede for them."[2] Thus when God looks at believing sinners who are just beginning to grow in grace, He sees not their immature defects of character, but only the spotless purity of the active and passive obedience of Christ that is being moment by moment reckoned as theirs.

Ellen G. White echoes these profound and comforting teachings of Scripture as she expresses the truth of the continual, justifying intercession of Christ in the following words:

"When He [Christ] sees men lifting the burdens, trying to carry them in lowliness of mind, with distrust of self and with reliance upon Him," the sinner's "defects are covered by the perfection and fullness of the Lord our Righteousness." Such a justified believer is "looked upon by the Father with pitying, tender love; He regards such as obedient children, and the righteousness of Christ is imputed unto them."[3] In another statement that speaks of the lingering effects of sin, even in the experience of believers, she claims that such trusting, penitent persons have their "unavoidable deficiencies" legally made up for them by the "imputed" righteousness of Christ.[4]

But probably we find her most radical expression of the concept of the ongoing reckoning of the "true believer" as legally just before God in her understanding of Christ as the believer's constantly interceding Advocate with the Father in the heavenly sanctuary. Carefully note how she unfolds this comforting and assuring concept:

"A daily and yearly typical atonement is no longer to be made, but the atoning sacrifice through a mediator is essential because of the constant commission of sin. Jesus is officiating in the presence of God, offering up His shed blood, as it had been a lamb slain. Jesus presents the oblation offered for every offense and every shortcoming of the sinner."

One paragraph later, Ellen White waxes even more profound in her teachings about Christ's intercession for "true believers":

"The religious services, the prayers, the praise, the penitent confession of sin ascend from true believers as incense to the heavenly sanctuary, but passing through the corrupt channels of humanity, they are so defiled that unless purified by blood, they can never be of value with God. They ascend not in spotless purity, and unless the Intercessor, who is at God's right hand, presents and purifies all by His righteousness, it is not acceptable to God. All incense from earthly tabernacles must be moist with the cleansing drops of the blood of Christ. He holds before the Father the censer of His own merits, in which there is no taint of earthly corruption. He gathers into this censer the prayers, the praise, and the confessions of His people, and with these He puts His own spotless righteousness. Then, perfumed with the merits of Christ's propitiation, the incense comes up before God wholly and entirely acceptable. Then gracious answers are returned.

"Oh, that all may see that everything in obedience, in penitence, in praise and thanksgiving, must be placed upon the glowing fire of the righteousness of Christ. The fragrance of this righteousness ascends like a cloud around the mercy seat."[5]

The implications for this understanding of justification are comforting beyond our fondest hopes and spiritual aspirations! The stunning implication is that not only do our sins need to be atoned for, but even our best works, which are the genuine "fruit" of the working of the Holy Spirit, also must be justified through the perfuming "merits of Christ's propitiation" that He constantly mediates in the heavenly sanctuary.

Thus, by way of summary, we can affirm that both the Bible and Ellen White teach that the justifying grace of God not only covers (1) the sins of the past, pre-Christian life, (2) the ongoing sins repented of by growing Christians (Rom. 3:21-25), but also (3) that Jesus as intercessor is always making up for the "unavoidable deficiencies" of "true believers." Moreover, Ellen White simply cannot leave it at that. She also explicitly makes the claim that (4) even the best things that emerge from "true believers," including their prayers, praise, penitence, and the Holy Spirit-induced fruits of genuine obedience (the precious "incense" arising from "earthly tabernacles"), are all in need of the cleansing effects of the justifying "drops of the blood of Christ." Amazingly, even the very best things that those filled with the Spirit of God will manifest as the "fruit of the Spirit" are also in need of God's justifying grace!

The radical nature of the "by faith alone" concept must surely lay in the dust any lingering thoughts of self-glorification of even the most sanctified of "true believers." Furthermore, for those who have trained their hearts and minds to focus on Christ as their mediating intercessor, there are profound implications for genuine Christian assurance.

Justification by Faith Alone and Christian Assurance

Most definitely, if Christ is atoning for the "unavoidable deficiencies" that cling to even the most precious fruit of the Spirit produced in "true believers," He can also, in all of these graces (for all cases), steadily lead His humble and trusting children through to glorification. Because of such an effective and constant advocate, mediator, and intercessor, a genuine child of God has no reason ever to give into despair and distrust. Quite obviously, when we place justification by faith alone in the context of Christ's high-priestly intercession in the heavenly sanctuary, the implications of assurance for believers are powerful. In fact, we will later argue that such a concept should even become the default key for the faith of believers when spiritual failure has ravaged their assurance and a sense of profound condemnation seems to be descending from the judgment bar of God.

Yet in the face of all such good news, the reader needs to be aware that many sincere believers regard such glorious blessings with great suspicion. Such individuals often sense the scent of "cheap grace" and the dreaded aromas of presumption and lawlessness. Furthermore, the writer is well aware of such sobering concerns and how some can distort the gospel of justification by grace through faith alone. Yet the truth of the matter is largely determined by the quality of the believer's faith. And if such a faith is truly genuine, we will see that fact demonstrated by a life overflowing with obedience to all of God's requirements.

Most assuredly, then, the solution to any lurking threats of "cheap grace" will emerge from a careful exposition of the right relationship that converting and justifying grace has with transforming (sanctifying) grace and how such a relationship will lead to Christian perfection (both character growth in the present life and glorification at the Second Coming).

Summation

God's regenerating grace produces personal conviction of sin and assures the repentant individual of God's goodness and mercy. And when one fully embraces and receives such convictions, conversion, or the new birth, will be the inevitable result. Genuine conversion's sure accompaniments will include (a) forgiveness of sins, (b) a new legal standing that declares the believer to be perfect for the sake of Christ's justifying merits, and (c) the beginnings of a life of character transformation (sanctification).

Furthermore, God's avid pursuit of sinners assures them that He who first sought them while they were still in sin, will also be the Christ who will continue to convince them of their sin and assuredly lead them by His Spirit all the way to the everlasting kingdom. We must never forget that the One who constantly leads to ongoing conviction of sin is the very same Jesus who, through His intercession, will constantly reckon them to be legally perfect, even from the very first moment of their claiming faith to the momentous moment of glorification.

With these thoughts kept steadily before the eyes of faith, the time has now arrived to give careful consideration to the various facets of transforming grace and their vital contributions to Christian assurance. And it is to these delicate issues that we now turn.

---

[1] Is God trying "to prevent" anybody from being saved? Of course not! See the ensuing definition.

[2] George Knight, *Exploring Hebrews: A Devotional Commentary* (Hagerstown, Md.: Review and Herald Pub. Assn., 2003), p. 124.

[3] Ellen G. White, *In Heavenly Places* (Hagerstown, Md.: Review and Herald Pub. Assn., 1967), p. 23.

[4] Ellen G. White, *Selected Messages* (Washington, D.C.: Review and Herald Pub. Assn., 1980), book 3, p. 196.

[5] *Ibid.*, book 1, p. 344.

Chapter 5

Regeneration, Justification, Sanctification, Perfection, and Personal Assurance

In a Seventh-day Adventist context, probably no three subjects have the potential to stir up more anxiety relative to the believer's personal assurance of salvation than the investigative judgment, sanctification, and perfection. Too many believe that only when someone becomes sinlessly perfect in character can they be ready to face the excruciatingly detailed searching of the pre-Advent investigative judgment. And of course there always looms the thought *Woe be to anyone who shows up with any spots on their garments!*

What, then, is the proper connection between the assurance of salvation, the theme of perfecting grace, and the investigative judgment? This chapter seeks to explore the appropriate relationship between conversion, forgiveness, and sanctification. As we do so, we will note any implications for assurance. Then in the following chapter we will focus more particularly on the issue of perfection. And finally, in the last two chapters of this book, we will return to an exploration of the connection between character change, the judgment, and Christian assurance.

We are now at the point in our pilgrimage on the "Way of Salvation," or the highway to heaven, at which we need to move out from the healing confines of God's comforting "Love Inn" and commence a new phase of Christian experience that will unfold amid the shifting twists and turns on the way to the kingdom. The healing imparted at the "Love Inn" has given us a significant change of attitude toward sin and grace and has placed us upon the solid footings of justification by faith alone. Armed with these special graces and the sensitive perspectives that they engender, we are now prepared to advance, in the power of the Holy Spirit, to a dynamic life of growth in character change and greater usefulness in God's service.

But first we need to examine the proper relationship existing between the blessings already received and those yet to come. And it is to those considerations that we now turn as we seek to get a handle on the theme of "union with Christ by faith." It will provide us with valuable insights as to how the earlier way stops of regeneration, conversion, and justification prepare the way for a richer understanding of sanctification by faith and Christian assurance.

Union With Christ by Faith

As previously hinted at in our discussions about conversion, justification, and the early experience of sanctification, an intimate connection exists between these various aspects of Christian experience. Furthermore, we suggest that we can best grasp those linkages within the biblical theme of the union of the believer with Christ by faith. Within the parameters of this theme we will explore the legitimate relationship that should exist between the dynamics of converting, justifying, regenerating, and sanctifying grace.

In fact, this overarching theme, though prominent in the writings of John and Paul, is one of the most neglected and misunderstood concepts in Christian thought. And not only do misconceptions abound in biblical interpretation—we also find them manifested in the traditional teachings of Protestant theologians. Thus, what follows is a summary of the key concepts contained or enfolded in this strategically important concept.

When the sinner begins to feel the convicting and drawing power of the Holy Spirit in the heart, it is really the work of Christ drawing the lost one to Himself. The Spirit of Christ (in other words, the person of the Holy Spirit) utilizes the benefits of Christ's life, death, and resurrection as He seeks to reconcile and unite the needy person to Christ. And when the convicted one responds with trusting faith in Christ, then our Savior begins to impute and impart the blessings of His grace to the penitent and responsive sinner.

But as we carefully and prayerfully explore the concept, we must never forget that we have defined conversion as including the whole process that leads to the new birth and justification. What then normally emerges in the experience of conversion and the new birth is a life of dynamic, active cooperation with the Holy Spirit. Moreover, this life in the Spirit includes the early stages of the guiding and transformative work that we normally

74

call sanctification, a phase of the process that we have defined as regeneration. But what are the appropriate interrelationships among all of these varied benefits of grace?

Perhaps we should approach the topic in the following way: while a certain logical sequence plays out between God's love as manifested in the conviction of sin, penitence, confession, new birth, justification, sanctification, perfection, and glorification, there is also a sense in which all of these blessings come in one complete, total package. Thus, when a penitent sinner receives Jesus by faith, the Savior comes to the needy convert as the sole source of all His varied, saving *benefits*. Faith in Christ is a "package" deal: you receive Him by faith, and in doing so you get all the benefits of His grace.

It is not so much that someone becomes converted because he or she has simply undergone repentance, or that the believer experiences justification because of conversion, or that justification causes sanctification, or that sanctification produces perfection and perfection glorification. Rather, it is just that all of these blessings are but different *facets* of the total package that we refer to as the redemptive grace of Christ. Thus when the penitent sinner accepts Christ as Savior from the guilt of sin, that same trusting person also receives Him as transforming Lord of their new life in Christ.

When any child enters a normal family, it is his or her privilege to receive all of the benefits of family membership. It is not that the newly minted parents begin to say to themselves, "Well, if this kid will just learn to drink milk, then we will give him or her the privilege of eating some cottage cheese loaf and mashed potatoes." Or "if he or she will do well in elementary school, then we will send him or her to the best academy and college that Adventism has to offer."

Quite obviously, the dreams of most caring parents include not just kindergarten and elementary school, but that the newly minted child will eventually receive all of the education needed for a successful life—vocationally, socially, and spiritually. And so it is with Christ when any newly converted believer is united to Him by genuine faith: all of the blessings come with the package!

Consider a medical or healing analogy. Normally, when a person gets sick and comes under the care of a physician, a good medical practitioner will begin by surveying the whole physical and mental status of the patient. Sometimes, that will include emergency treatment of the most obviously serious symptoms. Usually, however, when physicians have dealt with the most threatening symptoms, they will then search for the root causes of the key syndromes in order to prescribe a broad course of treatment. It is just good, sensible wholistic medicine being exercised to bring about the full restoration of mind and body.

And so it is with Christ, the Great Physician. When people are drawn to Him and place their sin-sick souls in the care of His healing ministry, He commences a most comprehensive course of spiritual and moral restoration.

Obviously, the first thing that Christ has to do is to get our attention so that we fully realize that He truly does love us and that He understands what our needs are. And it is then that His convicting grace draws us to Himself so that He can lift even the most terrible burdens from our flagging spiritual shoulders. Certainly, not much will take place until He has performed those initial steps.

Thus, in a most practical way, sinners are not going to be able to walk with Christ in the experience of transforming grace until He has lifted the load of guilt and meaninglessness from the backs of each needy, newly begotten child of God. Therefore, it just makes sense that justification, or the forgiveness of sin, is one of the essential initial benefits that the responsive and dependent soul needs to experience.

While, however, the experience of justification prepares the way for the transformative grace of sanctification (which will lead to genuine Christian perfection), we cannot necessarily say that justification causes sanctification. Only Christ, the newly installed merciful and loving heavenly "caregiver" (parent, physician, or whatever image that appeals to you), causes forgiveness and character change to take place. And when the believer responds by faith, then Christ becomes Lord of every aspect of their life. It just therefore makes sense that our Lord wisely commences a comprehensive, all-out campaign to bring into play the full range of the *benefits* of His atoning, reconciling grace.

Now, the reason we make such a strong wholistic emphasis is that it best reflects the overall thrust of Scripture. Both the Old and New Testaments provide abundant evidence that this way or manner is how Christ and His Spirit deal with any needy person. And while the basic sequences are quite similar, God seems to adapt to the specific requirements of each individual.

For instance, I have never had much of a problem with meaninglessness or lack of spiritual direction in my life. I have, however, been endowed with an extremely sensitive conscience. Therefore, when I began to mature and come to a more sober realization of my particular needs (besetting sins), the knowledge that Christ was my constantly justifying advocate with the Father especially comforted my guilt-ridden soul. As I have continued to grow in grace, however, I have had a much more appreciative experience with Christ's persistent and effectual grace that not only has delivered me from the guilt, but also has been progressively freeing me from the power of the sins that constantly beleaguer me (including my most persistently taunting and unlovely character traits).

Furthermore, while the knowledge of merciful forgiveness has greatly contributed to my receptiveness to all of Christ's saving benefits, it is not necessarily true that I experienced sanctification because of justification. No, that is not how it works. I experienced sanctification because I received Christ as my personal Savior and in so doing I accepted Him in all of His complementary *offices* or *benefits*. I might not have been aware of all that He had in store for me, but I have come to realize that what He has always intended for me was a complete package of redemptive blessings.

What follows in the balance of this chapter and the next is the key to our understanding of the more subjective work of Christ in the soul. And when we receive Christ, it is not our option to pick and choose what particular benefits we will allow Him to bring into the mix of our spiritual growth. Since Jesus is now Lord, He has become king of the entirety of our lives. And when He has established His rulership, it is then that we begin to yield to what His Lordship benevolently offers. It is like getting married. When anyone unites with that specially chosen "significant other," it is not just about all the privileged joys of the bed, but it is also about the blessings of sharing the challenges of raising the bundles of joy that have resulted from the privileges of the bed. O, maybe it is possible to establish the same principle by reversing the metaphor of the marriage relationship (even standing it on its head).

When we "get married" to Jesus, His role as the bridegroom in our lives demands a certain level of exclusiveness. Should a potential spouse announce the night before the wedding that he or she is going to bring all of their old flames along on the honeymoon and that they are all going to share the nuptial bed, it will surely trigger indignation and dismay in the stunned groom or bride-to-be. And thus will it be with our faith-marriage, or union, with Christ. When we unite with Him, we agree to leave all of the old passions and loyalties of the flesh behind and give ourselves completely over to all of the blessings of our new, exclusive relationship with His gracious Lordship. Either He is exclusive Lord of all our desires and affections, or He can be Lord of none! It is just that simple.

A Real Christian Character Portrait

With the key perspectives of the previous section clearly in mind, we need to begin to explore more carefully the relationship between the dynamics of converting, justifying, and transforming grace (sanctification, perfection), and the great investigative judgment. And the best way to do this is to answer the following question: What should a "saved" Christian look like?

The basic answer is that such Christians will manifest telling characteristics that the character-changing power of God's grace (which we normally refer to as sanctification by faith in Christ) has been consistently transforming them.

While we will treat this subject in greater detail in the next chapter, we want to make some preliminary suggestions to make clear that truly saved and assured Christians are those who love and practice obedience to God's revealed will. Thus, their testimony is not just some verbal celebration of salvation but includes a life of faithful obedience and service.

The parable of Jesus regarding the contrasting houses built on the sand and the rock affirms the virtue of the man who constructed his house upon the rock. He "does the will of My Father in heaven" while Jesus censures the "sand" house builder who "practices lawlessness" (Matt. 7:21, 23).

The apostle Paul (often appealed to for alleged evidence that faith does away with the law) even makes the astounding statement that "not the hearers of the law are just in the sight of God, but the doers of the law will be justified." Later on he asks if "faith" "[makes] void the law"? With bold directness he hastens to say that such is "certainly not" the case; to the "contrary," "we establish the law" (Rom. 2:13 and 3:31). Elsewhere he declares that "what the law could not do in that it was weak through the flesh, God did by sending His own Son in the likeness of sinful flesh, on account of sin: He condemned sin in the flesh, that the righteous requirement of the law might be fulfilled in us who do not walk according to the flesh but according to the Spirit" (Rom. 8:3, 4). Thus, Paul is not in any way at variance with James when it comes to the simple fact that those who have true faith will evidence this fact by obedience to the law of God, including the Ten Commandments (James 2:8-24).

And finally there are the familiar words of the apostle John, who said that those who claim to believe "that Jesus is the Christ" and "is born of God" will be known by their love for God, one clearly evidenced by the doing of "His commandments" (1 John 5:1-3). John makes it unmistakably plain that such a person is filled with "the love of God" and that their love will lead to the keeping of "His commandments." Furthermore, he declares that "His commandments are not burdensome" (verses 1-3). Need

78

I remind the reader that this same John was shown in vision God's end-time people to be those "who keep the commandments of God and the faith of Jesus" (Rev. 14:12; cf. Rev. 12:17).

It is an indisputable fact that the Bible envisions a people who exercise the faith of Jesus, and their faith in Him will lead them to be command-keeping disciples whose lives of obedience will match their profession of faith and love, the fruit of the sanctifying grace of God. Yet the reader is probably wondering, "What is the purpose for the sanctified obedience of God's professed people?" And it seems that the best answer to this important question emerges when we clarify what sanctification is and why it is that God subjects His believing followers to the transformative discipline of grace-induced obedience.

So What Is Sanctification?

Sanctification is what Christ does in the minds and hearts of all true believers to transform their characters. It changes them so that instead of harboring the attitudes and habits of sin (selfishness and rebellion), they begin to manifest such virtues as unselfishness and loyalty to God. And those virtues result in lives filled with habitual obedience to the known will of God. It is the work of the Holy Spirit, who produces an abundance of spiritual fruit.

Furthermore, it leads to a radical change in the mental attitudes of Christ's followers. Service then becomes joyous, and obedience to God, along with witness to others, will emerge as the hallmarks of all that they do and say.

The process of character change, while it has a definite beginning point in conversion, is not just the experience of a moment, or a day, but the privilege of a lifetime. Both the Bible and Ellen White make it abundantly evident that there is no such thing as "instantaneous" sanctification. Repeatedly, inspiration declares that sanctification is the "work of a lifetime," not just the raptures of a fleeting moment, a point that Paul makes clear in Philippians 3:12-15. The apostle's imagery is that of a patient distance runner who steadily presses "toward the goal for the prize of the upward call of God in Christ Jesus," with the ultimate objective of being spiritually mature ("perfect" in the KJV) like Christ (verse 15).

Why Is Sanctification a Drawn-out Experience, Not Instantaneous?

Many may wonder why it is that God does not just instantaneously sanctify, or perfect, us. Most likely the major reason for His more gradual, or protracted, strategy is so that believers will be led naturally and habitually to learn to trust Christ in all of the vicissitudes of their pilgrimage to the kingdom. After all, the entire sweep of Christian experience features an intensely personal love relationship. And most of us have come to sense that the best love-matches are those nurtured during a significant period of dedicated, quality time. It just seems obvious that most quick affairs of the heart do not feature long-haul, staying power.

Thus, undergirded by the justifying assurances of the Word of God, the newly minted disciple settles in for a gradual and persisting relationship of give and take. Christ steadily leads His followers to give their all to Him in successive phases of surrender, service, and gradual growth. He constantly imparts the blessings of His Holy Spirit so that believers come to a settled and steady responsiveness to God's ways and will.

But we need to consider additional important questions. For instance, what are the purposes and goals of sanctifying grace, and what does it mean when Christians claim that sanctification leads to a state of spiritual and moral maturity called "Christian perfection"? Perhaps the best way to answer such questions is to fill out a fuller portrait of sanctification's effects, purposes, and goals.

Why Does God Sanctify His Disciples?

First, we need to make clear what sanctification is *not*. It is not the purpose or the goal of sanctification to make sinners good enough to be justified. Scripture and Ellen White both explicitly testify that we are not justified when we become good enough in character. On the contrary, the only foundation from which anyone can launch into a fruitful program of developing character maturity is the solid, legal platform of divine justification. The only ones who will become good in character are those first forgiven and accepted for Christ's sake through His imputed righteousness—all bestowed by faith alone! Hence, sanctification is not some attempt to gain merit for the purposes of acceptance with God. Therefore, if sanctification is not to make us good enough to be justified, what then are its legitimate roles in the life of the true believer?

Maybe we should pose the question in an even more graphic manner: if transforming grace is not for the purposes of producing justifying merit, why then does God seek to make His followers holy and righteous? Or to state it another way, if the faithful people of God are justified only by the imputed merits of Christ, why then does God have a judgment according to their works that examines both their good and their bad acts?

The short answer to the latter question is that God will have a judgment according to works so that He can vindicate us (and His decision to justify us) by revealing to the entire, intelligent universe that our faith in His imputed merits was genuine. Furthermore, it will become evident that our spiritual fruit was the sure result of the Spirit's work in our lives. It will thus be made apparent to all that it was not just some "fake fruit."[1]

Yet it seems that God also has a number of other providential reasons for our experience of learning to walk with Him in the sanctified life, something often referred to as "life in the Spirit." And within the dynamics of such new life in graced obedience, the relationship of sanctification to the true believer's emerging experience of assurance more clearly unfolds.

The Six Key Reasons for the Experience of Sanctification and Perfection

Reason 1: The believer should submit to the process, or discipline, of transforming grace for the simple reason that God commands it: "For this is the will of God, your sanctification" (1 Thess. 4:3). We urge the reader to contemplate the context of this verse's simple command to experience sanctification. The essential point unfolds as it accents new life in Christ through obedience to the "commandments" of the Lord Jesus.

Reason 2: God wants to teach His people about the source of true happiness and joy in life. One of the initial fruits of love is "joy" (Gal. 5:22). What Paul refers to here is the deep satisfaction that comes to believers from the knowledge that they are accepted and continually sustained by grace as they grow in the richness of God's will and ways. In fact, the Greek words for "grace" and "joy" come from the same root: "grace" is *charis* and "joy" is *chara*. Now, all such "fruit" of the Spirit stands in stark contrast with the "works of the flesh" (verses 19-21).

The simple truth of any genuine Christian's experience is that the true depths of joy and happiness spring from the sanctified life, not from any supposed "fleshly" pleasures of sin for a proverbial season of selfish gratification. John Wesley, the greatest exponent of sanctifying grace in the eighteenth century, repeatedly declared that "holiness is happiness!" Therefore, while the pleasures of sin are the natural inheritance of our fallen, corrupt natures, their rewards are not all they are cracked up to be. If one will be responsive to God, the patiently acquired tastes of transforming grace will ultimately impart a life of the truest and most lasting joys and pleasures.

Reason 3 has to do with another deep pleasure that only those who know transforming grace can truly grasp. It involves the privileges of being an effective servant of God through the exercise of particular spiritual gifts (or even just one). We will further elaborate this witness and service aspect of sanctification in a later chapter devoted to life in the Spirit. But at this juncture, suffice it to say that one of the key characteristics of the Spirit-filled servants of God is their sense of assurance in God's love. It is quite evident that there exists a law of the mind that states that the greater one's service to God is, the greater will be such a believer's confidence in His love.

Reason 4 deals with the fact that our experience of character growth has been designed to bring greater glory to God. Beyond all other believing Christians, Seventh-day Adventists should be foremost in seeking to live for the glory of their great Creator/Redeemer and vindicating Judge. Certainly those who profess to be fulfilling the first angel's message of Revelation 14:6 and 7 (including the command to "Fear God and give glory to Him") should be leading the way in their concern to glorify their great God and King! We will return to this aspect in a later chapter when we will more carefully reflect on the perfection experience of the last-day saints. This issue has certainly both haunted and challenged Seventh-day Adventists for more than 160 years. And if for no other reason than its enduring presence in the Adventist mind-set, it does deserve some solid answers to the persistent questions it has generated. But for right now it is enough to suggest that it is one of the privileges of the sanctified, visible servants of God to honor and glorify Him in all that they do and say (1 Cor. 6:20 and 10:31).

Once again, I assure the reader that we will return to the question of the providential purposes of God's last-day followers and their perfection experience. But before we do that, we need to make one more highly practical point regarding living perfectly for the glory of God.

One of the most faith-affirming exercises that any sanctified Christian can engage in is to be living (even unconsciously) in such a manner that they are bringing glory to God in all of their words and acts and even their facial expressions and bodily postures. To live in such a way is to be reminded of how much we owe to God's abundant grace. It is truly a lifestyle that begets a rich sense of usefulness and the growing realization of the goodness of the glorious God we serve and worship.

Reason 5 is one of the most subtle yet profoundly obvious factors as to why God grants believers the discipline of transforming grace. Quite possibly our Lutheran friends most clearly articulate it: "Sanctification helps us to appreciate the privileges of our justification!" For Seventh-day

Adventists the core ideas undergirding this explanation for the necessity of the experience of sanctifying grace are a variation on the traditional evangelistic sermon often entitled "The Unpardonable Sin."

Since it is the role of the Holy Spirit to convict of sin and God's love, it thus becomes problematic when any professed believer begins to frustrate the special work of the Holy Spirit by willful, premeditated acts of sin and attitudes of excuse for any known sin(s) in the life. Such attitudes quite naturally lead not only to a growing insensitivity to sin but also to a further, strange blindness to the saving efficacy of God's unmerited love. A couple illustrations can help to make the former point.

One of the most noxious odors in the world comes from pigpens. Yet what is truly striking is that people who work around porkers much of the time become so accustomed to the horrific fumes that the creatures normally produce that the stench becomes ironically comfortable, even inexorably normal or "natural" to the sense of smell. A somewhat analogous phenomenon was my adolescent experience of working with my father in his honeybee business: the older I got, the more indifferent I became to the inevitable bee stings associated with such activity. They always brought pain, but the more stings I experienced, the tougher I got. In fact, I reached the point at which I would simply swat away the offending insect, scratch out the stinger, and keep on working as if nothing unusual had taken place. The sad truth is that the more a person indulges thoughts of sin and plays with temptation, the greater will become the indifference and insensitivity to the enormity of the sin being indulged in and the effect it may have on others.

Maybe one last illustration will further clarify the point. For those who have had some experience with boomerangs, it is important that the person flinging it keep in mind the possibility that it could curve back around and punch out his or her eyes. High-handed sinning and casual excuses bring on a strange spiritual blindness of the most tragic dimensions.

Most obviously, our Lutheran brothers and sisters are onto the following practical truth: if anyone takes the attitude that they can willfully ignore the convictions of conscience in the name of the promised forgiveness of justification by faith, they slip into spiritual bankruptcy and make a mockery of grace. The more that anyone indulges in willful sin and tries to excuse sin, the more blinded they become to the blessings of justifying and forgiving grace.

With these considerations in mind, we perceive that the more terrible that sin appears, the more wonderful the grace of God will be to the perfected one! That is why the Bible teaches that one of the most special bless-ings that the Spirit of God grants to true believers is the gift of repentance. Such an attitude of humility will be one of the hallmarks of all genuine Christian experience.[2]

When the idea that penitence will be the believers' "daily meat and drink"[3] first hits our spiritual ears, it has an odd ring to it. Yet when any-one really thinks about it, it acquires a ringing sound of sensible truth. The closer that we come to Christ through growth in grace, the more terrible sin will appear to us. Yet even more important, the greater will be our ap-preciation of the assurance of our salvation that both forgiving and trans-forming grace respectively impute and impart. The less penitence manifested, the greater will be the insensitivity to the subtle, deadening dangers of sin and the priceless value of God's grace.

Reason 6 is the last and, in fact, one of the most simple and obvious understandings of why God leads believers into a richer, more mature ex-perience of character transformation. Yet in one sense it is essentially a spe-cial variation of reason 5: just as unrepentant sinners become increasingly more insensitive to God's love, so those growing in grace become progres-sively more conditioned to His presence and glory.

And what is the practical outworking of such growth? It is that the closer that believers come to God, now in earthly time, the more readily and thoroughly will they be prepared to enjoy the pure and glorious atmo-sphere of heaven in eternal time. To put it as simply as possible, sanctifica-tion by grace through faith prepares believers in Jesus to begin to appreciate better the anticipated joys of heaven. And the greater the antic-ipation of celestial joy, the greater will be the assurance of God's sustain-ing love. Clarity of spiritual vision brings clarity of assurance that with God's goodness the way to the kingdom is a highway festooned with the waymarks of an expanding confidence in the boundless love of the Trinity. And such buoyant thoughts inspire a couple of further reassuring implica-tions for Christian believers.

If the key blessing of heaven is to be personally united with the three great Persons of the Holy Trinity, then all Christians had better commence sharing the Trinity's sacred attitudes and adjusting their spiritual eyesight to the glories that the Godhead will be perpetually shedding on heaven's landscape. Moreover, even these very facts bring us face to face with the further ironic truth that God's final justice (hell) takes on a certain aura of divine mercy: unrepentant sinners would be utterly miserable in heaven, and annihilation is a much more merciful alternative for them.

A Concluding, Transitional Thought

So here we have six sensible and spiritually logical reasons that God grants His children the assuring graces of sanctification and holiness in Christ. But they raise still one more vital question that always lurks just around the corner in most Seventh-day Adventist discussions of sanctification and the assurance of salvation: What about the issue of sanctification's ultimate goal—Christian perfection? Thus with a sense of anticipation we now turn to the issue of perfection and its implications for genuine perseverance in the faith of Jesus.

---

[1] I am indebted to Morris Venden for this wonderful little turn of phrase that he invoked in one of his recorded sermons from the early 1970s.

[2] Referring to the experience of the apostle Paul, Ellen White claims that "when the spiritual character of the law was discerned, he saw himself a sinner. Judged by the letter of the law as men apply it to the outward life, he had abstained from sin; but when he looked into the depths of its holy precepts, and saw himself as God saw him, he bowed in humiliation, and confessed his guilt. . . . When he saw the spiritual nature of the law, sin appeared in its true hideousness and his self-esteem was gone" (*Steps to Christ* [Mountain View, Calif.: Pacific Press Pub. Assn., 1956] , pp. 29, 30).

[3] Terminology appearing in Ellen G. White manuscript 35, 1903, published as "Repentance—the True and the False," *Review and Herald,* Aug. 19, 1971.

Chapter 6

Perfection and Assurance— The Reassuring Implications

Introduction

We have now come to one of the most delicate subjects we could encounter during our theological pilgrimage along the way of salvation. But some would probably mutter that "delicate" is too genteel of an adjective for the subject, suggesting such things as "controversial," "fanatical," or even "too prone to extremism to handle in polite, evangelical company" would be more appropriate.

Would it be too optimistic to hope that the more Bible-believing Christians (including wary Adventists) think about this issue, the greater will be the likelihood that they will get over their history of allergic reactions to the word "perfection"?

The Adventist Church has had its various species of false teachings and fanaticism associated with the subject. But such extremism and fanaticism are no excuse to keep believers from squarely facing the fact that both the Bible and the writings of Ellen G. White are quite comfortable with perfection terminology and the truths contained in its genuine manifestations. And in the spirit of a more optimistic search for theological balance, I would suggest that the best way to get at the truth of this volatile issue is to take two vital steps.

1. The first step is to realize the wisdom of an often neglected element of human experience: the truism "that abuse does not cancel legitimate use," especially any truth that could possibly aid in the recovery of any genuine facet of Christian thought and experience.

Just because we encounter bad doctrines of Christian perfection, such perversions do not automatically cancel out the existence of any true teaching that could be beneficial in its balanced, saving purposes. After all, food is an essential gift of God, and the people of God should not give up

86

eating just because of those professing Christians who struggle with gluttony. Moreover, Christians should not go negative about conjugal relations just because of a world filled with prostitution, romantic betrayal, and sexual addiction.

2. The second step is to clarify the biblical and Ellen White understanding of the experience of perfection. We suggest that six essential facets will inevitably emerge from such a careful analysis. Furthermore, when we see the six important aspects in all of their beauty and complementary dynamics, perfection will appear not as some horrible cross to bear or theological swearword, but a blessed gift to embrace intelligently and joyously. Thus the following thoughts encompass what Adventist author George Knight has described as an illuminating "taxonomy of perfection."[1]

In a manner similar to the work of a good botanist who seeks to place plants or animals in appropriate phyla, orders, families, species, and so forth, the student of God's grace should be able to classify and then clarify the varied aspects of the genuine article of Christian perfection. This becomes especially evident when such analysis reveals the complementary aspects of perfection. Or to use another analogy, the more experience we gain in polishing such a diamond in the rough, the more facets of hidden glory we will discover. And in the course of this cutting and polishing process, unanticipated refractions of brilliance, never before experienced or anticipated, will be revealed in all of their wonderful complexity.

Therefore, what follows is an exposition of the multiple hues that emanate from this much misunderstood subject. While it will involve some repetition of previously made points, we urge the reader to be patient, for our review of one of salvation's key accomplishments, reflected in perfection's overall contours, will enable us to grasp more fully the entirety of God's forgiving and transforming work. Moreover, we hope there will emerge a clearer realization of perfection's implications for a more enriching experience of the genuine assurance of salvation.

Perfection's Six Essential Facets

The first perfection facet flows from the experience of forgiveness and justification by faith. When converted believers claim the justifying merits of Christ, they are declared to be legally perfect in the sight of God, all for the sake of the imputed righteousness of Christ. And once more, we need to remind ourselves that this experience forms the solid legal foundation for all yet to unfold in sanctification and its resultant character growth.

As healing and growth continue to occur after initial justification, not only does the plan of salvation cover the sins of the past and dispose of them, but it makes up for all of our ongoing, unwitting "unavoidable deficiencies" through the constant imputation of Christ's forgiving merits (2 Cor. 5:21; cf. *Selected Messages*, book 3, pp. 195-197). Christ effectually provides this wonderful "safety net" of legal perfection through His continuous intercessory ministry as the great high priest in the heavenly sanctuary. Furthermore, "safety net" is one of the best metaphors for the assurance that inheres in the work of justification. Maybe we could express it in the following manner.

Those who are truly "in Christ" have no desire to indulge in sin by recklessly presuming on God's mercy. But they do unwittingly "fall short of the glory of God" (Rom. 3:23). Therefore, when any growing believer unintentionally "falls short" of the divine ideal, Jesus catches that person with the safety net of His justifying grace.

One of the marvelous reasons Christians should be able to progress in Christian service and character development is that they will always have the inspiration of the reassuring safety net of the merits of Jesus who faithfully underwrites their faith pilgrimage across the gaping, death-dealing gorges of the "Way of Salvation." Those who positively live "in Christ" via their growth in perfection are well aware that they can "fall short." But they also realize that when they do their best by faith in Jesus, He will be there for them to atone for their deficiencies in His role as their great advocate with the Father.

While we are practicing the arts of Christian perfection, we need to know that Jesus always has His watchful eye on us in order to pick us up when we feel spiritual slippage. A couple other illustrations will hopefully shed further helpful light on this issue.

When little children begin to practice walking, we need to grant them the freedom to sally forth in the actual experience of toddling. But parental experience has taught us that when they do so, it is a no-brainer that there will be falls. What is the best way for a wise parent to relate to such lapses? Will they think it best to scold? Of course not! The best approach is simply to reach out to them when they fall with encouragement to persevere in their little walking adventures.

A vivid metaphor comes from the common North American experience with fire insurance. Most of us are always glad to have it in case of an electrical short, natural gas leak, or a lightning strike. But it would be pure mania, even an act of wanton criminal arson, purposefully to set the house on fire in order to collect the fire insurance. Thus, those who are in Christ will simply not be setting their respective spiritual experiences on fire. Rather, they will be grateful for the assurance that Jesus is constantly invoking His faithfully ministered merits as they pass through the fiery ordeals of unwitting failure during their earthly pilgrimage

The second perfection facet encompasses dynamic growth in grace. Its best description appears in Philippians 3:1-15. In the wake of some practical comments on Christian living, Paul begins to share his own remarkable testimony. He reminds the Philippians that if they think they have the right to be confident in the flesh, they really cannot begin to match the possibilities for self-confidence that Paul could boast about (verse 4).

Beginning with the reminder that he had been "circumcised" (a fundamental act of obedience for any Jew), he then proceeded to lay out an impressive litany of his other "fleshly" advantages. He was, after all, an Israelite (the chosen people of God), of the tribe of Benjamin (the tribe that, with Judah, remained faithful to God the longest and gave Israel its first king, Saul), he was a Hebrew's Hebrew (not just some pretend or nominal Jew), and as "concerning the law, a Pharisee" (the sect of the Jews most zealous for obedience to the letter of the law). And then follows the claim that he was filled with "zeal," as powerfully evidenced by his fanatical persecution of the church. Then he concludes with what should have been the real clincher: if anybody really wanted a demonstration of the "righteousness which is in the law," he was one who was "blameless" (verses 5 and 6). In other words, when it came to moral and spiritual advantages and accomplishments, Paul was loaded!

Yet in the light of his new understanding of life through Christ and His righteousness, Paul had begun to sing a radically new version of his salvation song. All that was "gain" he now "counted loss for Christ" (verse 7) and reckoned it all to be mere "dung" (KJV; "garbage,") in the light of winning Christ as his great, all-surpassing spiritual treasure (verse 8). And where was such a treasure to be obtained? Through being located by faith "in Him"—Christ.

Once again we encounter our central righteousness by faith perspective: being "in Christ," united to Him and the entire complement of His righteous benefits. It is, however, a union not attained through our "own righteousness, which is from the law, but that which is through faith in Christ, the righteousness which is from God by faith" (verse 9).

What Paul is here saying is that we really do not have the resources in our natural spiritual natures to be able to produce any species of righteousness that would ever prove acceptable or effectual in meriting our personal salvation. But what is even more instructive is how the apostle so smoothly transitions from the primacy of justifying grace to the inevitable fruitions of sanctifying grace. He recognizes that the two can never be separated when we are in Christ, continually united to Him in living, trusting, appropriating faith that works by love and steadily manifests "perfect" obedience. Yes, perfect, but perfect in what sense?

Verses 10 through 15 are the most powerful exposition of sanctifying and perfecting grace in all of Paul's writings. He begins with another metaphor that speaks of union with Christ by faith: "to know him" (verse 10). The phrase echoes our Lord's words in John 17:3: "This is eternal life, that they may know You, the only true God, and Jesus Christ whom You have sent." Truly knowing God, in or through Christ, also points to a dynamic, intimate relationship of constantly giving and receiving. We give up all of our fleshly "advantages" that engender pride, and in return we receive "the power of His resurrection, and the fellowship of His sufferings" which effectually crucify all our prideful, fleshly advantages through conformity to "His death" (Phil. 3:10). And what is the ultimate goal? It is attaining to the "resurrection from the dead" (verse 11).

Then in verses 12 through 15 there unfolds a stirring presentation of how to have such a spiritual resurrection. It is in this passage, so filled with word pictures of advanced, forward moving faith in Christ, that Paul unfolds one of the most powerful biblical portraits, or definitions, of genuine, dynamic Christian "perfection."

First of all, he claims that he has not yet attained his goal nor has he become "already perfect" (KJV). That, however, does not deter him from pressing the issue as he continues to "follow after" (KJV) in order to "take hold of that for which Christ Jesus took hold of me" (verse 12, NIV). Not only has he not attained, but he humbly admits that he has also not fully taken hold of all that Christ has on offer for him (verse 13). But he stubbornly refuses to give up! He continues to reach for the things which are yet in front of him and ignores "those things which are behind" (verse 13).

What is it that he is reaching forward to? It is "the goal for the prize of the upward call of God in Christ Jesus" (verse 14). And what is it that he has left behind in sanctified forgetfulness? Most obviously it included his fleshly pride and ambitious, ill-conceived zeal, especially his persecution of the church.

Right here we need to pause to make a vital point about spiritual growth toward the perfection ideal. Not only should believers be positively pressing forward, but everyone should also be constantly leaving pride and failure behind in the miracle of divine amnesia. One of the most dangerous obstacles to spiritual growth and Christian assurance is to be always dredging up the past personal failures or the discouraging defects of others. Such a negative mind-set or focus can never lead to any victory.

Growth and joyous experience are mainly found in keeping our eye on the prize and the glory of the One who gives that prize. There is certainly a time for taking stock of self through some good introspection; but such inventories should never degenerate into a sick preoccupation with our or others' flaws and defeats. Paul is right when he declares that growing believers need to forget what is behind and then positively "press toward the goal for the prize of the upward call of God in Christ Jesus" (verse 14).

With his past failures in proper perspective, Paul then proceeds to give one of the great passages in the whole history of the debates over how to define Christian perfection: when believers are dynamically *growing* in grace, it is then that they are declared to be *perfect:* "Let us therefore, as many as be perfect, be thus minded" (verse 15, KJV).

So, then, what is perfection? Paul's definition is that if any believer is growing in grace, advancing in union with Christ, he or she can be declared to be perfect.

Once more we must clearly highlight the dynamic nature of Paul's classic teaching in Philippians 3. The various verbs of knowing, claiming, taking, following, forgetting, and pressing on are all part and parcel of what it means to be perfect in Christ. What is the result? Suffice it to say, the moment we come to Christ is the moment we begin to experience the process of growth in grace through cooperation with His imparted, transforming power. And as we grow, we are in a special sense perfect at every advancing stage of our unfolding development.

Often parents speak of perfect babies and of children who are perfect at whatever stage of development they are passing through. And what they mean by such language is that their wee ones are unfolding in a natural and normal way for their age and their current stage of development. They are not yet fully mature, but they are "maturing" (we technically call this process "maturation"). The Bible describes growing believers as perfect at every stage; that is, as long as they keep maturing. This is certainly a "relative perfection," but it is nonetheless an important stage, or waymark, on the path of the perfection pilgrimage.

The third perfection facet features the absence of acts of willful sinning or attitudes that involve the excusing of any known sinful act and thought.

Early on in any experience of the regenerative work of the Holy Spirit, each believer must begin to reach the point at which they become aware of the danger of premeditated acts of sin and attitudes of indulgent excuse-making for any sinful attitude or character defect.

We have already explored the deadly aspect of presumption in our earlier discussion as to why it is that God subjects believers to the graced discipline of sanctification. But let's remind ourselves of the seriousness of this aspect of growth in perfection so that we can avoid the miasma of spiritual deadness and insensitivity to the enormity of sin as well as the precious gift of God's love. No genuine Christian assurance ever masquerades under the deceptive guises of presumption and the excusing of sin in any form.

Someone might say to us that we just have to deal with their offensive behavior ("it's just my way"), but Ellen White declares that we are not to tolerate any such excuses.[2] To be quite blunt, this attitude falls in the same category as premeditated sinning. And it is patently evident that both have proved to be a deadly blow to the spiritual life of any professed believer. Falling short is one thing, but refusing to take responsibility is quite another matter.

The fourth and fifth perfection facets concern the experience of the people of God in the final crisis of earth's history (facet 4) and the saints' experience at the moment of glorification (facet 5). Since both subjects have had such challenging and confusing overtones for many Seventh-day Adventists, we will devote most of a subsequent chapter to a more extended treatment of the controversial and closely related issues. Yet suffice it to say that whatever we will find out about the sealed saints of the endtime, it will only be the practical extension of all that has gone on previously in their personal experience of God's forgiving and transforming grace. And ultimately, it will be these practical, daily aspects of grace that will assuredly see God's last-day people safely through history's greatest test of faith for the followers of Jesus.

The sixth perfection facet includes the endless character growth through - out eternity with Christ. In other words, the dynamic growth that began here in time will continue forever. But only then will the advancing spiritual maturation of the redeemed be totally removed from the context of sin and all of its baleful effects. The infinity of love in the nature and character of God will endlessly charm and challenge our mental, social, and spiritual capacities.

If eternity is going to be so great, can we not then be assured that our present privilege is to be the continuous recipients of the most abundant grace as we, right now, this very day, stand on our tiptoes in anticipation of the glories to come? If the goodness of God can grant such blessed prospects of growth for all eternity, why should we not be confident that He can effectually carry us through all of the ups and downs of growth in grace and service here on earth during our present walk with God?

Conclusion

God has provided wonderfully encouraging resources for personal Christian assurance. They emanate from all aspects of His transforming grace, including the heights of earthly Christian maturity that we call Christian perfection. Thus we suggest that the key issue involving converting and transforming grace, in relationship to Christian assurance, has to do with the fact that the more we grow into the likeness of Christ's character, the more sensitive we become to the greatness of God's love and the terribleness of sin.

Without this vital working of the subjective, internal effects of transforming grace, there will be no deepening appreciation of the marvels of God's justifying grace and the need to eliminate the blinding aspects of sin from our experience. Far from placing sanctification and perfection into a category of legalism and pride, they are to be claimed as indispensable to a proper experience of forgiving and justifying grace. Such transformative graces most certainly do not, in any way, add to the merit of Christ's justification. But they certainly do highlight the glories of justifying grace and offer a deeper appreciation of its powers to generate genuine Christian assurance. Thus justification and sanctification are, on both a theoretical and practical level, truly inseparable.

Now that we have established the basic inspired facts of the dynamic interrelationship between justification and sanctification (and perfection, the earthly goal of sanctification), we still face another practical and positive aspect of the Christian's experience of the assurance of salvation. And this has to do with how each individual can know that all of the benefits set forth in the Bible and Christian teachings on the doctrines of conversion, justification, and perfecting sanctification can actually become a reality in our personal experience of God's saving grace.

Therefore, with these challenges firmly in hand, we can now turn our attention to the manner in which the Holy Spirit "witnesses" to each believer that they are personally an assured child of God. So what are we to make of the biblical teaching of the "witness of the Spirit"?

---

[1] Comments made by Knight in 1989 when reviewing my doctoral dissertation on Ellen White's doctrine of salvation, with special attention given to the controversial issue of Christian perfection.

[2] The following references document the "It is my way" excuse or special pleading that fellow believers must overlook such bad character traits. Clearly stating that sin has no excuse, she rejected such attitudes. While there is an atonement for sin, there is no excuse for any true believer to be tolerating their known sins. We will speak to this issue in more detail when we discuss the perfection of believers during the time of the end. See *Youth's Instructor*, June 7, 1894, and Oct. 2, 1902; *Signs of the Times*, Feb. 8, 1892.

The Witness of the Spirit

Chapter 7
The Spirit Witnesses to Our Spirit and
With the Witness of Our Spirit—
Can There Be Perceptible Assurance?

Chapter 7

The Spirit Witnesses to Our Spirit and With the Witness of Our Spirit— Can There Be Perceptible Assurance?

Introduction

The key question of the present chapter deals with the highly subjective matter of just how it is that God effectively communicates the reality of people's personal salvation directly to them. To be even more precise, the question is How can we have the personal assurance that what Scripture says about salvation really applies to us? Perhaps we could restate it in the following manner: How can we know that God intends that all the wonderful provisions of salvation (described in the previous chapters, the a priori factors that form the foundation of personal assurance) are not just nice word pictures, but are actually intended to enable each individual believer to join the family portrait of God's redeemed children?

Another closely related aspect involves just how "perceptible" or truly knowable a conviction of a genuine assurance of personal salvation is. This question greatly preoccupied John Wesley. He had explored all sorts of well-worn paths that claimed to lead to the assurance of salvation (including direct mystical union with God, good works, strict use of time, and faithfulness in religious observances). His desire to possess the genuine article of personal salvation had turned into a relentless spiritual pilgrimage. And when he finally came to the phase of his religious experience that he felt that his "heart had been strangely warmed," he still struggled to find some sort of practical balance between the extremes of an unhealthy subjectivism and an overly rationalized idea of personal salvation.

In Wesley's case, as in that of many others, a most important aspect of the whole issue of an assured acceptance with God occurred when he came to a more informed, mature understanding of justification by faith alone (and its proper relationship to sanctification by faith in Christ, a key component of the a priori factors). But even after finally gaining such biblical clarity and uncovering confirmation of his convictions in the key doctrinal standards of his very own Anglican heritage, it became clear that he had been blinded by an unhealthy overemphasis on "holy living." His failure to grasp the simple basics of gospel assurance was compounded not only by his own unhealthy accent on holy living but also by a pronounced lack of any clear-cut grasp of justifying grace (both practical and theoretical).

While there were many positive aspects of the holy living tradition (despite its imbalance), Wesley's immersion in its writers almost seemed to shield him from the aforementioned proper understanding of justification by grace through faith alone.[1] So where did Wesley go from there, and what can we learn from his frenetic search for the perceptible evidence of his own assurance of salvation?

At the very foundation of any experience of genuine Christian assurance lies an important aspect of calling and convicting grace ("prevenient grace"). And this special facet of grace is the "illuminating" work of the Holy Spirit that leads and guides believers into a solid understanding of Bible truth, especially those truths regarding the basics of salvation. Therefore, the Spirit of God not only convinces believers that the Bible is a truly inspired source of truth but also leads to a personal saving knowledge of the great principles of salvation.

And while the process is inherently quite subjective, it does open the way to further doctrinal and ethical clarity, and such truths also take on a "self-authenticating" (or self-evident) aura. Furthermore, such basic clarity is especially essential when it comes to the great aspects of converting, regenerating, forgiving, and transforming grace. Without such a foundational grasp of saving truth (including a personal ownership of the issues), many believers will have a hard time arriving at a genuine experience of the direct witness from the Spirit that they are truly children of God. Once more, let's remind ourselves that what we are here talking about when we speak of the facts of Christian experience are the factors mentioned in the introduction to this book, ones that we have called the a posteriori elements of assurance. Thus when one reflects on their personal experience of grace, there will be some after the fact (a posteriori) experiences that give evidence that the believer has been truly and assuredly redeemed. The Spirit brings such facets of experience to their consciousness.

Wesley had to deal with one further complicating factor in his desperate search for the conscious, or perceptible, witness of the Spirit to his own mind or "spirit." It was an attitude prevalent in his day and one that still infects a significant portion of Christian believers, including many conservative Adventists. It includes an inordinate fear that if the direct witness of the Holy Spirit is granted to our individual "spirits," it will lead to religious fanaticism. The eighteenth-century term for it was the dreaded smear word "enthusiasm."

Now, what always seems to be lurking in the background of such suspicions is the specter of spiritual presumption and its cheap-grace claims: "I am saved and free in Jesus, and thus I am free from obedience to the laws of God and the varied ethical principles of the Word of God and the standards of the church." And most certainly the danger of such fanatical excesses does exist. As a pastor and college religion teacher, I do recall painful episodes in which "saved" church members and students have manifested such attitudes, and it has proved difficult to wean them away from such a deadly frame of mind.

But Wesley did not let such fears hinder him in his search. He determined to be a "biblical and real Christian" and was not about to allow the fear of cheap grace and fanaticism to cancel out what he felt was the biblically described "use" or experience of the "witness of the Spirit." And the main reason for his persistence was his sense that without such a sense of assuring grace, believers would not be able to know the fullness of grace that is their privilege when God's Spirit speaks directly to the soul.

Most certainly Wesley felt that the Spirit of God was leading him into a deeper understanding of the illuminating work of the Holy Spirit when it came to a clearer grasp of basic Bible teaching on the issues of salvation. He was, however, doggedly persistent in claiming that there was more to the work of the Holy Spirit than just the area of doctrinal truth. And what was it that drove him to such a conviction?

For Wesley the key text that led him to the basic concept of the perceptible, personal "witness of the Spirit" was the biblical "witness" of Romans 8:14-17: "For as many as are led by the Spirit of God, these are sons of God. For you did not receive the spirit of bondage again to fear, but you received the Spirit of adoption by whom we cry out, 'Abba, Father.' The Spirit Himself bears witness with our spirit that we are children of God, and if children, then heirs—heirs of God and joint heirs with

Christ." And in Wesley's understanding of the passage, the core expression was that "the Spirit Himself bears witness with our spirit that we are children of God."

Furthermore, his interpretation was quite simple. Indeed, he felt that Paul was obviously claiming that the Person of the Holy Spirit speaks directly, or perceptibly, to the individual's soul or spirit (mind or consciousness). And what the Spirit seeks to communicate is that the believer is an adopted child of God and joint heir with Christ. Was Wesley correct in his rather simple yet controversial interpretation of the biblical expression the "witness of the Spirit"?

I would suggest that he was essentially correct not only in his basic interpretation but also in his theological thrust or emphasis. Obviously God is intensely loving and personal as He reveals Christ through the internal, subjective workings of the Holy Spirit. The loving Father will also not leave His blood-purchased children without a deeply personal witness of His love for them and His intense desire to adopt them and grant the clear assurance that they are His reconciled and adopted sons and daughters. Now I ask, What is wrong with such an interpretation?

Absolutely nothing is wrong as long as we keep this special experience in proper perspective, especially with the caution that such a direct and personal communication must be safeguarded by further experiences of "witness." And such a further witness is closely associated with the more rational notion of the Spirit's leading the believer to experience "the witness of our spirit," as revealed in 2 Corinthians 1:12: "For our boasting ["rejoicing" in the KJV] is this: the testimony of our conscience, that we conducted ourselves in the world in simplicity and godly sincerity, not with fleshly wisdom but by the grace of God, and more abundantly toward you."

Thus for Wesley, we have not only the direct witness of the Spirit to our minds that we are the children of God, but also the biblical teaching that "our spirit," or mind, is influenced by the Holy Spirit through our Spirit-informed conscience so that we can rationally identify, or infer, the signs or marks of our personal experience of election, including the answer of a conscience that is "devoid of offense toward God." In other words, there will be the obvious, outward evidences of the manifestation of the workings of the Spirit in our lives, especially the "fruit of the Spirit." And such "fruit" indicates not only that we can claim a personal revelation or a "witness" from God of our adoption, but that we can also actually act like somebody growing in the likeness of Christ's character.

We will say more about this "witness of our spirit" and its relationship to personal assurance a bit later. But first we must explore a little more fully the direct witness of the Spirit to our individual conscious minds.

Some Thoughts on the Direct "Witness of the Spirit"

Could it be that Wesley's basic interpretation of Romans 8:14-17 is essentially correct? I would suggest four basic reasons in support of his essential convictions and conclusions.

The first reason stems from the fact that the Bible tells the story of a triune God whose most basic characteristic is interpersonal, self-sacrificing, other-oriented creative and redeeming love. And if the members of the triune Godhead have personally and eternally manifested such love, is it all that strange that we could or should expect that such a deeply loving, interpersonal God would want to directly share the same experience with His created and redeemed children? When seen in this light, it would be extremely strange that God would not in some way "speak directly" to us by "the witness of the Spirit" that we are His blood-purchased children.

Second, all Bible-believing Christians will readily admit that God has personally and directly communicated to His prophets through dreams, visions, and other means of inspiration that have produced what we call the canonical Scriptures. Though not all should expect that God will speak to every Christian in this manner, it is still powerful evidence that God has communicated to humanity in the past and may continue to do so in the present. Does this fact of personal revelation have any implications for our issue?

If the loving God has spoken in such a way to prophets in the past and more recent church history, why then cannot He personally communicate to believers regarding their newly revealed status as redeemed sons and daughters of God? We are not calling for all believers to be prophets in either the canonical or the Ellen White sense of the word (though I think we should be open to this, especially as a corporate body). But such a deeply personal revelation is certainly an instructive precedent that strongly suggests that God can speak directly to individual believers in order to grant them a perceptible, or direct, witness of the Spirit that they are God's personally adopted children.

The third line of evidence concerns the longings that so many individual Christians feel as they hunger for a deeper personal relationship with God. Such desires may manifest themselves through participation in corporate worship, the ordinances of God (the Lord's Supper and baptism), and other spiritual devotions. The latter phenomenon holds a very special place in the convictions of most deeply spiritual Seventh-day Adventist and other genuinely spiritual Christians. Such spiritual devotional practices include private worship, personal prayer, reflective Bible reading, fasting, and solitude.[2]

Furthermore, such exercises are obviously based on the assumption that any sincere believer can commune with God and that God is open to the personal and directly interactive communication of His grace to all believers. Therefore, if God can speak to us through prayer, Bible reading, and so forth, why would it seem strange for Him to infuse a conviction of salvation into the minds and hearts of those who respond to His leading?

The final line of evidence in support of Wesley's contention that there is a "perceptible witness of the Spirit with our spirit" is the analogy of those who fall in love. Most couples sooner or later manage to articulate some version of "I love you!" When there is a deep reciprocal involvement, these are some of the most exhilarating words found in any human language! In fact, I would suggest that they are absolutely essential and must continue throughout the entire life of all such relationships.

But most mature lovers realize that their relationship requires more than just words. In fact, words without loving acts can become a devastating mockery.

Any lover with even a bit of sense will test the object of their love to see whether they mean what they say. But such testing would never deny the importance of the verbal expressions of affection that are such an essential aspect of all loving relationships. As a pastoral counselor I have on occasion sought to coach couples or individuals who have found it difficult to verbally express affection and affirmation. Almost universally, such persons acknowledge that when such verbal skills emerge from hearts moved by genuine love, it greatly enriches the relationship.

Thus if verbal affirmation is absolutely essential to interpersonal human love relationships, why would it seem so strange if those made in God's image would also feel the need for Him to speak His message of love more directly to their spiritual senses? If the Christian life is any reflection at all of the deepest love experiences of human beings, it should not seem out of line for God to speak to His beloved ones regarding His deep, yearning, saving affection for them.

Other Inspired Evidence of the Witness of the Spirit
Before dealing with the actual manner in which God communicates to us through the witness of the Spirit, we should mention that the basic con-

cept of the witness of the Spirit is not exclusive to Paul in Romans 8:14-17. John also seems to speak to the experience, and Ellen White confirms the testimonies of both Paul and John.

First John 5:9-13 clearly addresses the "witness of God" to believers. John affirms that they may have the testimony "that God has given us eternal life, and this life is in His Son." It is particularly striking to note the way that John speaks of his own ministry: "These things I have written to you who believe in the name of the Son of God, that *you may know that you have eternal life*" (verse 13).

"The Holy Spirit is a person, for He beareth witness with our spirits that we are the children of God," Ellen G. White comments. "When this witness is borne, it carries with it its own evidence. At such times we believe and are sure that we are the children of God. . . . The Holy Spirit has a personality, else He could not bear witness to our spirits and with our spirits that we are the children of God. He must also be a divine Person, else He could not search out the secrets which lie hidden in the mind of God. 'For what man knoweth the things of a man, save the spirit of man which is in him? even so the things of God knoweth no man, but the Spirit of God' [1 Cor. 2:11, KJV]."[3]

In What Manner Does God Speak to Believers?

We have previously affirmed that God communicates through His inspired Word of Scripture when we prayerfully read the Bible or other spiritual writings, and also through the taught or proclaimed Word. This we refer to as illumination. But it does not prevent Him from directly communicating His love to each believer's individual heart and mind.

Now as to just how God speaks, we cannot be overly dogmatic. Wesley left many of the details up to actual experience. He argued that just as we cannot fully explain the mystery of the new birth in a totally rational way, so it is with the ongoing ways that God speaks to the soul of each believer. Yet I would urge that it will be hard to improve on Wesley's succinct definition of the witness of the Spirit:

"The testimony of the Spirit *is an inward impression on the soul*, whereby the Spirit of God directly 'witnesses to my spirit that I am a child of God'; that Jesus Christ hath loved me, and given himself for me; that all my sins are blotted out, and I, even I, am reconciled to God."[4]

While we naturally must be tentative in interpreting what Wesley was getting at in his statement, it does seem safe to assume that his concept of "witness" includes all of the deep moments of spiritual conviction. Such events would include responding to an altar call to embrace salvation or to reconsecrate ourselves, receiving deep personal convictions of the sense of God's care in times of stress and danger, and stirring impressions regarding personal actions appropriate to new practical or moral duty. Such seem to be the major aspects of God's "inward impression on the soul." But the Holy Spirit also aids in bringing to the personal consciousness of believers God's assuring witness to His love through a more indirect, rational means.

"The Witness of Our Spirit"

Subsequent to the experience of the "inward impression on the soul" granted by the "witness of the Spirit," there is also the confirming witness of "our own spirit." In an interesting twist, Wesleyan scholarship has called "the witness of the Spirit" the "objective" witness and the "witness of our own spirit" the "subjective" witness. But we suggest that it might better be defined in a reverse manner. Not surprisingly, such have been the traditional instincts of the Seventh-day Adventist experience with the workings of the Spirit of God in direct or indirect communications to individual souls. Such reluctance to see the "witness of the Spirit" as primarily objective has been the result of numerous bouts with perfectionistic fanaticism in our history.

Beginning right after the Second Great Disappointment and throughout the subsequent decades of the ministry of Ellen G. White, many claimed that the Spirit of God had declared them to be saved and perfected. Unfortunately, such persons have usually proved to be self-deceived hypocrites. Thus we have felt a need to examine carefully the experience of all claimants to perfection by subjecting them to the more objective testing of their characters and the larger contours of their overall Christian experience.

But are there biblically informed character indicators that manifest themselves in every instance of genuine Christian experience by which the people of God can reasonably evaluate any claims to more direct, or special, Christian experiences (including the claim to be saved)? We believe that the following tests will help us examine any claim to salvation and Christian perfection.

The Objective, Rational Tests of the Spirit

As earlier suggested, one of the clearer signs that the new-birth process has been taking place in a person's experience is that there will be the visible fruit of the Spirit. In Galatians 5:16-18 and 22-26 Paul describes the Christian virtues that become the inevitable spiritual result of the Holy Spirit's regenerating work.

His language seems to draw on the imagery that Jesus gave in His illustration of the vine and the branches (John 15:1-11). Christ compared the Spirit to the life-giving sap of the grape vine and suggested that if any branch is not bearing "much fruit" (verse 5) it is clear that such a branch is not properly connected to the Vine (Christ). And most obviously the "much fruit" that Spirit-fed branches produce is the same as the "fruit of the Spirit" spoken of by Paul in Galatians 5. Therefore, those receiving the true witness of the Spirit will manifest the divine love being shed in their hearts by the Holy Spirit (Rom. 5:5).

Furthermore, closely related to the virtues mentioned in Galatians 5 (love, joy, peace, etc.) are descriptions found in 1 John 5:1-4: those "born of God" will (a) love God, (b) keep His commandments, (c) overcome the world, and (d) "love the children of God." It is a pretty comprehensive list that needs little detailed or technical interpretation. Most of these character traits are quite apparent to others. Thus, those born of God will verbally testify to their love for God, they love to obey His commandments, they are experiencing real victory over the world, and they are persistently discovering a renewal of love for their brothers and sisters in the faith.

Further Testimony From James and Paul on the Witness of Our Spirit

James declared that "faith by itself, if it does not have works, is dead" (James 2:17). No deeds, no real living faith! If there is the "fruit" of works, then it is most likely that there will be the healthy "root" of living, trusting faith. Clearly James does not contradict Paul.

In Ephesians 2:8-10, one of the great salvation passages of the Bible, Paul demonstrates a most fundamental agreement with James. But what is truly remarkable about the passage is that it couples the concept of "by grace you have been saved through faith . . . not of works" (verse 8) with the very practical observation that "we are His workmanship, created in [or by] Christ Jesus for good works, which God prepared beforehand that we should walk in them" (verse 10). The apostle's meaning here is just too obvious to be misunderstood: salvation by grace through faith alone will always be evidenced by "good works." Genuinely converted believers will overflow with the fruit of God's regenerating grace.

A Vital Objective Evidence

Quite possibly the greatest possible demonstration of a genuine conversion experience manifests itself when an individual readily acknowledges and confesses sin(s). It surely takes a deeply converted and truly spiritual person to admit to sin and then own up to it.

David's great acknowledgment and confession, recorded in Psalm 51, is the classic exhibit. Paul portrays a similar spirit in Romans 7: "For we know that the law is spiritual: but I am carnal, sold under sin" (verse 14). "For I know that in me (that is, in my flesh) nothing good dwells; for to will is present with me, but how to perform what is good I do not find. For the good that I will to do, I do not do; but the evil I will not to do, that I practice" (verses 18, 19). "O wretched man that I am! Who will deliver me from this body of death?" (verse 24). If anyone is truly converted, there will be confession, overt sorrow for sin, and the taking of full responsibility for all transgression and its evil results.

Can there be objective evidence that Christians have been born again? It appears that there is. Such believers are (1) free from the condemnation of sin (yet heartily acknowledge and confess their sinful condition and acts), (2) manifest the fruit of the Spirit, (3) gain victory over character defects, (4) love their fellow believers, and (5) obey God's commandments.

Two Additional Evidences of Saving Assurance

Furthermore, two other factors of subjective spiritual evidence witness to our personal salvation. First, not only do genuine Christians consciously manifest the fruit of the Spirit, but they can find some assurance in the very fact that they are consciously exercising faith in God's grace. If you are a person of faith, its exercise should be consciously realized as an evidence that God is saving you.

The second factor involves what theologians have called Christian *lucta* (a term derived from the Latin word for "to wrestle, to strive"). It refers to the Christian's struggle, or literally any personal wrestling with the power of sin, temptation, and the lusts of the flesh. Thus, one of the evidences that I am being assuredly saved is that I am experiencing the opposition of the great adversary. My conflict with and victory over satanic forces reveals the power of God in my life to deliver me from them.

Some Concluding Comments

While the intricacies of personal experience can take many unique forms, yet the portrait of any genuine Christian will clearly stand out, especially when contrasted to that of deceptive, and self-deceived, religious pretenders. As Ellen White observes: "The character is revealed, not by occasional good deeds and occasional misdeeds, but by the tendency of the habitual words and acts." She acknowledges that "there may be an outward correctness of deportment without the renewing power of Christ." But then she lays out a simple, but searching test that any sensible Christian should be able to apply to their own religious experience: "By what means, then, shall we determine whose side we are on?" she asks. She answers with a series of questions: "Who has the heart? With whom are our thoughts? Of whom do we love to converse? Who has our warmest affections and our best energies? If we are Christ's, our thoughts are with Him, and our sweetest thoughts are of Him."[5]

There will most certainly always be challenging subtleties when we deal with the issues of the subjective workings of the Holy Spirit in the personal experience of Christians. But we should not allow such mystery to prevent us from sensitively exploring the issues, even at the risk of the charges of fanaticism. The only way we could avoid dealing with them would be to take some sort of totally deterministic route in which all things are under the arbitrary control of God. Thus the most relevant question that we need to raise regarding the witness of the Spirit is: What is the contribution that such a "witness" makes to a deeper experience of being assured of salvation?

One senses that any answer must build on the implications of freely chosen love. In the biblical sense of this matter we are talking about God's "covenant" love, which very much includes the issues of forgiveness and the fruit that results from having the law "written on the heart."

The clear message of both the Bible and Ellen G. White is that the Holy Spirit gives a direct witness to our spirit that we are forgiven. Thus it is our privilege to be obedient and loving Christians who bear the marks of the abundantly evident fruit of the Spirit in all that we do, feeble and defective though we may be. And just as love in any normal human relationship grows and deepens in ways that bring interpersonal assurance and relational stability, thus it may be with all true believers who give themselves over to the lordship of Christ. His Spirit will witness to and with our own individual spirits in such a manner that it will produce a deepening sense of God's love for us.

But what does the matter of the witness of the Spirit have to say to certain special challenges brought against the Arminian version of the assurance of salvation? To answer it, we must consider certain issues raised persistently by the Calvinistic/Reformed claim that their version of Christian assurance, based on a special understanding of irresistible election and "once saved, always saved" teachings, grants them a far greater degree of confidence than does the Arminian version. We will deal with that claim in the next chapter.

---

[1] This shielding included Wesley's godly parents, who were also avid readers of the key classics of the Anglican emphasis on personal holiness.

[2] We will explore the practical functions of spiritual disciplines in the devotional life of the believer in chapter 12.

[3] Ellen G. White manuscript 20, 1906, cited in *Evangelism* (Washington, D.C.: Review and Herald Pub. Assn., 1946), pp. 616, 617.

[4] A. Outler, *Sermons*, vol. 1, p. 274. (Italics supplied.)

[5] E. G. White, *Steps to Christ*, pp. 57, 58.

Section Four

Special Adventist Challenges

Chapter 8
Do the "Once Saved, Always Saved"
Calvinists Have an Assurance Advantage?

Chapter 9
The Latter Rain, the Close of Probation, and the Time
of Trouble—Who Will Assuredly Thrive and Survive?

Chapter 10
The "Final Generation" Perfectionist
Explanation of the Time of Trouble

Chapter 11
Ellen G. White on the Assurance of Salvation:
Are Her Writings a Help or a Stumbling Block

Chapter 8

Do the "Once Saved, Always Saved" Calvinists Have an Assurance Advantage?

During my first two years in high school my brother Ivan and I became friends with a Baptist classmate. One day he invited us to a special series of meetings held at his church, one of the most active Baptist congregations on the east coast of Florida. The services that we attended were mostly revivals that featured one of the best Baptist preachers in the southeast United States, the up-and-coming Adrian Rogers (1931-2005). Rogers would go on to pastor one of the largest Baptist churches in the world, serve three terms as president of the Southern Baptist Convention (the largest Protestant denomination in the United States), and become one of North America's leading televangelists.

Although my brother and I enjoyed the lively preaching, rousing singing, and doctrinal stimulation, I still recall as clearly as yesterday the first time my brother Ivan told me about the common Baptist belief regarding the assurance of salvation. I was, at that time, more theologically and biblically naive than my brother, but I was alert enough to be quite taken aback as Ivan explained to me the gist of the doctrine known commonly as "once saved, always saved," or "once in grace, the believer can never lose his or her saving relationship with Jesus."

As already mentioned in the introduction to this book, the teaching is nothing but the popular version of the Reformed/Calvinistic tradition's concept of what is more technically known as irresistible perseverance. While we will explore it in more detail later, first I want to share my initial reactions to it.

To be perfectly honest, I thought that my brother was kidding me, seeking to make some sort of theological joke. In reality, my reaction was quite natural for someone nurtured within the Seventh-day Adventist perspective that has consistently taught that salvation can, indeed, be lost. But upon further exposure to my brother's investigations, the witness of our Baptist friend, and the preaching of Adrian Rogers, I became convinced that the issue of personal salvation and the "once saved, always saved" version of it was not a joke. To the contrary, it is a deeply held, central component of the theology (and evangelistic outreach) of most Baptists, Presbyterians, and other Calvinistic-oriented Christian groups. So where did the whole idea come from?

The Origins of "Once Saved, Always Saved" Teachings

The three greatest of the sixteenth-century European Protestant Reformers, Martin Luther, Ulrich Zwingli, and John Calvin, were all strong advocates of the doctrine of election, especially the version of it that taught that God irresistibly predestines most human beings to damnation and a small minority to be among the elect (the saved). While Luther was convinced of the doctrine of irresistible, particular election, his Lutheran tradition did not hold to it very strongly. Luther's understudy and most influential successor, Philip Melanchthon, ultimately rejected this more deterministic form of the doctrine of election.

However, Zwingli and Calvin, leaders of what theologians usually label as the Reformed tradition, enthusiastically embraced the doctrine of irresistible election. And the person most responsible for shaping the Reformed tradition was John Calvin. As a result the tradition has continued to be called not only Reformed but also Calvinistic. Thus scholars have used the terms *Reformed* and *Calvinistic* interchangeably to describe the theology of this highly influential Protestant tradition. Moreover, the various Baptist and Presbyterian denominations have emerged as the most numerous members of the Calvinistic/Reformed tradition in North American Protestantism.

It should therefore not surprise us that Calvin's writings shaped the teachings of the groups that often bear his name. One of the tradition's strongest teachings has been his doctrine of election and its concomitant doctrine of irresistible perseverance. We therefore need to explain what theologians have meant when they invoke the rather technical-sounding word "perseverance."

The basic concept involved in the teaching is that since God has irresistibly elected or predestined some to salvation, it is thus necessary for Him also to provide for their continuing "perseverance." In other words, since God elects the redeemed, He must then also keep them safely saved. The logic here is really quite simple: if God forcefully, even irresistibly, elects them, then He also must ceaselessly maintain them among the elect.

What has happened, however, in the history of the Reformed/Calvinistic tradition is that the majority of its believers have given up the doctrine of irresistible election, or deterministic predestination. It is, however, quite apparent that they have not abandoned election's somewhat logical corollary of irresistible perseverance. They include large numbers of the previously mentioned Baptists and Presbyterians as well as others, such as the Dutch Calvinist denominations (the Christian Reformed Church and the Reformed Church in America), and numerous other independent groups strongly influenced by the long reach of Calvin's teachings. And at a practical level, the Reformed-oriented believers probably include some Seventh-day Adventists who have either come from a Reformed background or have chosen the teaching as the best solution to the challenges they have struggled with in their personal search for the assurance of salvation.

Some Preliminary Observations on Irresistible Election

But before we explore the rationale of the popular doctrine of perseverance any further, we need to make some preliminary observations on the issue of irresistible election and the assurance of salvation. Once more, we must emphasize that most contemporary Reformed/Calvinist Christians resist the idea of irresistible election. But for those who do hold the concept, it reduces any ultimate assurance of salvation. If the vast majority of sinners are irresistibly predestined to be damned, it immediately and significantly reduces the number of possible candidates for election to salvation, which most deem to be but a small group anyway.[1]

Since the Arminian view claims that God has always intended the benefits of Christ's atonement potentially to save all sinners, it then becomes abundantly clear as to which teaching is inherently more optimistic about the possibility of more sinners being saved. In fact, one could argue that the classic Calvinistic doctrine, which teaches a greatly restricted number of individuals irresistibly elected, is thereby more inherently negative about the possibility of salvation for the many.[2]

To put it more bluntly, if the pool of candidates is so small, then the chances of anyone being among the elect, with its alleged assurances of salvation, are quite minimal. Therefore, even though Arminians also admit to a small segment that will ultimately receive salvation, they at least teach that every sinner has a chance of ending up among the redeemed. And this is simply because Arminians understand the Bible to teach that the choice of salvation ultimately depends upon the decision of every individual person.

Here we find an obvious contrast between the Arminian and the Calvinist positions, especially when the latter teaches that salvation and damnation are totally and irresistibly determined by the inscrutable wisdom of God. Clearly Arminian believers will be much less prone to worry about reduced statistical chances or even arbitrary rejection (the Calvinists call it reprobation), since they are convinced that God desires, even longs for, all to be saved. Thus they should then be more optimistic about their chances to receive not only salvation but also the assurance that such a great salvation (offered on such a universal scale) will prove so alluringly desirable that the saved will be loath to mishandle such a gift. We therefore suggest that Arminian believers should logically be the most assured Christians in the world.

Once more, let's keep in mind that the vast majority of modern Calvinists have dropped the classic doctrine of irresistible election and also want to say, in good Arminian fashion, that all sinners can be saved. But they then declare that those who do respond to God's universal offer will suddenly find themselves in His irresistible clutches once they say yes! In other words, once God lovingly "hooks" any responsive sinner, that person is in the gospel boat to stay whether they want to or not.

The question then immediately presents itself: Why would God respect any believer's freely chosen decision to be initially saved but then immediately deny him or her the option of voluntarily choosing to leave His "loving" embrace? That question raises still another: What is it that is truly at the heart of the "once saved, always saved" concept?

The Basic Rationale of the "Once Saved, Always Saved" Teaching

At the risk of some repetition, we need to make clear the basic rationale undergirding the "once saved, always saved" position. What it boldly, even confidently, asserts is that God simply will not allow those who have responded to His call to salvation to slip away from His grasp. Thus the Lord providentially makes it impossible for any of His initially responsive children (defined as those who have accepted Him as their Savior) to fall away from their saving relationship with Him. Two basic versions of the idea have gained widespread acceptance.

The first version, already outlined, teaches something to the effect that

God will so forcefully hem in or surround the responsive believers with compelling, saving influences that they will find it virtually impossible to backslide. Thus they effectively cannot renege on their salvation commitment to the Lord. Moreover, if alleged believers should begin to stray from their saving relationship with God, the Godhead either will irresistibly protect them from the temptation to apostasy or will chastise them with a chain of providential circumstances so as to discourage any ultimate slippage away from their assured status among the saved.

But what about those alleged believers who give the appearance of losing their salvation or drifting away from the Lord's irrevocable embrace? The most common explanation is also the second popular version of irresistible perseverance. What this version claims is that such believers were never truly saved in the first place. Contemporary Reformed theologian Millard J. Erickson has articulated a good example of such a claim.

Erickson begins by clearly affirming "once saved, always saved": "The practical implication of our understanding of the doctrine of perseverance is that believers can rest secure in the assurance that their salvation is permanent; nothing can separate them from the love of God. Thus they can rejoice in the prospect of eternal life. There need be no anxiety that something or someone will keep them from attaining the final blessedness that they have been promised and have come to expect."

But not surprisingly, Erickson then feels the need to face up to the nettlesome issue of sinful presumption that so often accompanies the idea that such a salvation is so secure that it cannot be lost. "On the other hand, however, our understanding of the doctrine of perseverance allows no room for indolence or laxity. It is questionable whether anyone who reasons, 'Now that I am a Christian, I can live as I please,' *has really been converted and regenerated.*"[3] In other words, if someone manifests persistent evidence of apostasy, that person was simply never truly converted in the first place. As a result, Erickson has summarily rendered the argument almost impossible to deal with at any truly coherent, practical level. What should we make of such logic?

An Arminian Response

First of all, we must admit, even from the Arminian perspective (which says that salvation can be lost), that it could well be true that there are believers whose tendency toward apostasy suggests that they were never genuinely converted in the first place. Jesus' parable of the sower speaks of "believers" who are "wayside," "rocky," or "thorny" ground types of professed Christians whose faith lacks deep rootage, and such wavering individuals can ultimately succumb to evil influences in their salvation pilgrimage (Luke 8:11-15).

But Calvinists reject the possibility of apostasy. And such a denial simply begs the question as to whether any given believer can be genuinely converted and then either heedlessly wander away by careless neglect or be led away by strong temptations and go on to openly renounce the saving power of God in their lives. After all, Jesus did plainly say that the great adversary works in such a way as to snatch the "word out of their hearts, lest they should believe and be saved" (verse 12).

Furthermore, many Reformed teachers conveniently ignore the fact that our Lord also declares that a person can "believe and be saved." And finally, the context explicitly states that the seed that fell on the rocks did "receive the word with joy" and "for a while" did "believe," strongly implying that their belief did effectually save them, if only temporarily.

If Jesus' teaching about "believing" and being "saved" has any merit, the question then becomes, Does such an experience of belief, one that ultimately fails or languishes, prove to be no belief at all? Or were Jesus' "rocky" variety of believers simply mentioned in order to put forward a sensible, cautionary warning to all Christians to be watchful lest they carelessly fall into such circumstances? For the Calvinist teachers (such as Erickson) the answer is that such individuals were never saved in the first place. But for the Arminian interpreters it seems obvious that such struggling believers could have been truly saved but just were not vigilant enough in their walk with Jesus. Thus their failure did not result from the secret will of the electing God, but simply because of a lack of attentiveness on the part of careless believers who still had the distinct possibility of finding healing for their backsliding ways.

So what about the believer who enters the stormy waters of intense struggle without having achieved the fuller trust of a persevering child of God? Should such a person be told that they were never saved in the first place? From an Arminian perspective such believers should receive the benefit of the doubt and then be strongly encouraged to look again to the Lord in faith for the healing of their propensity to backslide.

Now, let's assume (for the sake of discussion) that the truth claims of both positions (Reformed and Arminian) could justifiably go either way. At this point the Calvinist faces a critical question. If the "once saved, always saved" teacher is even close to being correct, this immediately raises another problem: Do not the Calvinist teachers share a common predicament with all Arminian believers? Think about it in the light of one more pressing yet illuminating issue.

If it is true that when God elects a person to salvation, the individual receives the gift of irresistible perseverance, how then can Reformed believers truly know that they have been either genuinely saved or lost? The problem becomes especially urgent when the battle with sin becomes especially intense and the temptations to apostasy seem almost overwhelming. Are we then to tell them that they were never truly saved in the first place?

No matter what the response may be from either camp, all believers, whether the "once saved, always saved" Reformed/Calvinist or the Arminian who is experiencing salvation from sin, face the real challenge of figuring out whether they are truly among the saved or among the unknowingly damned! We can only conclude that the Calvinist really has no built-in advantages over the Arminian, especially when it comes to any sort of genuine assurance from God regarding the status of their salvation. Put another way, both Calvinists and Arminians need to be able to discern the marks or evidences of their election to salvation if they are to have genuine assurance!

And thus we are back to the basic issues of the previous chapter, which dealt with the biblical teaching of the illuminating power of the Spirit—the "witness of the Spirit" and His work of communicating to our own spirit that we do have the evidences of election. Therefore it should not surprise us that the avowedly Calvinistic Erickson immediately declares that "genuine faith issues (manifests itself) . . . in the fruit of the Spirit. Assurance of salvation, the subjective conviction that one is a Christian, results from the Holy Spirit's giving evidence that He is at work in the life of the individual. The Spirit's work results in conviction on biblical grounds that God will enable the Christian to persist in that relationship—that nothing can separate the true believer from God's love."[4]

Both Calvinists and Arminians must seek subjective evidence that they are assured of their salvation. In actual fact, I have yet to meet any Calvinist believers who could share with me that they have found their names explicitly written in the Word of God, including the caveat that they had been specifically prophesied to be among the elect. Thus it seems most obvious that all professed believers (Calvinist or Arminian) have to figure out individually whether their particular names will be in the book of life.

Furthermore, the process inevitably demands a personal sorting out of the ways in which the Spirit illuminates the Word of God and speaks directly to believers, all for the purpose of personally convicting and guiding them into the path of ongoing assurance of salvation. And once more, not surprisingly, Erickson and other informed Calvinist writers and thinkers have explicitly had to deal with this aspect.

Besides Erickson, one of the most eminent twentieth-century Calvinist theologians, G. C. Berkouwer, has made a similar point. In his book *Divine Election* he devoted most of his chapter entitled "Election and the Certainty of Salvation" to the issues of what have been called the *syllogismus mysticus* and the *syllogismus practicus*.[5]

These clumsy-sounding Latin terms deal with the question of whether believers should be able to draw logical, syllogistic conclusions regarding the evidences of the genuineness of what is "actually present in the believers" as their personal experience of election and salvation unfolds.[6] Such terminology, of course, is just different language referring to two aspects of the a posteriori evidences that we discussed in the previous chapter. To put it another way, Berkouwer is here wrestling with the question of the Spirit's saving illumination of the Word of God and the more direct "witness of the Spirit" (the *syllogismus mysticus*) in raising believers' personal awareness that they are actually having a genuine experience of salvation. The key issue that Calvinists have always struggled with involves whether it is a denial of election to be seeking to discover any subjective evidences of the work of the Spirit in the experience of individual believers.

Berkouwer, after a torturous discussion of all the objections raised in the anguished debates over the *syllogismus practicus* and *mysticus* in the Reformed tradition, finally comes to the studied conclusion that it is indeed legitimate for any believer to engage in sanctified self-examination for the subjective marks, evidences, or signs of election (again, the a posteriori evidences of personal experience) to salvation and ongoing perseverance.

And in his affirmation Berkouwer explicitly recognizes a number of factors that contribute to the legitimacy of any such search. He believes that personal faith always receives some direct "witness of the Spirit" that the believer is indeed a child of God. Furthermore, he makes his claim not only from Scripture but also on the basis of John Calvin's powerful teaching that when any truly elected believer responds to the converting work of the Holy Spirit, it mystically and personally unites that individual with Christ by faith.

Moreover, the normal result of a personal faith union is not only that Christ imputes justifying righteousness to the believer by faith alone, but that the Lord of salvation also imparts the sanctifying or transforming power of the Spirit into their hearts and lives. That is, not only does the Spirit of God lead the believer to receive and confirm His forgiving grace, but also He "witnesses" directly to the person's "spirit" that the imputation of Christ's righteousness has actually taken place.

But the Spirit's witness does not end with His confirmation of forgiveness. The believer is also comforted with the direct experience of the presence of the transforming Christ who, through the same Spirit, comes to dwell in the heart of the saved sinner. Such a transforming or sanctifying presence will become subjectively quite self-evident to the elect, trusting soul led to recognize the fruit of the Spirit in his or her personal experience (the so-called *syllogismus practicus*).

To state the issue as plainly as possible, both the Calvinistic way of salvation and the Arminian view have unavoidable personal, subjective elements. Calvinistic believers expect such evidence to be just as "evident" as the Arminian believers do. And if such evidences are not abundantly and ultimately made clear, a serious crisis of faith will ensue. To put it another way, the Calvinist believers are very much in the same boat with the Arminians when it comes to the need for the evidences of election and perseverance. Thus it is only logical to conclude that Calvinist believers have no ultimate advantage when it comes to assurance of salvation in Christ!

Jerry Moon claims that the "doctrine of 'once saved, always saved' is simply a theoretical guarantee of eternal security, not an actual guarantee, since in that theological system (Reformed/Calvinistic), *one cannot infallibly know that one was 'once saved.'*"[7] Once more we find ourselves reminded of the common privileges and challenges of all (both Calvinist and Arminian) who would be united to Christ by a saving faith that justifies, sanctifies, and assures. Moreover, an important aspect of such privileges is that the Spirit of God will not leave any believer bereft of the illuminating power of the Spirit's direct witness and its more indirect working that sparks the witness of our own spirit.

Who Has the Better Biblical Evidence?

Perhaps the reader wonders why I have not engaged in an extended discussion regarding the Bible evidences for or against the respective claims of the Calvinist and the Arminian positions as to whether salvation can be lost or not. But if what we have already suggested is true, then that whole discussion is, for the ultimate purposes of this book, made somewhat moot. But a few sample comments about the respective biblical strengths and weaknesses of both theological schools would provide some helpful background.[8] Though not exhaustive, the following arguments are quite representative of each position.

The key evidence commonly put forth by Calvinists revolves around such verses as John 10:27-29: "My sheep hear my voice, and I know them, and they follow Me. And I give them eternal life, and they shall never perish; neither shall anyone snatch them out of My hand. My Father, who has given them to Me, is greater than all; and no one is able to snatch them out of My Father's hand." The typical Calvinist interpretation concludes that since "no one is able to snatch them out of" the "Father's hand," believers are eternally secure against apostasy.

The Arminian response normally unfolds along the following lines. While it may be true that no other being in the universe can ultimately cause someone to lose their salvation, this does not apply to those who decide to ignore the saving graces that placed them into the saving hand of the Father in the first place. Is God's fatherly love such that He forces them to stay with Him against their will? For the Arminian the answer seems patently obvious, or we turn God into some deterministic overlord of the universe. Such an interpretation as the Calvinists normally give to this text seems more typical of the brutish love of a "caveman" sallying forth to find a lover and promptly hits the "elected one" over the head and drags her into his "loving" lair. Carl Bangs is quite correct when he claimed that James Arminius' objective in refuting the Calvinist claims was to present "a theology of grace which does not leave man" to be reduced to the status of a "stock or a stone." For Arminius and all Arminians, "grace is not a force; it is a Person" who lovingly draws sinners to embrace His saving love.[9]

One hesitates to sound so dismissive of the Calvinistic position, but when we have assessed the arguments for various other texts cited in support of the concept, it reminds one of the sign that hung outside of the old blacksmith shops of yesteryear: "All sorts of fancy twisting and turnings done here." We are not here suggesting that the Calvinistic position totally lacks any evidence, and we do acknowledge that some of their arguments involve a certain type of persuasiveness. But they ultimately seem to be largely based on a type of logic that has to assume some sort of deterministic, irresistible presupposition. Unfortunately, such presuppositions just seem to distort the overall biblical portrait of God as a savior who employs persuasive love, not forced affection borne of an intensely controlling determinism.

Another common Calvinistic argument is their use of logical conclusions drawn from parallelism. Robert Shank examines this approach, including the commonly used reasons employed in its support, and then offers the following critique.

"A popular and serious error is the assumption that an equation somehow exists between physical birth and spiritual birth: whatever is intrinsic in physical birth is equally intrinsic in spiritual birth; whatever may be predicated of one may likewise be predicated of the other. Laboring under such erroneous [assumptions], many have concluded that spiritual birth, like physical birth, is necessarily irrevocable. 'If one has been born,' they ask, 'how can he possibly become unborn?' 'I may be a wayward, disobedient son,' say they, 'but I must forever remain my father's own son.' In defense of what seems to them to be an obviously logical conclusion, they have proceeded in good conscience to impose unwarranted and fanciful interpretation upon many simple discourses of Jesus and upon many plain, explicit warning passages in the New Testament. After all, the Scriptures must agree!"[10]

Shank then proceeds to outline "three essential differences between physical and spiritual birth:" "1. Physical birth effects the inception of the life of the subject *in toto*, whereas spiritual life involves only a transition from one mode of life to another." "2. In physical birth, the subject has no prior knowledge and gives no consent, whereas in spiritual birth, the subject must have prior knowledge of the Gospel and must give consent." "3. In physical birth, the individual receives a life independent of his parents. They may die, but he lives on. But in spiritual birth, the subject receives no independent life. . . . In view of obvious essential differences, it cannot be considered strange that spiritual birth, unlike physical birth, is not irrevocable. . . . Physical birth and spiritual birth are equally real, but essentially different. While an analogy exists between the two, there is no equation whatever."[11]

The strength of the Arminian interpretation of their key supporting passages is that their proof texts so obviously suggest the possibility or even the historical reality of spiritual apostasy for genuine believers. For instance, the parable or illustration of the vine and the branches, found in John 15:1-11, exhibits abundant evidence that a well-connected "branch" (the believer) attached to the "vine" (Christ) can be cut away and burned up. The parable is simply strong evidence that those once entwined with Christ can be cut away and lost forever.

In addition to the teachings of Jesus, we find in Scripture numerous other warnings of the possibility of apostasy. Here one immediately thinks of 2 Peter 2, in which the apostle speaks of those who "have escaped the pollutions of the world through the knowledge of the Lord and Savior Jesus Christ" and "are again entangled in them and overcome" (verse 20). Then he adds that "the latter end is worse for them than the beginning. For it would have been better for them not to have known the way of righteousness, than having known it, to turn from the holy commandment delivered to them" (verses 20, 21). Paul writes to Timothy urging him to "wage the good warfare, having faith and a good conscience, which some having rejected, concerning the faith have suffered shipwreck, of whom are Hymenaeus and Alexander, who I delivered to Satan that they may learn not to blaspheme" (1 Tim. 1:18-20).

One of the most explicit passages regarding the possibility of apostasy comes from the words of Jesus in His letter to the church at Sardis: "He who overcomes shall be clothed in white garments, and *I will not blot out his name from the Book of Life*; but I will confess his name before My Father and before His angels" (Rev. 3:5). Jon Paulien's succinct comments speak right to the point at issue: "It seems clear from this text that Jesus didn't believe in the popular version of 'once saved, always saved.' Remaining in the book of life is the result of an ongoing process of 'overcoming' (a Greek participle in the present tense). Thus remaining in the book of life rests on continuing relationship with Jesus, not some arbitrary decree on God's part. While our works are never the basis for our salvation, good works are the ongoing evidence that people are saved (Rev. 19:7, 8). Righteous deeds are the garments of the righteous. The promise that God gives to those who continue to overcome—that He will not blot their names out of the book of life—is a warning to all Christians who think that mere profession or church attendance will be sufficient to ensure their salvation."[12]

The final exhibits are the sad histories of Lucifer, the angels cast out of heaven with him, and Adam and Eve, the first humans who fell into sin. What are we to make of the apostasies of these once-perfect beings?

Lucifer was the highest of all created beings in the universe, yet somehow became the devil and Satan (see Eze. 28; Isa. 14; and Rev. 12). Can anyone really believe that the loving triune God created Lucifer and his rebellious angelic compatriots with the specific intention for them to morph into the beings we refer to as demons and devils? The answer appears so obvious as not even to merit a reply! Thus if the highest of all the created beings in the universe could be subject to the possibility of apostasy (and do it in the very presence of the loving triune God), who is to say that sinful human believers would be exempt from the same possibility?

The case of Adam and Eve is similar. In their sinless state in Eden, can we say that they began life in a "saved" condition? It seems that, in a special sense, they started life by being initially saved from the death-dealing bloodlust of Lucifer and his fellow fallen angels. God not only protected them from Satan's power, but warned them about his presence at the tree of the knowledge of good and evil. But God did not irresistibly guarantee them safety from the temptations of the devil. They, like us, though we were born sinful and fallen, needed to heed the instructions of God's grace and trust in His warnings about the demonic dangers lurking in Eden. If it was possible for the sinless Adam and Eve to fall from their state of sinless grace (which was given to them and retained on condition that they exercise a protecting faith in God's gracious warnings and guidance), who is to say that it is somehow impossible for saved sinners to fall from their state of favor with God? To state it more directly, would it be fair of God to give an ironclad guarantee to lost sinners saved by grace, but not grant the same gift to the sinless and unfallen Lucifer, one third of the heavenly angels, and Adam and Eve?

It was these scriptural passages and stories, along with many others that we could cite, that finally convinced the arch-Calvinist Baptist theologian Clark Pinnock to give up on the teaching of irresistible perseverance ("once saved, always saved") and embrace conditional perseverance. During the 1970s, while teaching at Trinity Evangelical Divinity School in northern Illinois, the doctrine of irresistible perseverance began to crumble in his mind. His loss of conviction regarding "once saved, always saved" transpired while he was engaged in sustained reflection on the biblical evidence, especially the witness of the New Testament book of Hebrews.

"If in fact believers enjoy the kind of absolute security Calvinism had taught me they do, I found I could not make very good sense of the vigorous exhortations to persevere (e.g., Hebrews 3:12) or the awesome warnings not to fall away from Christ (e.g., Hebrews 10:26), which the book addresses to Christians."[13] Pinnock then went on to tell how he began to conceive of an alternative version of perseverance more attuned to the larger narrative of God's dynamic way of salvation.

"It began to dawn on me that my security in God was linked to my faith-union with Christ and that God is teaching us here the extreme importance of maintaining and not forsaking this relationship. The exhortations and the warnings could only signify that continuing in the grace of God was something that depended at least in part on the human partner. And once I saw that, the logic of Calvinism was broken in principle, and it was only a matter of time before the larger implications of its breaking would dawn on me. The thread was pulled, and the garment must begin to unravel, as indeed it did.

"What had dawned on me was what I had known experientially all along in my walk with the Lord, that there is a profound mutuality in our dealings with God. . . . For the first time, I realized theologically that the dimension of reciprocity and conditionality had to be brought into the picture of God's relations with us in creation and redemption and that, once it is brought in, the theological landscape would have to change significantly. The determinist model cannot survive once a person starts down this road."[14]

Some Final Considerations

I want to affirm that Pinnock touched on a vital principle of the assurance of salvation when he claimed that his "security in God was linked to" his "faith union with Christ and . . . the extreme importance of maintaining and not forsaking this relationship." Does not the Bible and our own personal history of faith in Christ resonate with this realization?

As I have reflected on these issues, the concept has gradually evolved in my own mind that our beloved Calvinistic brothers and sisters, in their longing for a secure relationship to Christ, have overemphasized the importance of the moment of redemption, leading to a neglect of salvation's long-term relational dynamics. And it is the long-haul relational dynamics, not so much the initial moment of the realization of redemption, that truly generates the critical core of the Christian's assurance of salvation. Most certainly the initial moment and its deep commitments are absolutely foundational, but it does not negate the personal choices of faith's ongoing responsibilities in the believer's saving walk with the Lord.

The initial moment of saving faith is the beginning of the Christian's pilgrimage, not an experience of being irresistibly "hooked" by Christ. To the contrary, it is the start of a lifetime of responsive and responsible give-and-take that steadily grows and deepens into the mutuality of a dynamic loving relationship. Therefore, this more relational vision (version) of salvation seems truer to the biblical portrait that portrays a God who is lovingly self-giving in the interest of our reconciliation. It clearly stands in contrast to the questionable vision of God being some sort of relentless manipulator deity intent on kicking in the doors of our hearts and forcefully binding us to Himself. Once more, it seems that Carl Bangs was correct: "Grace is not a force; it is a Person"!

It is true that God's pursuit of us does have some sovereign aspects to it. As I mentioned in chapter 3, God must always take the initiative in our salvation. And in this sense, He does come knocking at the doors of our hearts—whether we want Him to or not. But the truth is that He simply does not knock our doors down! Instead of irresistible force, He offers winsome appeals and motives that seek to elicit a positive, love-engendered response from our grace-transformed "freed" wills.

Furthermore, I would suggest that many Arminians will readily attest that God's persistent pursuit of us can, on occasion, feel downright compelling (though it never ultimately forces anyone's will). Contemporary Methodist theologian Geoffrey Wainwright has sagely recalled an old truism: "When push comes to shove in Christian experience and witness, Arminians preach the assurance of salvation in a manner worthy of a Calvinist and Calvinists seek salvation through prayers which sound very much like those of a free-will Methodist."[15] Indeed, many can testify to the persistence with which God has sought and nurtured them. On occasion, it feels as if He is a watchful mother bear. Moreover, the persistent, prayerful intercessions of many Calvinists evoke the need for human cooperation with divine providence in seeking the salvation of the lost. But neither position necessitates either a doctrine of irresistible, deterministic election and perseverance or some bald doctrine of humanistic, natural free will.

With a proper emphasis on the central importance of salvation being understood or conceived of as a complete process of cooperative interaction between the Savior and the individual believer, all the way from initial belief until glorification, we offer the following cautionary caveats regarding the "once saved, always saved" version of Christian assurance.

A Cautious Critique of Irresistible Perseverance

First of all, our hope is in Christ, not ultimately in a once-for-all decision made in response to an altar call during some local church revival, evangelistic series, summer camp, or camp meeting. The important thing is to remain constantly attentive by keeping our focus on Jesus and His abundant graces and thus nurture the spiritual discipline of responsive sensitivity to the leading of the Spirit through the ministry of the Word.

Second, the focus of the Reformed version of perseverance is on faith itself. But important as faith is, its primary focus is not to be on itself. Faith is a gift of God that has no real virtue in and of itself, except that its great efficacy is found in the One it lays hold of. Furthermore, saving faith is not to be primarily defined as an exercise in giving mental assent to an abstract or theoretical guarantee of irrevocable assurance. Rather, biblical faith is better defined as a heartfelt trust in Christ that embraces Him as the one and only person capable of keeping believers effectively convinced that their salvation is steadily assured. Herbert Douglass has succinctly expressed it this way: the "secret" of Christian assurance is that "we are not to trust in our faith, but in God's faithfulness."[16]

Therefore, any present blessings of the assurance of salvation have much more to do with the believer's current faith focus on Christ than it does in what faith did in some supposed "once for all time" claiming of salvation during a particularly moving altar call. Any initial exercise of faith that claims salvation at the instigation of the Spirit is of vital importance. But it is only a conscious beginning. Therefore, persevering assurance is much more the result of an ongoing focus on Christ rather than on faith itself and its past exercise.

Third, as acknowledged earlier by Millard Erickson, the "once saved, always saved" version of assurance has had a checkered history of presumption and antinomian attitudes on the part of many Calvinists. And it was this troubling tendency that provoked John Wesley and the vast majority of later Arminian Christians to oppose so strongly and persistently the Calvinistic version of Christian election, perseverance, and assurance.

Moreover, at an elemental level of pastoral concern, I can personally attest to the wisdom of the long-standing Wesleyan/Arminian aversion to Calvinistic inspired versions of assurance. Such troubling cheap-grace attitudes are still all too evident among Reformed-oriented believers.

The idea that believers can go on knowingly transgressing God's law and still consider themselves saved is currently very much alive and well among many professed believers who seek to excuse themselves from confronting their lingering sins. Furthermore, the issue includes not just indulgence in known defects, but an all-too-common refusal to embrace the Spirit's call to incorporate new moral and practical duties into their personal Christian walk. The fruit of the irresistible grace teachings is simply not good.

In the face of such persistent attitudes of "cheap grace," antinomian excuses for sin,[17] and the self-evident fact that the Calvinists have no real built-in advantages (either theologically or practically) when it comes to the assurance of salvation, we would suggest the following:

On balance, the Wesleyan/Arminian (and Adventist) version of the personal assurance of salvation is the preferred biblical, theological, and practical route to take in our walk with the Lord. But we hasten to acknowledge that the Arminian way also has had some distinct challenges of its own. And they have generally manifested themselves in Adventism as a response to the perfection challenges raised by the prospect of the future end-time crisis of faith. What then are we to make of the sobering prospects raised by the biblical and Ellen White teachings on the close of probation and the rigors of the great time of trouble? We now turn our attention to these fascinating questions and their implications for personal assurance of salvation.

---

[1] Calvin claimed that the pool of candidates for divine election to salvation included only "that little number whom he [God] has reserved for himself," or "only a few people" (cited from Francois Wendel's classic analysis of Calvin's theology entitled *Calvin: Origins and Development of His Religious Thought* [New York: Harper & Row, Pub., 1963], pp. 279, 280).

[2] Most certainly Arminians also need to admit that only a relative few (compare I Tim. 2:3, 4; Titus 2:11; and 2 Peter 3:9) will embrace Christ's offer of salvation. Jesus clearly states that the vast majority of humanity will not accept His gracious offer of redemption (Matt. 7:13, 14). But that is a far cry from the Calvinist concept that claims that the small number results from God's sovereign decision instead of those who could have chosen to be in the kingdom.

[3] Millard J. Erickson, *Christian Theology*, 2nd ed. (Grand Rapids: Baker Books, 1998), pp. 1007, 1008. (Italics supplied.)

[4] *Ibid.*

[5] G. C. Berkouwer, *Divine Election: Studies in Dogmatics* (Grand Rapids: Wm. B. Eerdmans Pub. Co., 1960), pp. 278-306.

[6] *Ibid.*, p. 286.

[7] Moon's observation is just one key point of his wonderful lecture regarding Ellen White's true teachings on the issue of assurance of salvation. His lecture forms the heart of chapter 11, "Ellen G. White on the Assurance of Salvation: Are Her Writings a Help or a Stumbling Block?" Furthermore, Moon's point about "once saved, always saved" being a "theoretical guarantee, not an actual guarantee" of the assurance of salvation will be further elaborated at that point.

[8] Erickson gives a spirited summary in his *Christian Theology* (pp. 997-1003) of the key arguments normally used to defend both the Calvinistic and Arminian concepts of perseverance. Of course, he sees the resolution as falling on the Calvinistic side of the issue (pp. 1003-1008). The classic defense of the Arminian position (and refutation of the Calvinistic arguments) on perseverance appears in Robert Shank, *Life in the Son*, 2nd ed. (Springfield, Mo.: Westcott Pub., 1961). For the more recent editions, the reader can readily locate them on the internet.

[9] Cited by Roger E. Olson, *Arminian Theology: Myths and Realities* (Downers Grove, Ill.: IVP academic, 2006), p. 164.

[10] *Ibid.*, pp. 89, 90.

[11] *Ibid.*, pp. 90, 91.

[12] Jon Paulien, *The Gospel From Patmos: Everyday Insights for Living From the Last Book of the Bible* (Hagerstown, Md.: Review and Herald Pub. Assn., 2007), p. 79.

[13] Clark Pinnock, gen. ed., "From Augustine to Arminius: A Pilgrimage in Theology," *The Grace of God and the Will of Man* (Minneapolis: Bethany House Pub., 1989), p. 17.

[14] *Ibid.*, pp. 17, 18.

[15] The quotation is Whidden's rough paraphrase of comments made by Wainwright, though he could not locate the actual source of the quotation in Wainwright's *Methodists in Dialog* (Nashville: Kingswood Books, 1995).

[16] Herbert E. Douglass, *Should We Ever Say, "I Am Saved"? What It Means to be Assured of Salvation* (Nampa, Idaho: Pacific Press Pub. Assn., 2002), p. 26.

[17] We do want to make it clear that not all Calvinist/Reformed Christians manifest such attitudes, but it is all too evident in their corridors of influence, including the experiences of numerous Seventh-day Adventists who have been either implicitly or explicitly affected by the popular preaching and publishing venues of Calvinsitic/Reformed teaching. We sense that the Arminian viewpoint offers, on balance, a better way.

Chapter 9

The Latter Rain, the Close of Probation, and the Time of Trouble—Who Will Assuredly Thrive and Survive?

Introduction

The subjects of the latter rain of the Holy Spirit, the close of probation, and the time of trouble (also called the great time of trouble or the time of Jacob's trouble) are biblically based Seventh-day Adventist terms used to describe events immediately preceding the second coming of Jesus. Furthermore, they form part of the legitimate interpretation of important Bible prophecies and have received detailed attention from Ellen White.[1]

But they have also been the objects of sustained fascination for those interested not only in eschatology (final events) but also with interpretations of both the Bible and Ellen White that have implications for Christian perfection. And some of the perfection-oriented interpretations have not been all that balanced. Thus it is in the connection between closing events and the issue of Christian perfection that we find the apparent source of the considerable anxiety that has emerged when these themes enter any Adventist discussion of personal Christian assurance.

First of all, however, we must clearly define the terms and their place in the sequence of final events in earth's history. At the same time we need to remind the reader that the most important facet of these issues has to do with the legitimate redemptive purposes that God intends for such events to have in the pilgrimage of His faithful last-day followers (Rev. 12:17 and 14:12). If we can clarify this latter issue, it is most probable that we can demonstrate better how the conclusion of the pre-Advent investigative judgment at the close of probation and the time of trouble could or could not be negative for any genuine experience of Christian assurance. Thus the real question is: *What should be the chief characteristics of the faith experience of those people of God who face history's last great pre-Advent crisis?*

But before we address the issues introduced in the previous paragraphs, we must make some preliminary observations about the close of probation and the fact that the Bible clearly teaches that the history of our world, as we now know it, will come to a cataclysmic end. So what is essential for any understanding about the close of probation and the end of the world?

The End of History—The Implications for All Christians

In a general sense, the somewhat complex set of issues surrounding the pre-Advent investigative judgment and the close of probation are not unique to Seventh-day Adventists. Such challenges confront all Bible-believing Christians who take the scriptural teaching of the second coming of Christ seriously, including evangelicals who have promoted a dispensationalist interpretation of the final events of earth's history. Dispensationalists speak of the secret rapture (or the "great snatch"), a two-phase version of the second coming of Christ, and regard contemporary events unfolding in Israel and the Middle East as the epicenter of end-time prophetic fulfillment. In addition, they predict a great "tribulation period" just before God puts into place some earthly millennial rule at the glorious, visible phase of the Second Coming.

Thus while Seventh-day Adventists do have some significant doctrinal disagreements with many of our Bible-believing fellow spiritual travelers (including dispensationalists), all Christians who believe in Christ's return still recognize that a serious crisis of faith lies ahead for all of us. Furthermore, these common agreements include the fact that the vast majority of Bible-oriented Christians believe that our world will end with an irreversible division between the faithful who will be saved and the unbelievers who will be eternally lost. Thus when the time of the end of all things emerges, there will be no changing sides, and all those living will have settled their eternal destinies either through belief or unbelief in Christ and His gospel.

Let's make the previous point absolutely clear. If there is going to be a time when every case will be eternally decided, with no more opportunities for switching allegiances, then God must have a basic series of redemptive events that include the following: (1) a final warning; (2) a decisive, completed process of investigative judgment that reveals who will be saved or lost; and (3) a final cosmic battle in which the forces of righteousness will decisively triumph over those of Satan and evil.

Furthermore, if any person does not believe in such a decisive sequence of final events, the chances are quite good that they will also not be overly concerned with issues of personal salvation (including personal assurance) and how they will be involved in any final, eternal settlement during the end time. For example, if you were Daniel and you did not believe that lions were a serious threat to your life, you would not worry much about them or see any need to exercise faith in God when thrown into a den of them. But if there are real prospects of having to face a set of dangers associated with the final events of world history, then that very thought should raise serious concerns about being ready to meet the impending crisis.

Moreover, we should not regard such ideas as inherently destructive to any real position of Christian assurance. To the contrary, *the anticipation that God will one day soon defeat the adversaries of truth, righteousness, and justice and eternally save and vindicate His faithful and loyal servants should generate a fervent experience of genuine Christian assurance!*

But What About Fear as a Motivator?

Many Christians (including concerned Adventists) are somewhat leery of end-time issues because they feel that fear should not be a major factor in motivating people to get ready for heaven. Such cautions do contain an element of truth that both the Bible and Ellen White have wisely affirmed. But while they do not present the threat of punishment and the frightful prospect of a fast-approaching end-time crisis as the primary motivational factors for serious preparation, both sources of inspiration do teach that the end is soon to come and that every believer in Christ should take this sobering reality seriously. Perhaps a simple illustration will help.

Suppose you have reliable information that an arsonist will burn down the house that some friends live in. They will not appreciate it if you fail to warn them! To do otherwise, in the name of not using fear as a primary motivational factor, is simply criminal and has little to do with any commonsense understanding as to what constitutes merciful sensitivity.

A final preliminary reflection related to the fear motivation concerns one other eschatological issue starkly relevant for all Bible-believing Christians who do not indulge in "second-chance" fantasies.[2] It involves another simple Bible truth: when someone dies the first death, that person's eternal destiny will be eternally sealed at the moment of expiration.

Therefore, all those who will not live to see the coming of the Lord will have already faced a "close of probation" and sealed their eternal destiny sometime before or at the moment of death. Their life histories are forever settled, and they await the final revelation of the just judgments of God on the last day. Thus for all who are now alive, their close of probation could come at any moment when they draw their last earthly breath. So what are we to make of these obvious Bible facts?

The most appropriate Christian response is to conclude that "now is the day, now is the time" of salvation. Especially for convinced, active Adventist Christians, every moment is fraught with eternal consequences as to the quality of the faith they are developing (and exercising). Therefore, no wise Christian (Adventist or otherwise) will put off serious spiritual and moral decisions to a more "convenient season" (Acts 24:25, KJV). The only truly "convenient season" for the critical decisions of faith is right now, this very day, when the Holy Spirit is wooing, convincing, convicting, and leading to a deeper experience in God's grace.

Thus every moment of the present life is crucial in determining each and every one's unchanging eternal destiny. Is this fearmongering? The reader will have to make that call, but it seems that the wisest course for all who profess the name of Christ is right now to commit themselves unreservedly to make their calling and election eternally sure!

Now that we have clarified the larger contours of the end-time concerns shared by a wide range of Christians, we will begin to grapple with the practical challenges of what proper readiness entails. But first we need to lay out the basic Adventist understanding of how the sequence of end-time events will unfold.

The Basic Sequence of Closing Events

As eschatology is not the primary concern of this book, the following comments will be a somewhat summary review. Furthermore, space does not permit extensive discussion of the biblical support for such interpretations. Our comments, however, will be sufficient to set the appropriate chronological and spiritual contexts of the basic Adventist teachings on eschatology so that the reader can gain a better idea as to how its events will affect any genuine believer's personal assurance of salvation.

Seventh-day Adventist end-time teachings unfold a scenario in which global events will continue to gather momentum as the time for the second coming of Jesus approaches. Fundamental in these teachings is the conviction that God never judges (either in investigation or in its executions) without sending a message of merciful warning. Moreover, the warning/mercy terminology has normally been associated with the events of the loud cry.[3]

The loud cry will feature a concluding worldwide gospel appeal initiated and empowered by the "latter rain" of the Holy Spirit (compare Rev. 7:1-3; 14:6-12; and 18:1-4).[4] This mighty Spirit-led work is the dramatic occasion when the whole world will definitively divide into two distinct, irreversible groups, those who receive the "mark of the beast" and those graced with the "seal of the living God."[5]

Therefore, those receive the seal of God will compose the living saints who will see the coming of Christ without experiencing death, and those who receive the mark of the beast will become the human agents of Satan in the great and final global crisis. The brightness of Christ's second coming will destroy the latter, while angels gather up the former to take them to heaven to meet their Savior.

Now when the final, universal division, precipitated by the loud cry, reaches its completion, the pre-Advent judgment in heaven ceases and the close of probation[6] takes place. Then, immediately following the close of probation, the time of trouble, also called the time of Jacob's trouble, commences (Dan. 12:1-3 and Rev. 13). Furthermore, the time of trouble will also be the occasion for the pouring out of the seven last plagues on those that have received the mark of the beast (Rev. 15 and 16).[7]

Seventh-day Adventist prophetic interpretation teaches two clear-cut challenges for God's sealed and loyal people. They will go through the solemn period of Jacob's trouble. But to do that, they will need to have a faith that shields them from (1) the terrors threatened by Satan and his agents and (2) the horrors of the seven last plagues that successively fall on Satan's people who seek to destroy the faithful saints.[8]

And finally, when it looks as though the forces of evil will overwhelm God's beleaguered people, the sovereign Lord spectacularly intervenes to deliver them at the second coming of Jesus.[9] At the same time the brightness of Christ's appearing annihilates those with the mark of the beast (Rev. 19:17-21), the righteous dead will be resurrected, and they, along with the living faithful, will be caught up together to meet their Lord in the air. God transports the vast multitude of the redeemed of all ages to heaven where they will spend the millennium with the Trinity and the unfallen angels (John 14:1-3; 1 Thess. 4:13-5:4; and Rev. 20:6).[10]

Furthermore, during the heavenly millennium God will clarify all of His judgments on both the living saints and the lost of all ages (the bodies of the latter group lie moldering back on earth during the millennial period [Rev. 20:1-5]). When the millennium concludes, the entire host of the redeemed descends to the earth in the new Jerusalem. It is at this time that the final great "white throne" investigative and executive judgments take place. Satan and all of his followers (both angelic and human) receive their conclusive judgment and destruction in the lake of fire (Rev. 20:7-15). God re-creates our purged world, and it will become the abode of the redeemed for all eternity (Rev. 21:1-8).[11]

What then should be the proper attitude and response of those who face the possibility of living through the sobering events of the last great crisis of earth's history? Furthermore, what does the salvation experience of God's people during it have to do with Christian assurance?

Key End-time Events—the Implications for Assurance

Without a doubt, it appears that the most serious and relevant questions orbit around the spiritual status of God's people as they face the final deliberations of the pre-Advent investigative judgment, the close of probation, and the time of trouble.

Most certainly it is during the pre-Advent investigative judgment, before the close of probation, that a final determination will take place as to who shall receive the seal of God (Rev. 22:12, 13). Moreover, what follows the determination and revelation of those sealed is that they will then immediately be engulfed in the horrors of the crisis called the great time of trouble. But what kind of faith experience will typify those who will receive the seal of God, and how can believers now be assured that they possess such a faith?

What Is True "Sealing" and "Time of Trouble" Faith?

It seems quite obvious that the type of faith needed to carry any true believer through such decisive end-time events (the close of probation and the time of trouble) will be the same kind of saving faith referred to in the earlier chapters of this study. Therefore, the hallmarks of such a faith will be that it will claim rich drafts of justifying and sanctifying/perfecting grace, including the optimistic prospect of glorifying grace—all of which find their source in Christ. It will feature constant, affirmative responsiveness to Christ's convicting, leading, guiding, forgiving, and transforming grace. Furthermore, Christ's grace is, and will also continually be, mediated to the faithful through the working of the Holy Spirit.

Therefore, all that we have previously established up to this point in our study still applies in any discussion of the end-time issues—especially as they relate to the personal assurance of salvation. But the end-time contexts of faith and assurance do raise some unique questions.

Some Further Questions on Faith and God's Fairness

For instance, do the faith descriptions of the previous paragraphs include a special preparation required of those who will face the end-time events we have been examining? Some have suggested that if the response is yes, God's fairness gets called into question. Or to put it another way, do those who die before the time of trouble have it easier than those who go through this great test of faith? Could it really be true that the faith of the sealed saints will trump or transcend the faith of those believers who will have to only face death and a friendly, personal wake-up call at the Second Coming? While I will certainly seek to answer such questions, I will before doing so offer the following caveat about the issue of divine fairness in sparing some from the time of trouble while sending others through such a fiery affliction.

A Question Not of Fairness but of Mercy

From the perspective of the Bible and Ellen White, it is really not a matter of simple fairness but one of God's mercy that seems to be in play in this instance. The Bible hints at such a thing when it proclaims a blessing on those who die in the context of the great seal of God versus the mark of the beast crisis: " 'Blessed are the dead who die in the Lord from now on.'

" 'Yes,' says the Spirit, 'that they may rest from their labors, and their works follow them' " (Rev. 14:13). Ellen White, in the same spirit, comments that infants and certain physically weakened believers (perhaps because of age, disease, or injury) will be laid to rest to await the appearing of Jesus. Such physical disabilities will preclude their being able to endure the rigors of the time of trouble.[12]

Therefore, it is not that great of a stretch to suggest that if God then allows others to go through the time of trouble, He must see something in them that will work out to His greater glory and their personal blessing. Does it seem fair? We sense that it is and will very much highlight divine mercy in this context. The basic idea of fairness emerges from the principle that if God is willing to supply special grace for special circumstances, this fact would justify or vindicate His fairness in allowing some to go through the time of trouble while sparing others from it.

With these thoughts in mind, let's return to our original question: Does the faith of the sealed, end-time living saints trump that of those who die before the Lord comes (with the latter being granted the comforting assurance of an imminent bodily resurrection)?

What About Translation Faith and Resurrection Faith?

Could it be that the answer is both a qualified yes and no? The reasons for the no unfold along the following lines of thought.

The faith that saves those facing death and those about to endure the crisis of living through the close of probation and the time of trouble are both manifestations of one that shares the same essential quality. What is common to both faith experiences is that they will require a trust that features (1) genuine, implicit dependence on Christ alone and (2) a willingness to receive everything that the entire range of God's grace has to offer.

Such a faith experience includes not only ongoing penitence, forgiveness, and character transformation, but also a complete willingness to experience a radical change of sinful human nature. In other words, those who will die before the Second Coming need a faith in Christ equaling that of the "sealed."

On the other hand, those who will possess a persevering faith through the close of probation and the time of trouble will need a "translation faith." It is clearly of the same basic nature as "resurrection faith." The difference, however, is that those who experience "translation faith" will have to endure (Except for Jesus' passion in Gethsemane and death on Calvary.) the most terrible crisis in the history of the world.

We will speak in more detail later on about the instructive parallels between the faith of Christ during His ordeals in Gethsemane and at Calvary and the faith of those who will survive through the close of probation and the time of trouble. But perhaps an illustration can help to make an important preliminary distinction between translation faith and resurrection faith. And it has to do with the difference between the more ordinary experience of early courtship and the later more serious phase—engagement to be married.

While both periods require a trust that features openness, responsiveness, and honesty, the act of engagement thrusts any couple into a crucial period with permanent consequences. Moreover, its seriousness is quite apparent to anybody who has experienced it.

To put it in the symbolic terms of appropriate attire for special occasions, it is one thing for a couple to get dressed for a balmy day picnic or a stroll in the park, but quite another matter what they wear as they walk up the aisle to the altar during a real wedding ceremony. A wedding involves the type of finality that requires the most serious considerations and the greatest of care in the preparation of each and every detail. One seldom sees pictures of picnics on living room or family room walls, but wedding photo galleries are common.

The picnic requires a social commitment analogous to the spiritual sense of responsive trust and cooperation, while a wedding, in marked contrast, includes much that reflects the experience of the latter-rain power of the Holy Spirit. Dressing for a date is one thing, but an engagement includes a preparation that has much higher stakes. And perhaps the key metaphor that we need to draw from biblical wedding plans involves the putting on of wedding garments (see Matt. 22:1-14 and Rev. 19:7, 8).

Most certainly appropriate spiritual garb is one of the primary goals of the experience of the latter rain of the Holy Spirit. Only those who are fully and appropriately dressed with the wedding garment of Christ will be able to face the close of human probation and the time of trouble. The difference between the two examples, though one of some subtlety, will be qualitatively significant in actual experience.

Maybe we can stretch the illustrations a bit further. It might be true that both of our dating couples could love each other enough to get married. Furthermore, if lightning should strike one of the individuals dead at the park, the survivor might even wish that he or she could have been married to that person. But while this is all that it should be in any experience of true love, there is still the stubborn fact that the wedding simply did not take place. Thus, it is one thing to love with such intent and quite another actually to experience that latter rain called covenant love—a love that actually makes the pilgrimage to the altar!

What can we reasonably conclude? Every stage in faith development is foundational and has saving significance. But the faith that will be latter-rain conditioned will uniquely prepare those who experience it to endure or persevere through the second greatest crisis in human history: the investigative judgment, the close of probation, and the time of trouble, all of which will more directly usher in the second coming of the heavenly Bridegroom.

Once more, I must emphasize that "dating faith" has redeeming effects. But "engagement faith" is a further maturation of the experience of love that will lead to marriage. Moreover, the "marriage" here contemplated will enable the partners to endure a uniquely terrible crisis before their love match emerges into a covenant of heavenly love that will be eternally sealed (settled once for all). The faith that leads to resurrection salvation is, in principle, the same as the faith that leads to translation salvation. It is just that translation faith will be tested in the context of the time of trouble.

As one of my perceptive students recently put it: "Different degrees of crisis call for greater degrees of grace, which are to be appropriately claimed by a more mature faith!"[13] Therefore it seems fair to conclude that the context that calls for various degrees of crisis faith ultimately has one, and only one, quality precedent.

The Gethsemane and Calvary Precedent

When one considers the great stresses the sealed saints will be forced to endure before the close of probation and during the time of trouble, the whole experience mainly seems to turn on one key Ellen White phrase: her claim that the people of God will have to "live in the sight of a holy God without an intercessor."[14] What does it mean to live "without an intercessor"? It sounds sobering, even ominous! But let's ratchet things up another notch or two. Consider the following from the pen of Ellen White:

"Now, while our great High Priest is making the atonement for us, we should seek to become perfect in Christ. Not even by a thought could our Saviour be brought to yield to the power of temptation. Satan finds in human hearts some point where he can gain a foothold; some sinful desire is cherished, by means of which his temptations assert their power. But Christ declared of Himself: 'The prince of this world cometh, and hath nothing in Me' (John 14:30). Satan could find nothing in the Son of God that would enable him to gain the victory. He had kept His Father's commandments, and there was no sin in Him that Satan could use to his advantage. This is the condition in which those must be found who shall stand in the time of trouble."[15]

Evidently, what will transpire during this time is that God's sealed, faithful people will be severely tested. That immediately raises the question of the nature of this terrible crisis. Once more we need to point out that the testing of the sealed end-time saints has to do with the quality of their faith. And it is at this juncture that the analogy of their experience with that of Christ in Gethsemane and on Calvary becomes absolutely critical.

I still recall the thrill I felt the first time that I encountered it.[16] I instinctively knew that I was onto something of profound spiritual and theological significance. And in reality, it was only during the preparation of this chapter that the depths of this perspective have unfolded in a fuller and most rewarding way.

What I am proposing consists of a carefully drawn analogy involving the experience of the Old Testament patriarch Jacob and our Savior Christ in their respective times of testing and trouble. Furthermore, it extends, or applies, to the ordeal of the sealed saints of the final time of trouble. And finally the analogy will provide the crucial keys for a better understanding of the "how" and "why" of God's providences in leading His last-day saints into the final furnace of affliction—the great time of Jacob's trouble.

Justification by Faith—Right Now—Becomes the Key Factor

What we are here suggesting contains a profoundly intimate tie-in between the experience of Jacob in his night of wrestling by the river Jabbok, the passion crisis of Christ in Gethsemane and on Calvary, and the fiery ordeal of the tried and tested end-time remnant. Each example clearly places the spotlight on the believer's premier asset for Christian assurance: the experience of justification by grace, through faith alone!

But even more specifically, the question is this: What do all three incidents have in common when it comes to justification by faith alone?

First of all, the salient feature of Jacob's struggle by the Jabbok concerned his fear that his repentance for the deceits and injustices inflicted against his brother, Esau, and his father, Isaac, had not been acceptable to God. In other words, Jacob's ultimate struggle with the Angel of the Lord rose from his desire for assurance that his penitence was genuine and his sins had been forgiven.

It is therefore strikingly relevant that the guilt-ridden but penitent Jacob refused to let his wrestling partner go and finally blurted, "I will not let You go unless You bless me!" (Gen. 32:26). Ellen White comments, "Through humiliation, repentance, and self-surrender, this sinful, erring mortal prevailed with the Majesty of heaven." And what was the blessing he so fervently sought? Jacob ultimately desired one thing—that "his life" would be "mercifully preserved." His desire for the preservation of his life and that of his family was obvious, but somewhat less so was the one clear condition that had to be met.

"Had not Jacob previously repented of his sin in obtaining the birthright by fraud, God would not have heard his prayer." Yet Ellen White cannot leave the issue as just applicable to Jacob. She then promptly goes on to make a sobering comparison: "So, in the time of trouble, if the people of God had unconfessed sins to appear before them while tortured with fear and anguish, they would be overwhelmed; despair would cut off their faith, and they could not have confidence to plead with God for deliverance. But while they have a deep sense of their unworthiness, they have no concealed wrongs to reveal."[17]

The Prime Purpose for the Time of Trouble

So what is the purpose for the time of trouble? It is so that now (even during this very day in probationary time) God's faithful people will make sure that their experience of genuine repentance and justification by faith is fully settled. But what relationship does this have with Jesus during His great final affliction?

Jesus and the Time of Trouble

Ellen White's interpretation of closing events regards the experience of Jesus, especially as He endured the struggles of Gethsemane and the terrible tortures of Calvary, as having powerful parallels with the trials and faith of God's end-time followers during the close of probation and the great time of trouble. As the reader carefully studies the key passion chapters in *The Desire of Ages*, especially "Gethsemane," "Calvary," and "It is Finished," they will find that the great crisis of Christ's life reveals the following instructive points:[18]

As Jesus entered Gethsemane, the searing trials began to unfold as a literal struggle to the death (Matt. 26:36-56; Mark 14:32-51; and Luke 22:39-53). The cumulative weight of the world's sin and guilt had begun, with unimaginable horror, to sink into the consciousness of our suffering Savior. The sense of condemnation became so heavy that His sweat was like great drops of blood and He appealed to His disciples to watch with Him in intercessory prayer. Three times our Lord cried out with the groaning request that the "cup" of His imminent suffering and death be removed from His quivering lips. And three times He received not one indication that His suffering would be relieved.

In a very special sense, Christ had reached the decisive moment of the great plan of salvation. Would He or would He not go ahead with the solemn covenant between Himself and the Father that they had entered into ages before in the heavenly "Council of Peace"? The question had become whether or not the Son would remain true to His agreement with the Father to become the atoning, sacrificial victim. Indeed, the crucial moment of testing had finally arrived!

As the struggle reached its climax, Christ made His final and irrevocable decision. He would persevere all the way to Calvary.

Our suffering Lord chose to give His all and die a death that would effectively create a terrible separation between Himself and His privileged fellowship with the Father. Yet at that same moment Christ received the assurance from the Father of His paternal acceptance of all that the Son had hitherto accomplished during the Incarnation, including His decision to keep on the bloodstained path to Calvary's act of atoning sacrifice. Truly it was the most momentous decision ever made in the entire history of the universe!

Until that moment Christ had prostrated Himself in agony on the ground. Now He calmly arose in an aura of full assurance, suffused with a confidence that braced Him to move through successive betrayals, condemnations, and finally crucifixion. The revelation of the Father's acceptance of His decision would be the last conscious communication of affirmation and comfort that Christ would receive before His death.

In fact, I would be so bold as to suggest that Gethsemane turned out to be both Christ's version of the latter-rain sealing of the Holy Spirit and His intensely personal close of probation. As His suffering abated, the Father then showered Him with the refreshing power of the Spirit, and Christ promptly commenced His final pilgrimage to utter rejection and condemnation on the cross. In effect, what followed was that the Savior then entered His time of Jacob's trouble—including His betrayal by Judas, abandonment by the rest of His disciples, condemnation by the Jewish and Roman authorities, cruel physical scourging, relentless mocking and cursing, and finally the actual crucifixion itself. The final crushing blow of the entire atonement process was the seeming utter abandonment of Christ by His Father.

He received not one conscious indication of affirmation and support from His heavenly Father. How did our Lord survive this most crushing of all blows? He simply had to endure by "faith alone"! Furthermore, His only solace was to recall the previous manifestations of His Father's assuring acceptance of His person and work before His jolting "close of probation" in Gethsemane.

According to both Scripture and Ellen G. White, Christ had absolutely no continuing sense of the Father's sustaining words and power as He entered upon His greatest time of trouble—His condemnation by the Jewish authorities and death at Calvary. And what was His greatest test? That He could only consciously sense the outpouring of the Father's wrath against

Him, the sin-bearer. How was it that He was made to be sin for us (see 2 Cor. 5:21)? It was solely because our sin and guilt had been fully imputed to Him!

In other words, Christ could move forward only by "faith alone" in His appointed work of making the atonement as our vicarious sacrificial victim. Furthermore, all that sustained Him were the affirmations of the Father that Christ had previously received by faith before His "probation" had closed in Gethsemane. Most certainly we must hasten to add that the Father was surely there, via the ministrations of the Holy Spirit, to uphold and sustain His oppressed Son. Yet the suffering Jesus had no conscious awareness or any perceptible sense of the sustaining power of His Father that was flowing forth for His benefit!

The Parallels Between Christ and the Sealed Saints of the End-times

Only from the perspective laid out in the preceding paragraphs are we now in a position to grasp the profound parallels and dissimilarities between the experience of God's end-time people during their fiery time of trouble ordeal and that of the faith and sufferings of their Savior as He came to the "end-time" of His earthly sojourn.

Once more, please keep in mind that the core of the crisis of faith for Christ focused on the previous affirmations of the acceptance of His work by His Father, including the final words of assurance that issued from the Father at the climax of Jesus' experience in Gethsemane. During this climactic moment Christ finalizes His ultimate decision to go on to Calvary! In essence the last moments in Gethsemane were our Lord's final baptism of the Spirit (the fruition of His own personal latter rain). It became the means by which the Spirit "sealed" Him for His work and walk of faith during His own unique time of trouble. And by way of some instructive parallels for God's faithful, sealed people during their final earthly time of trouble, they will have been sealed by a latter rain that will have prepared them to walk by faith alone in Christ.

His atoning merits will be granted to the sealed ones through their experience of justification by faith alone before their collective probation will close. The sobering, even unsettling, truth is that if their faith in His justifying merits has not been effectively settled before probation closes, they will be overcome with despair during the terrible temptations of the time of trouble.

Christ had to have a faith that trusted the affirmations of the Father before He finally went to Calvary as the sin-bearer, while the end-time saints must have a sealed, settled faith that trusts their acceptance of Christ's forgiveness before their probation closes. Christ had to trust by faith alone in the words of affirmation from the Father as He bore our sins and was "lost," while we will have to trust by faith alone in the divine forgiveness before our probation closes and we are saved. On the one hand, we have Christ who underwent His test by bearing our sins with no word of affirmation from the Father (from the betrayal in Gethsemane until He finally died on Calvary). And on the other hand, the sealed saints of the end-time must meet their test by faith alone, something they have had and will continue to exercise in the forgiveness that flows from the atoning life and death of Christ, their by-faith-alone sin-bearer.

What we have here suggested is that this whole panorama is about as Christ- and faith-centered as it gets. And this applies with particular force to the issues of justification by faith alone as probation closes and the great time of trouble envelops God's faithful, sealed followers. Most *assuredly*, the thought that Christ has gone through the same essential crisis experience of faith in the Father's words of affirmation and acceptance should give to every Christian a keen sense that their trust in Christ as their sin-bearer is a faith that will endure any stresses that may arise during their end-time test!

Some Further Thoughts on the Providential Purposes of the End-time Testing

Aside from these clear implications for the experience of justification by faith alone, including a faith that must be fully settled before probation closes, there is really only one other specific purpose that Ellen White assigns to the time of trouble trials of those who bear the seal of God: the sealed saints and the entire onlooking universe will witness one last manifestation of satanic evil, especially as a cruel and unjust death decree spreads around the world. And it is this demonstration of Satan's principles that will once and for all alienate them from any lingering sympathies that they may still retain for Satan's deceptive claims. The "severe trials" of the persecuted believers are "designed to lead the people of God to renounce Satan and his temptations. The last conflict will reveal Satan to them in his true character, that of a cruel tyrant, and it will do for them what nothing else could do, uproot him entirely from their affections."[19]

Thus the justification-by-faith-alone principle is the key positive side of the coin that makes the people of God as eternally secure. But their exposure to Satan's final, masterful cruelties will unfold as the negative side of the same coin. Will sin ever arise again? It will not! And the reasons are that the sealed ones will be so settled into God's merciful love and so alienated from Satan's perversion of that love (especially his claim that happiness can be found only in self-love) that they will always have an allergic reaction to any thought of ever rebelling against the God of patient, redeeming love. Stated more positively, they will be so enveloped into the Godhead's redeeming love that all other pretenders to their affections will be totally inadequate to meet their deepest spiritual and relational needs!

There is, however, one other alternative explanation for God's subjecting the sealed saints to the severe testing of the time of trouble. And that is the "final generation," perfectionist demonstration thesis. And it is this fascinating subject that we now turn to in chapter 10.

---

[1] We will base most of the discussion in this chapter on these topics in the teachings of Ellen G. White. This is not to deny that her teachings are biblical, but simply to recognize that most of the anxiety over the issues of assurance arises out of her commentary on the latter rain, the close of probation, and the time of trouble. For Ellen White's comments on the whole range of closing events, the best place to begin is the helpful compilation entitled *Last Day Events* (Nampa, Idaho: Pacific Press Pub. Assn., 1992). As we move through our rather brief summary and more extensive commentary on the aforementioned subjects, we will reference key sections and chapters of *Last Day Events*. As they see the key references in this concise Ellen White compilation, it will enable readers to continue to study in more depth.

[2] Such ideas include that of purgatory and a number of Protestant scenarios about a last chance to opt for salvation during an earthly millennium.

[3] *Last Day Events*, pp. 197ff.

[4] *Ibid.*, pp. 183ff.

[5] *Ibid.*, pp. 215ff.

[6] *Ibid.*, pp. 227ff.

[7] *Ibid.*, pp. 238-270.

[8] *Ibid.*, pp. 253ff. Dispensationalists claim that those who are Christians will be "raptured away" to heaven and will not need to face the frights and scourges of the seven last plagues and the great tribulation (the term they use to describe what Adventists usually refer to as the time of trouble).

[9] *Ibid.*, pp. 271ff. To put the issue more succinctly: the faithful remnant, the sealed children of God, will be preserved through the time of trouble (or earthly tribulation), not raptured away before its commencement. This has been God's biblical pattern, as we see during the Flood, the 10 plagues in Egypt, and the Babylonian captivity.

[10] Ellen White describes the events, both earthly and heavenly, that take place during and at the end of the millennium, beginning on page 645 in her book *The Great Controversy* (Mountain View, Calif.: Pacific Press Pub. Assn., 1911) and continuing through to page 673.

[11] *Last Day Events*, pp. 283ff.

[12] *Ibid.*, p. 255.

[13] Pastor Joseph Olstad, at the time of this writing, was a Master of Arts in religion student at the Adventist International Institute of Advanced Studies in the Philippines.

[14] *The Great Controversy*, pp. 613, 614. She states again on page 649 of the same volume that the sealed saints, now referred to as the 144,000, "have stood without an intercessor through the final outpouring of God's judgments" (the seven last plagues during the time of trouble).

[15] *Ibid.*, p. 623.

[16] The source of this line of thought was the Australian midtwentieth-century evangelist and prolific writer, Louis Were. Though looked upon as a gadfly by his fellow Australians in the 1940s and 1950s, Were would later be substantially vindicated in many of his insights into prophetic interpretation. Professor Hans K. LaRondelle, of the Seventh-day Adventist Theological Seminary during the 1970s and the 1980s, was able to raise our awareness of the thinking of Were and his numerous publications.

[17] *The Great Controversy*, pp. 617, 620.

[18] At this juncture we urge the reader to spend a few thoughtful hours with these important chapters from *The Desire of Ages*. As you read, keep asking yourself the question: How does the experience of Jesus parallel that of Jacob and what the sealed saints will go through during the close of probation and the time of trouble?

[19] *Review and Herald*, Aug. 12, 1884, and *Our High Calling* (Washington, D.C.: Review and Herald Pub. Assn., 1961), p. 321.

Chapter 10

The "Final Generation" Perfectionist Explanation of the Time of Trouble

Introduction

In the previous chapter we considered what we could call the justificationist explanation of the time of trouble experience of God's people. In this chapter we will consider the major alternative, the "final generation" perfectionist concept. It has probably created the most Adventist anxiety about the time of trouble.

The advocates of this interpretation essentially teach that God needs a "final generation" of perfectly obedient believers, whom they identify as the 144,000 of Revelation 7 and 14 and the faithful survivors of the time of trouble. According to their thesis, God will use such "sealed ones" as a final demonstration that perfectly sinless obedience to the law of God is possible for His people, even under the worst of circumstances. It will once and for all refute Satan's charge that total obedience to divine law is impossible for human beings.[1] Such obedience will finally vindicate God during the time of trouble.[2]

So what should we make of the thesis? A fully adequate response is beyond the scope of this chapter.[3] What follows are a few suggestions for reflection and further study.

First of all, the thesis itself is not explicit in either the Bible or the writings of Ellen G. White. Satan made the charge that obedience is impossible, and we have no evidence that God depends on any Christians (including the 144,000) to refute the claim during the time of trouble.

Furthermore, the concept seems to want to ignore the fact that Jesus has already demonstrated such an obedience in His earthly life of faith and perfect obedience to the law of God. More especially our Lord's

146

obedience included His own severe testing in Gethsemane and on Calvary—His supreme version of the latter rain and times of trouble testing. Is not the faithful obedience of Jesus the most fitting refutation of Satan's charges?

What it seems that the last-generation advocates are unwittingly doing is suggesting that somehow Jesus had some sort of advantage over all the rest of us and thus He is not really the best example for perfectly overcoming temptation. Can we really say that those of the final generation are better exhibits of obedience by faith than Jesus? Such a suggestion seems to border on the truly incredulous when it effectively claims that Christ's followers are greater examples of a working faith than Christ Himself!

At the risk of some repetition, we need to reinforce the previous point. It is abundantly evident, from both Daniel and Revelation (see especially Rev. 14:1-5) and the writings of Ellen White, that God's faithful followers during the time of trouble will be without any consciousness of known, or "cherished," sins. They simply cannot find anything to repent of when it comes to such sins (though they still retain their sinful natures). But the question still needs to be pressed: Why would God need this type of obedience to vindicate His demands for perfect obedience when Jesus has already proved that such obedience not only is possible but is already a historical reality in His life of faith as our example par excellence?

As we have already painstakingly pointed out, the key issue for the sealed close-of-probation faithful is to demonstrate that they can fully trust in Jesus' power to sustain them. And their experience will be built around a faith based on their previous genuine penitence, forgiveness, and habituated trust in Christ's power to deliver from temptation.

But what about the quality of their sanctified obedience during the time of trouble? I would propose that such perfect obedience will be an ongoing evidence of the genuineness of the faith that they will have already been exercising before probation closes. But how perfect should that preclose of probation perfection be?

The Perfection Component of the Sealed Saints

In response, I would remind the reader of the exalted vision of godly living that Ellen White presented in the previously cited time of trouble statement from *The Great Controversy* (p. 623). Once more, let's carefully note her most crucial definition of the perfect obedience required before probation closes: "Now, while our great High Priest is making the atonement for us, we should seek to become perfect in Christ. Not even by a thought could our Savior be brought to yield to the power of temptation. Satan finds in human hearts some point where he can gain a foothold; some sinful desire is cherished, by means of which his temptations assert their power." Then she invokes the example of Jesus with the claim that He "had kept His Father's commandments, and there was no sin in Him that Satan could use to his advantage." Now, with this point clearly in place, Ellen White then promptly proceeds to make the practical application. "This is the condition in which those must be found who shall stand in the time of trouble."[4]

How should assured, justified Seventh-day Adventists relate to such a high calling? What does it mean not to sin "by a thought" and to cease cherishing "some sinful desire"?

What follows are some reflections that I tentatively put forth for the prayerful consideration of the reader. This is a most sensitive, even potentially volatile subject. Furthermore, we need to keep in mind two other considerations as we explore this area.

1. We are here dealing with only the issue of temptations that the believer will be fully conscious of, not propensities that lurk deep within the unconscious mind. While the latter aspect is of some relevance, we will never fully be able to grasp it this side of heaven. So this discussion addresses only the temptations consciously confronting the harried remnant.

2. In a somewhat nuanced sense, we are also dealing with unfulfilled prophecy. And while the details of the remnant's future victory are yet to unfold, the key principle that inspiration has consistently spotlighted is that believers need to learn to trust Christ right now (this very day) in their current response to temptation. Such a focus is far more essential than engaging in speculations about the subjective details of how they will act in the future time of trouble.

In the light of these two important considerations, what follows we put forth to stimulate further thought, not to be dogmatic. In the spirit of pastoral sensitivity we ask:

Can we settle once and for all that we all need to finish with known premeditated sins and our excuses for them? When overtaken by the Spirit's conviction of sin, will we (1) cease to make excuses for our weaknesses and shortcomings, (2) honestly flee to Jesus in childlike faith for forgiveness, and (3) determine anew to trust Him more implicitly when battling our most deep-seated sinful and cultivated propensities to sin? In sum, what we here suggest is the necessity of being brutally honest to God about these matters in an attitude of growing and sensitive responsiveness to the workings of the Spirit of God. Furthermore, (4) can we all agree that we need to be far more optimistic than we have collectively been about God's power to transform and perfect His professed people?

Now, if we can agree that positive answers can and should be given to all of the previous four rhetorical questions, then I think we might be in a position to consider what I am calling an honest yet optimistically realistic version of final-generation victory over sin.

So what about the question raised by Ellen White's statement found on page 623 of *The Great Controversy*: Is it truly a realistic possibility to cease from sinning "by a thought" and stop cherishing "sinful desires"?

The best way to understand such concepts is to grasp the simple fact that any temptation always involves some sort of alluring thought that can readily morph into sin when people deliberately nurture the sinful thought inherent in the temptation. Furthermore, some cultivated or inherited lust of the sinful flesh will make the temptation even more attractive. Do these conclusions seem fair and accurate? If they do, then we should be open to another important principle of temptation.

It needs to be made abundantly clear that the thought of sin suggested by any temptation is not a sin in and of itself. Such sinful thoughts become damnable "sin" only when we cultivate and indulge them. Does this last point accurately reflect at least one key aspect of the mental dynamics of temptation and sin? If it does, I would propose that when we view temptation and sin in this manner, we can take a more realistic and optimistic attitude about conscious victory over temptation and its power. Therefore, let us consider some more questions.

Just which of your sinful thoughts or desires do you think has God throwing up His hands and declaring that He cannot deliver us from such sinister seductions? Is it possible, by the grace of God, activated by a responding, trusting, claiming faith, to think new thoughts and be inspired to cherish righteous desires through the power of the Holy Spirit? Furthermore, do we really want to say that there is an excuse for sin when God has made such a powerful atonement for it—an atonement that can deliver from both the guilt and the power of any such sinful thought or cherished desire?

I pray that our collective response will be a decided yes to God's power to deliver us through living faith in the transforming presence of the Spirit of Christ!

Furthermore, I hasten to add that any such grace and Spirit-empowered obedience does not justify us before God. Only the imputed merits of Christ's forgiving grace can do that—and that "by faith alone." Additionally, I want to affirm that the faith that justifies is never alone and will always be accompanied by a faith that leads to transformation of the mind (the thoughts) and the character (the desires and normal acts) of any true believer who seeks the healing, sealing power of grace.

What do you think? Is this just too much? If it is, I respectfully grant you space to reflect and even object. But please permit me to suggest a couple other angles that might make the theme of perfect victory over sin more realistic and palatable.

Does it make good sense to say that if anyone has not learned to step off the back porch, it would prove foolish for that person to go sky-diving or bungee jumping? Clearly, yes is the appropriate reply. But on a more positive note, is it not reasonable to believe that if we take all of our maturing tests seriously (in athletics called "training"), we will then be enabled to do greater things in our lives? I would hope that your reply is positive. But consider one further aspect.

If you find yourself growing more responsive and responsible in the things of God, do you believe that He would suddenly send you some temptation that would be beyond your ability and His grace to bear? After all, the Bible has promised in no uncertain terms that He will not do this. "Therefore let him who thinks he stands take heed lest he fall. No temptation has overtaken you except such as is common to man; but God is faithful, who will not allow you to be tempted beyond what you are able, but with the temptation will also make the way of escape, that you may be able to bear it" (1 Cor. 10:12, 13).

Can it be that if we seek to grow by grace, God will either shield us from any temptations that would overwhelm us, or send the needed power appropriate to the tests that may assail us?

Please consider one more thing. Is it asking too much for all of the professed followers of Jesus to keep an open mind on the issue of perfection? I have recently discovered some practical insights on Christian perfection offered by James Arminius, the great Protestant theologian of the early-seventeenth-century Dutch Reformed church. What follows is a question often asked by Seventh-day Adventists: "Can believers under the grace of the new covenant perfectly observe the law of God in this life?"

Arminius sought to answer the question by making the following two points: "If it refers to God's requiring obedience 'according to rigor,' which would involve 'the highest degree of perfection,'" the answer is no. But if it refers to God's requiring obedience according to clemency, and 'if the strength or power which He confers be proportionate to the demand,' the answer is yes." Put more simply, Arminius felt that some sort of absolute sinless perfection was not possible. But on a practical level, in the spirit of 1 Corinthians 10:12, 13, the power to meet a straightforward temptation would be "proportionate to the demand."

Most clearly, Arminius was not one to make a hobbyhorse out of perfectionist advocacy. But his opponents would give him no rest on the issue, seeking to paint him as some sort of perfectionistic fanatic. Yet, in spite of such pressures, Arminius wisely kept his faith options open on the issue with both God and the people of God.

"But while I never asserted that a believer could perfectly keep the precepts of Christ in this life, I never denied it, but always left it as a matter which has still to be decided." Do you see optimistic yet cautious wisdom in his reply? Even if something is "higher than the highest human thought can reach,"[5] is it possible that grace-inspired perfection of a "higher" sort is more possible than we have been inclined to believe?

"I think the time may be far more happily and usefully employed in prayers to obtain what is lacking in each of us, and in serious admonitions that every one endeavor to proceed and press forward towards the mark of perfection, than when spent in such disputations," Arminius observed.[6] Does this seem practical and sensible for all Christians, whether wrestling with perfection in the contexts of either the seventeenth or the early-twenty-first centuries?

What I suggest is that if believers would take seriously the good counsel of Arminius, they will not be defeated in any time of trouble that may come their way. I hope you are thinking more optimistically and positively about growth in grace and what it can positively contribute to the assurance of our salvation.

Summation

So what can we say about preparation for the close of probation and the destiny of the sealed believers in the time of trouble? And what does it mean to live in the sight of a holy God without a mediator?

If any believer is now trusting in the present blessings of the justifying and sanctifying grace of God, when the moment arrives to be sealed and thrust into the fires of the time of trouble, there will be no failure. They will be able to rise to meet this momentous occasion on the wings of God's grace and embrace a final deliverance at Christ's coming. Should anyone prove faithful now as they run with the foot soldiers, they will then be enabled to run with the horses in the heat of the last battle (see Jer. 12:5). To live in the sight of a holy God without a mediator after probation closes means to live by faith in the Mediator right now, each and every day for the rest of time and then for all of eternity.

Therefore, one of the most assuring conclusions about the time of trouble is that if we are prepared now, we will not lose our salvation then. It is like getting onto an airliner that will face some rough weather during the upcoming flight. But if the responsive and sealed children of God have received their faith tickets and secured passports sealed with the righteousness of the King of heaven, they will then be enabled to board the flight that will assuredly take them to the eternal kingdom. Will the plane crash in the crisis of the time of trouble? Not if you are connected to the Captain of your salvation and have boarded His plane as it sets forth on its holy itinerary!

So the ultimate question is Do you have your "by faith alone in Christ" ticket and secured your passport for the stormy flight through the passages of the close of probation and the time of trouble?

---

[1] See E. G. White, *The Desire of Ages,* pp. 761-764.

[2] Interestingly enough, Edward Irving of early-nineteenth-century British Adventism initially developed the concept, and then it passed on to late-nineteenth- and early-twentieth-century North American Seventh-day Adventism. The person who most likely brought it to North America was E. J. Waggoner (of Jones and Waggoner, 1888 renown). The Waggoner connection has received confirming support from the recently completed (and carefully researched) dissertation of Paul Evans, "A Historical-Contextual Analysis of the Final-Generation Theology of M. L. Andreasen" (Ph.D. diss., Andrews University, Berrien Springs, Mich., 2010). The idea has received great prominence in the twentieth- and twenty-first-century experience of Seventh-day Adventism, especially in the writings of such well-known advocates as M. L. Andreasen, Herbert Douglass, Robert Wieland, Donald K. Short, and more recently, Dennis Priebe and Larry Kirkpatrick.

[3] For a fuller evaluation of such theology, see "The Vindication of God and the Harvest Principle," *Ministry,* October 1994, pp. 44-47. Probably the two most trenchant critiques have been offered by Eric Claude Webster in his *Crosscurrents in Adventist Christology* (New York: Peter Lang, 1984, and Berrien Springs, Mich.: Andrews University Press, 1992), pp. 422-424, and Angel Rodríguez, "Theology of the Last Generation" (a paper available from the Biblical Research Institute of the General Conference of Seventh-day Adventists). For a more detailed study of Ellen White's actual treatment of the time of trouble and the character status of the sealed saints, see chapter 15, entitled "Perfection and Closing Events," in Woodrow W. Whidden, *Ellen White on Salvation* (Hagerstown, Md.: Review and Herald Pub. Assn., 1995), pp. 131-142.

[4] E. G. White, *The Great Controversy,* p. 623.

[5] E. G. White, *The Desire of Ages,* p. 311.

[6] James Arminius, quoted by Carl Bangs in his classic biography, *Arminius: A Study in the Dutch Reformation* (Nashville: Abingdon Press, 1971), p. 347.

Chapter 11

Ellen G. White on the Assurance of Salvation: Are Her Writings a Help or a Stumbling Block?

Introduction

Many Adventists wrestle with the challenge of their personal assurance of salvation. According to one survey, less than 70 percent of Adventist members worldwide have a confident assurance of present salvation.[1] Ellen White herself said, "This I do know, that our churches are dying for the want of teaching on the subject of righteousness by faith in Christ, and for kindred truths."[2]

Yet many blame Ellen White herself for the fact that so many faithful Adventists lack assurance of salvation. A common perception holds that because of her well-known teaching that no one should ever say "I am saved," she has effectively denied church members the kind of salvation assurance that should be the privilege of all believers in the gospel. The authors of this chapter know from personal pastoral and teaching experience that many Adventists do not believe that Ellen White taught and affirmed the present assurance of salvation.[3]

Such a perception has led many sincere Seventh-day Adventists to varying outcomes. A few toil on in more or less conscious legalism, hoping against hope that everything will come out all right in the end. Many give up on finding any certainty of salvation and just decide to get what they can out of the present life. Others (correctly) reject legalism, choosing (wisely, we believe) to base their lives on Christ and the gospel, but see no further need for Ellen White and other distinctive Adventist beliefs, since such concepts seem to be the source of the problem.

Some, however, take a different path. They reason (correctly, we believe) that if the same Holy Spirit who inspired Paul, John, Peter, and James (with their obvious diversity as well as underlying unity) also guided

153

Ellen White, then there must be an essential harmony between them. Therefore, the views that seem to deny Christian assurance must not be the whole truth, but partial or distorted truth, and we must not quit seeking until we find the whole truth.

The Bible says that many believe they are saved, but they will find out in the judgment that they are lost (Matt. 7:21-23; 8:11, 12; Luke 13:23-27). Therefore Paul exhorts, "Examine yourselves as to whether you are in the faith" (2 Cor. 13:5). It is our conviction that what we find in Scripture is also evident in the thought of Ellen White. To this end the following study presents the results of our search for and the discovery of a clear teaching on the genuine assurance of salvation from the totality of the writings of Ellen White.

A Definition of Assurance and Its Biblical Basis

"Assurance" as used here means the assurance of salvation. Assurance may be biblically defined as the inward witness of the Holy Spirit (Rom. 8:16; Gal. 4:6) that one has present salvation in Christ. Assurance and salvation are not identical. Scripture and Ellen White agree that it is possible to be saved without being sure of it (Rom. 2:11-16),[4] and it's possible to think one is assured without actually being saved (Matt. 7:21-23).[5] That's why it is so important that every believer understand this crucial topic. Scripture and Ellen White are also clear that genuine biblical assurance is essential to the normal Christian life (Luke 10:20).[6]

The doctrine of assurance is based on Scriptures too numerous to exhaustively list here; but among them are John 3:16; 6:37; 1 John 1:9; 5:11;[7] 2 Peter 1:1-11; Luke 15:20; 1 Timothy 1:15; 2:4; Isaiah 1:18-20; 53:4-6, 11, 12; 55:6, 7; Jeremiah 31:3; and Ezekial 36:26, 27. The biblical doctrine, however, does not assume the Calvinistic teaching of "once saved, always saved." What we have argued in an earlier chapter regarding the supposed Calvinistic advantage is that such teaching is not only unscriptural but also very much opposed to the perspectives of Ellen G. White on assurance. And her rejection of this false doctrine of assurance was probably the reason for her caution that believers should not claim "to be saved." In other words, the theory that holds that if you are among the elect, you cannot be lost, and thus "once saved, always saved" is thought to be an irreversible guarantee of salvation.

As already pointed out, the problem with this view is that its most knowledgeable representatives admit that it is possible for individuals to think that they are among the elect when in fact they are not! We repeat, predestinarian theologians admit that persons who assume that they are among the saved must always face the possibility that God may actually count them as among the lost. Thus the doctrine of "once saved, always saved" is only a *theoretical* guarantee of eternal security, *not an actual* guarantee, since in the Calvinistic system one cannot infallibly know that one was "once saved."[8]

So what are the basic presuppositions of the Bible and Ellen White on genuine assurance? We believe that there is one true biblical perspective and three key concepts that undergird Ellen White's teaching on salvation and its legitimate article of genuine personal assurance. First of all, we will lay out the most foundational biblical perspective that permeated her thought.

Ellen White's Foundational Biblical Perspective

Salvation and assurance are grounded in God's unchanging character of other-centered love. "We love Him because He first loved us" (1 John 4:19). They further rest in His unwavering purpose and persistent initiative to save all (Rom. 5:8-10)[9] who will accept the salvation provided through the life, death, resurrection, and high-priestly intercession of Jesus Christ.[10] Once saved, it is possible to fall from grace, but it is not necessary. If Jesus loved us so much as to die for us while we were still enemies, how much more will He do whatever is required to save us, now that we have become His friends (Rom. 5:10, 19, 20).

Most certainly, God's unchanging character of other-centered love is also the central part of Ellen White's key perspective: "So ready, so eager, is the Savior's heart to welcome us as members of the family of God, that in the very first words we are to use in approaching God He places the *assurance* of our divine relationship, 'Our Father.' Here is the announcement of that wonderful truth, so full of encouragement and comfort, that *God loves us as He loves his Son*" (John 17:23).[11]

Three Essential Concepts or Elements

Furthermore, her concept of assurance includes three further essential elements: (1) "justification through faith in the atoning blood of Christ," and (2) "the renewing power of the Holy Spirit upon the heart," which result in (3) "bringing forth fruit in a life conformed to the example of Christ."[12] While the statement from *The Great Controversy* was originally part of her discussion of John Wesley's contributions to Christian theology, she clearly agrees with him, and uses the same words in other contexts often enough to prove that they were also her conviction. And it is our belief that most misconceptions about Christian assurance arise from misunderstandings of these three elements and their relationship to each other.

Each element has some similarities and some clear differences from the popular belief of "once saved, always saved."[13] Thus what follows is a fuller exposition of these three essential elements upon which the genuine article of assurance is based in the writings of Ellen White.

1. The primary objective basis of the assurance of salvation, the "root" and "ground" of salvation, is always and only justification through the work of Christ, received by faith alone (Eph. 2:4-10; Rom. 3:23, 24; 4:16; 5:1; 6:23; 8:1; 2 Cor. 5:14-21; Gal. 2:16, 21; John 1:29; 1 John 2:2; 1 Tim. 4:10; Titus 2:11). And what is embedded in these key texts is abundantly evident in the writings of Ellen G. White.

"By His spotless life, His obedience, His death on the cross of Calvary, Christ interceded for the lost race. And now, not as a mere petitioner does the Captain of our salvation intercede for us, but as a conqueror claiming His victory."[14]

"The blessings of the new covenant are grounded purely on mercy in forgiving unrighteousness and sins," and "all who humble their hearts, confessing their sins, will find mercy and grace and assurance."[15]

Those who come to Jesus must "believe that *He saves them solely through His grace.* . . . Through faith we receive the grace of God; but *faith is not our Savior. It earns nothing.* It is the hand by which we lay hold upon Christ, and appropriate *His merits, the remedy for sin.* And *we cannot even repent without the aid of the Spirit of God.* [Acts 5:31 quoted.] Repentance comes from Christ as truly as does pardon."[16]

"The thought that the righteousness of Christ is imputed to us, not because of any merit on our part, but as a free gift from God, is a precious thought. The enemy of God and man is not willing that this truth should be clearly presented; for he knows that if the people receive it fully, his power will be broken. If he can control minds so that doubt and unbelief and darkness shall compose the experience of those who claim to be the children of God, he can overcome them with temptation."[17]

The previous citations do raise the question as to how Ellen White's view of justification differs from the popular Calvinistic notion of "once saved, always saved." The following points seem clear: (1) she rejected Calvinistic predestination and (2) she never reduced faith to mere belief (cf. James 2:19). For Ellen White, faith includes intellectual *belief* in the facts of the gospel but extends also to a *trust* in the personal character of God and Christ that leads to voluntary *surrender* of the will to God. Faith that does not lead to surrender and trust is only a partial faith that has not yet matured to the point of assurance.

"A nominal faith in Christ, which accepts Him merely as the Savior of the world, can never bring healing to the soul. The faith that is unto salvation is not a mere intellectual assent to the truth. . . . It is not enough to believe about Christ; we must believe in Him. The only faith that will benefit us is that which embraces Him as a personal Savior; which appropriates His merits to ourselves. Many hold faith as an opinion. Saving faith is a transaction by which those who receive Christ join themselves in covenant relation with God. Genuine faith is life. A living faith means an increase of vigor, a confiding trust, by which the soul becomes a conquering power."[18]

"It is important that we understand clearly the nature of faith. There are many who believe that Christ is the Savior of the world, that the gospel is true and reveals the plan of salvation, yet they do not possess saving faith. They are intellectually convinced of the truth, but this is not enough; in order to be justified, the sinner must have that faith that appropriates the merits of Christ to his own soul. We read that the devils 'believe, and tremble,' but their belief does not bring them justification, neither will the belief of those who give a merely intellectual assent to the truths of the Bible bring them the benefits of salvation. This belief fails of reaching the vital point, for the truth does not engage the heart or transform the character."[19]

"The so-called faith that does not work by love and purify the soul will not justify any man. 'Ye see,' says the apostle, 'how that by works a man is justified, and not by faith only.' Abraham believed God. How do we know that he believed? His works testified to the character of his faith, and his faith was accounted to him for righteousness."[20]

"Christ . . . is anxious to be our Helper, to bear our griefs and carry our sorrows. Will you let Him help you? *Say to the world, 'Jesus is my Savior; he saves me today, making me his obedient child, and enabling me to keep all his commandments.' If you knowingly disregard one of God's commandments, you do not have saving faith.* Genuine faith is a faith that works by love, and purifies the soul."[21]

Please note that Ellen White *does not say* that one who struggles with a habit or with a deep-seated defect of character lacks "saving faith." Those without saving faith are those who boastfully claim exemption from the biblical requirement, for this is the opposite of repentance. But those who acknowledge the requirement, repenting and confessing their shortfalls, receive immediate forgiveness and cleansing. It is precisely when we have sinned that "we have an Advocate with the Father, Jesus Christ the [only one who is] righteous" (1 John 2:1).

2. The second essential element involves the *continuing experiential* aspect of the assurance of salvation. Thus when Christ is received by faith, the

Spirit of God produces a new life in the soul (Rom. 6:4, 11-14; 8:9-11; Gal. 2:20, 21; Eph. 2:5, 6; Col. 1:27; 3:1-10, etc.). This "new life in the soul" is the actual beginning of "the life eternal."[22] The insistence on the absolute necessity of the ongoing "life in the soul" constitutes the major distinction between the Adventist understanding of assurance and the popular notion that a one-time act of believing is enough to ensure eternal security. "We must not base our salvation upon supposition; we must know of a surety that Christ is formed within, the hope of glory. We must know for ourselves that the Spirit of God is abiding in our hearts, and that we can hold communion with God. *Then if He should come to us quickly, if by any chance our life should suddenly be ended, we should be ready to meet our God.*"[23]

This vital concept of the ongoing "life in the soul"[24] or "life of the soul"[25] is the difference between those who merely profess faith in Christ and those who truly know Him and walk by faith in Him. It is both the believer's highest privilege[26] and the most basic essential. "We may have the assurance today that Jesus lives, and is making intercession for us. We cannot do good to those around us while our own souls are destitute of spiritual life."[27] Describing her own conversion, Ellen White said, "I felt the assurance of an indwelling Savior."[28]

Life in the Soul and Self-crucifixion

Before we move on from the assurance implications of the theme of "the new life in the soul," a further aspect of genuine Christian experience merits our attention. It involves the question of the crucifixion of self. Paul states it very graphically: "For if you live according to the flesh you will die; but if by the Spirit you *put to death* the deeds of the body you will *live*" (Rom. 8:13). "Indeed I also count all things loss for the excellence of the knowledge of Christ Jesus my Lord, . . . that I may *know Him and the power of His resurrection,* and the *fellowship of His sufferings, being conformed to His death,* if, by any means, I may attain to the *resurrection* of the dead" (Phil. 3:8-11).

The vital matter of self-crucifixion involves the fact that, along with the process of "attachment" to Christ (John 15:1-8), we have a work of "detachment" from everything that is in conflict with Him. "We must feel our *utter dependence* on Christ. We must live by faith in the Son of God. That is the meaning of the injunction, 'Abide in me.' The life we live in the flesh is not to [serve] the will of men, not to please our Lord's enemies, but to serve and honor Him who loved us, and gave Himself for us. *A mere assent to this union, while the affections are not detached from the world, its pleasures and its dissipations, only emboldens the heart in disobedi-*

ence."²⁹ *That's the essence of false assurance.* Its *result* is to "embolden the heart in disobedience."

Many have grasped this, and in recoiling from "mere assent" have fallen into the opposite extreme: legalism, preoccupation with personal performance, and perfectionism. But notice that the dying to self is both *once for all* (with Christ on the cross, Rom. 6:3, 6, 11; 2 Cor. 5:14, 15), and *a continuing process* (2 Cor. 4:10). The continuing process means that it is never finished until we lay off the "body of death" (Rom. 7:24). That does *not* mean we go on intentionally, presumptuously sinning until then, but rather that *the conquest of sin requires a continual dying to its attractions.*

Here is the practical, personal experience of the cross. It is the essence of what it means to be a Christian. The original disciples didn't like it any more than we do. Peter's initial reaction to the cross was "Far be it from You, Lord; this shall not happen to you!" (Matt. 16:22). But through hard experience he learned the true glory of the cross. Near the end of his life he wrote, "Beloved, do not think it strange concerning the fiery trial which is to try you, as though some strange thing happened to you; but rejoice to the extent that you partake of Christ's sufferings, that when His glory is revealed, you may also be glad with exceeding joy" (1 Peter 4:12, 13). We see that the experience of dying to self and sin is central to following Jesus (Heb. 2:18; 5:8) in Paul's description of "the enemies of the cross of Christ" as those "whose end is destruction, whose *god is their belly,* and whose glory is in their shame—*who set their mind on earthly things*" (Phil. 3:18, 19).

And what we find so evident in Scripture about dying to self is also abundantly witnessed to by Ellen White:

"Why is it so hard to lead a self-denying, humble life? Because professed Christians are not dead to the world. It is easy living after we are dead."³⁰

But the process of *dying to self is not legalism.* It is not a work of merit, but a gift of grace. Thus she says, "No man can empty himself of self. We can only consent for Christ to accomplish the work. Then the language of the soul will be, Lord, take my heart; for I cannot give it. It is Thy property. Keep it pure, for I cannot keep it for Thee. Save me in spite of myself, my weak, unchristlike self."³¹

"He [Christ] is knocking at the door of your heart, asking for admittance. He longs to renew your heart, filling it with a love for all that is pure and true. *He longs to crucify self for you, raising you to newness of life in him.*"³² Please carefully note that self is what gets crucified, not the crucifier. Self cannot crucify self!

3. The third essential element of the assurance of salvation is that *the external evidence of salvation is fruit bearing in obedience and loving service* (John 15:1-8; Gal. 5:22, 23; Col. 3:1-11). Because "those who are in connection with God are channels for the power of the Holy Spirit," the *"inner life of the soul will reveal itself in the outward conduct."*[33] The human response of grateful love to God, bearing fruit in obedience and service, is in no sense the root or ground of salvation, but it does constitute visible evidence that there is life in the soul. "As the mother watches for the smile of recognition from her little child, which tells of the dawning of intelligence, so does Christ watch for the expression of grateful love, which shows that spiritual life is begun in the soul."[34] "If Christ is dwelling in the heart, it is impossible to conceal the light of His presence."[35] *Therefore, the impossibility of concealing the divine life in the soul is the consideration that explains Ellen White's frequent emphasis on the external evidences of salvation.* The lack of a visible change in the life of a professed Christian she regards as a demonstration that there is no divine life within; hence it should be clear that the new birth has not yet occurred. If the new birth has not yet taken place, the person does not have salvation, and any claim to assurance would be self-deception.

Of course, while "the inner life of the soul will reveal itself in the outward conduct," the external evidence may not be evident to an onlooking Pharisee. One who never knew the person before he or she met Jesus may judge him or her as unconverted, when those who know the individual well can tell unmistakably that a profound inner change has occurred.

By way of summary, we may say that (1) the *ground* of assurance is justification by grace alone through faith alone; (2) the *experience* of assurance is the ongoing life of the Holy Spirit in the soul; and (3) the *outward evidence* of assurance is fruit bearing in obedience and loving service. Where any of these is absent, assurance must be called into question. But when they are present, believers should rejoice and not let Satan steal away their sense of security.

Related Practical and Theological Aspects of Assurance
What follows are a number of closely related factors that emerge in any balanced treatment of Ellen White's teaching on assurance. First of all, we will deal with the basic factors involving how Christians should personally nurture their redeeming relationship to Christ.

Assurance Is Maintained by Daily Communion With Christ
It is just a simple rule of personal relationships that there needs to be

significant, dedicated time for intimate communication. And thus it is with the Christian's walk with Christ (John 15:4, 5; Phil. 4:13; Col. 2:6; 1 John 5:11-13). Ellen White strongly suggests that we should purposely take time to engage in those pursuits that nurture the spiritual needs of the soul. "Nothing is apparently more helpless, yet really more invincible, than the soul that feels its nothingness and relies wholly on the merits of the Savior. By prayer, by the study of His Word, by faith in His abiding presence, the weakest of human beings may live in contact with the living Christ, and He will hold them by a hand that will never let go."[36] "Sinful man can find hope and righteousness only in God, and no human being is righteous any longer than he has faith in God *and maintains a vital connection with Him.*"[37]

Christians Are Always Free to Turn Away From God

The biblical concept of security in Christ has inherent in it the reality that believers will retain for all eternity their moral freedom to turn away from God (cf. Eze. 33:12-20).[38] Therefore the daily renewal of conversion is the practical necessity and privilege of every believer (Luke 9:23). But for those who cultivate the habit of continually yielding to the Lordship of Christ through the Holy Spirit, daily responding to His love and seeking a more complete surrender to His will, there is abundant and solid security.

Therefore, it just makes sense that genuine personal Christian assurance is *not* the security of an irreversible guarantee *but the security that results from serving a God whose persistence in seeking the sinner goes far beyond the weaknesses of the believer's faith* (John 10:28; Luke 10:20; 15:4-7, 8-10, 20-24; 1 John 1:9; 2:1; Rom. 5:10; 8:28-30, 35-39). The one who keeps on responding to Him and His drawing power will *never* be cast out (John 6:37). Thus Ellen White writes, "*All* who have put on the robe of Christ's righteousness *will stand* before Him as chosen and faithful and true. Satan has no power to pluck them out of the hand of the Savior. *Not one soul* who in penitence and faith has claimed His protection will Christ permit to pass under the enemy's power"[39] (Zech. 3:4, 7; cf. 1 Cor. 10:13[40]).

Ellen White's Personal Pastoral Counsel

One of the better-kept secrets about Ellen White's understanding of Christian assurance concerns her powerful but deeply sympathetic communications to individual Christians who, for one reason or another, were finding it hard to trust in Christ for their personal salvation. In actual fact, her counsels offer arresting practical manifestations of the principles that undergirded her strong grasp of genuine Christian assurance. Please carefully consider the following exhibits of her sensitive pastoral nurture as she dealt with the spiritually discouraged.

One of her favorite texts on security was 1 John 2:1. In a letter to a woman in desperate need of assurance, White reported hearing this text in vision, quoted by an angel: "Said the angel, 'God leaves not His people, even if they err. He turns not from them in wrath for any light thing. If they sin they have an advocate with the Father, Jesus Christ the righteous.'" She continued, "He who so loved you as to give His own life for you will not turn you off and forsake you unless you willfully, determinedly forsake Him to serve the world and Satan."[41] In a more public setting, she wrote the following: "If any man sin, he is not to give himself up to despair, and talk like a man who is lost to Christ. 'If any man sin, we have an advocate with the Father, Jesus Christ the righteous' [1 John 2:1, KJV]."[42]

Confronting some ministerial delegates at the 1883 General Conference session who were anxious and worried, "talking fears and doubts" as to whether they would be saved, she put forth the following challenge: "Brethren, you have expressed many doubts; but have you followed your Guide? You must dispense with Him before you can lose your way; for the Lord has hedged you in on every side."[43] In much the same vein, she climaxed one of her most powerful appeals to trust in Christ by declaring: "Faith comes by the Word of God. Then grasp His promise, 'Him that cometh to me I will in nowise cast out.' John 6:37, KJV. Cast yourself at His feet with the cry, 'Lord, I believe; help *thou* mine unbelief.' You can never perish while you do this—never."[44]

To a mature Christian who, because of depression caused by illness, found it hard to believe, Ellen White wrote the following:

"The message from God to me for you is 'Him that cometh unto me, I will in no wise cast out' (John 6:37, KJV). If you have nothing else to plead before God but this one promise, from your Lord and Savior, you have the assurance that you will never, never be turned away. It may seem to you that you are hanging upon a single promise, but appropriate that one promise, and it will open to you the whole treasure house of the riches of the grace of Christ. Cling to that promise and you are safe. 'Him that cometh unto me I will in no wise cast out.' Present this assurance to Jesus, and *you are as safe as though inside the city of God.*"[45]

Despite the possibility of backsliding, Ellen White believed in present assurance and security. She could optimistically counsel that "if you are right with God today, you are ready if Christ should come today."[46]

Assurance Is Based on the Merits of Christ Alone, Not in Ourselves

What seemed to undergird all of Ellen White's practical counsels to those seeking assurance was her warning against the dangerous temptation of searching for some merit in themselves as a guarantee of their salvation. To such persons she declared: "It makes all the difference in the world with us spiritually whether we *rely upon God without doubt, as upon a sure foundation,* or *whether we are seeking to find some righteousness in ourselves* before we come to Him. Look away from self to the Lamb of God, that taketh away the sin of the world."

To others who "seem to feel that they must be on probation and must prove to the Lord that they are reformed before they can claim His blessing," she reassures "these dear souls" that they may *"claim the blessing of God even now. They must have His grace, the spirit of Christ to help their infirmities, or they cannot form Christian characters.* Jesus loves to have us come to Him just as we are—sinful, helpless, dependent."[47]

To those who doubt the reality of *present* assurance, she cautions, "*You are not to look to the future,* thinking that at some distant day you are to be made holy; *it is now* that you are to be sanctified through the truth. . . . *No one can make himself better,* but we are to *come to Jesus as we are,* earnestly desiring to be cleansed from every spot and stain of sin, and receive the gift of the Holy Spirit. *We are not to doubt his mercy, and say, 'I do not know whether I shall be saved or not.'* By living faith we must lay hold of His promise, for He has said, 'Though your sins be as scarlet, they shall be as white as snow.'[48] "Each one of you may know for yourself that you have a living Savior, that He is your helper and your God. *You need not stand where you say, 'I do not know whether I am saved.'* Do you believe in Christ as your personal Savior? If you do, then rejoice."[49] "It is God that circumcises the heart. The whole work is the Lord's from the beginning to the end. The perishing sinner may say: 'I am a lost sinner; but Christ came to seek and to save that which was lost. He says, 'I came not to call the righteous, but sinners to repentance' (Mark 2:17, KJV). I am a sinner, and He died upon Calvary's cross to save me. *I need not remain a moment longer unsaved.* He died and rose again for my justification, and *He will save me now.* I accept the forgiveness He has promised.' "[50]

The Danger of False Assurance

Ellen White's frequent attention to the external evidences of salvation is an expression of her concern that many who think they are saved will find out too late that they are lost. "Desires for goodness and holiness are right as far as they go; but if you stop here, they will avail nothing. Many will be lost while hoping and desiring to be Christians. They do not come to the point of yielding the will to God."[51] It is therefore not surprising that she repeatedly warned against any concept of false assurance. And here we encounter what is possibly the source of most of the misunderstandings regarding her concept of assurance.

Ellen White has written some strong warnings against false assurance. Some sincere believers, unaware of the larger picture of her teaching on the necessity of true assurance, have thought that she was against any suggestion of assurance. But, read in context, it is clear that her warnings against false assurance are not denials of true assurance.

For example, she warns that "we are never to *rest in a satisfied condition, and cease to make advancement,* saying, 'I am saved.'" Her opposition here is not against the words "I am saved," but against an attitude sometimes expressed by those words—that ongoing spiritual life and growth are unnecessary. "When this idea is entertained, the motives for watchfulness, for prayers, for earnest endeavor to press onward to higher attainments, cease to exist. . . . As long as *man is full of weakness—for of himself he cannot save his soul*—he should never dare to say, 'I am [eternally, irrevocably] saved.'"[52] She rejects such presumptuous claims of assurance because of the fundamental gospel fact that a human being "cannot save his soul." Believers who know that they can do nothing toward their own salvation except to respond to the wooing of the Holy Spirit will be the most careful not to resist the Holy Spirit.

On the other hand, a parallel statement supports the point that by "saved" in the quotations cited above, she refers to "once saved, always saved," not to genuine biblical assurance. "When the conflict of life is ended, when the armor is laid off at the feet of Jesus, when the saints of God are glorified, *then and then only will it be safe to claim that we are saved, and sinless.*"[53]

A similar admonition against false assurance cautions that "never can we safely *put confidence in self or feel,* this side of heaven, that we are secure against temptation. . . . Those who accept Christ, and in their first confidence say, I am saved, are in danger of trusting to themselves. They lose sight of their own weakness and their constant need of divine strength. They are unprepared for Satan's devices, and under temptation many, like Peter, fall into the very depths of sin. . . . 'Let him that thinketh he standeth take heed lest he fall.' 1 Cor. 10:12, KJV. Our only safety is in constant distrust of self, and dependence on Christ."[54] She here equates "saved" with putting "confidence in self" and feeling that one is "secure against temptation." But right in the midst of such cautions occurs the balancing promise that "when we give ourselves to Christ" we may "know that He accepts us," showing that her opposition is not against true biblical assurance, but against presumption leading to false assurance.

A Major Insight Into Ellen White's Salvation by Faith Teachings

The above quotations, with their closely connected counsels of encouragement and caution, are excellent examples of Ellen White's writings on salvation. And such thoughts lead us to two critically important considerations:

1. On the one hand, she is deeply concerned to protect believers against Satan's devices of self-confidence and self-dependence. It prompts her to caution against a certain kind of talk ("I am saved!") that is commonly misunderstood and when misunderstood leads to spiritual defeat.

2. On the other hand, she desires that believers have legitimate biblical assurance—that is, one based in Christ, not in self. And thus all need to be appropriately aware of the snares that Satan has prepared for Christ's true disciples.

The close combination of caution and encouragement is typical of her writings, especially those on salvation, spirituality, discipleship, and righteousness by faith. When we discover that she makes such balancing counsels occur practically everywhere, we realize that this is the way she thinks. While she knows the danger of going to the overconfident extreme (presumptuous assurance), she recognizes that believers can also fail by focusing on their own performance as the basis of their acceptance with God (legalism). So as soon as she warns someone against the one extreme, she thinks, *But what if they go to the other extreme?* and normally includes the balancing counsel to guard against swinging the other way.

Which category (caution or encouragement) predominates in a given passage seems to depend on whom she has in mind as the audience. In some letters to an individual the rebuke may predominate, but the encouragement is there also if you look for it. In other genres of her writing, such as *Steps to Christ* or *Thoughts From the Mount of Blessing,* the encouragement is often more predominant. In most cases, as noted above, the balancing counsel occurs in the same passage. But when the reader realizes that she is *always* thinking in these "both/and" categories, that she is *always* concerned for the dual or multiple dimensions of a spiritual issue, then if the reader does not find the balancing counsel in the immediate context, he or she soon realizes that it is very likely assumed, because in her mature writings she *always* approaches the subject from a dual perspective. So if you don't see it immediately, start looking for it, because it can always be found, either in the immediate context or in other places where she deals with the same issue.

Here is the *paradigm shift* that occurs when a person realizes that Ellen White is really a thoroughgoing believer in righteousness by faith. As one strong-willed believer in sanctification by stern effort late in life confessed, "I never used to find righteousness by faith in the writings of Ellen White, but when you see it, it's everywhere you look."

One of our greatest hopes for the readers of this book is that all will discover that righteousness by faith is pervasive in her books and articles. Those who recognize the balanced righteousness by faith concept in her writings will never again find condemnation there, but rather hope and courage and faith. What follows is a classic example of her balanced perspective on salvation by faith in Christ:

"*While the Christian's life will be characterized by humility, it should not be marked with sadness and self-depreciation.* It is the privilege of everyone so to live that God will approve and bless him. *It is not the will of our heavenly Father that we should be ever under condemnation and darkness.* There is no evidence of true humility in going with the head bowed down and the heart filled with thoughts of self. We may go to Jesus and be cleansed, and stand before the law without shame and remorse. 'There is therefore now no condemnation to them which are in Christ Jesus, who walk not after the flesh, but after the Spirit.' Romans 8:1, KJV."[55]

The Necessity of True Assurance

The broader context of Ellen White's writings on righteousness by faith (uniting caution with encouragement) shows that her warnings against false assurance do not by any means negate her strong teaching on true assurance. On the contrary, she insisted that "it is *essential* . . . to believe you are saved."[56] Of herself she wrote, *"Jesus has saved me,* though I had nothing to present to Him."[57] "The perishing sinner may say: '. . . I need not remain a moment longer unsaved.'"[58] Repentant sinners may "claim the blessing of God even now."[59] The believer "need not stand where you say, 'I do not know whether I am saved.'"[60] And the one who clings to Christ with present active faith can be "as safe as though inside the city of God."[61]

What Happens to Assurance When We Fall Into Sin?

"My little children, these things I write to you, so that you may not sin. And if anyone sins, we have an Advocate with the Father, Jesus Christ the righteous" (1 John 2:1). Note that it is precisely "if anyone sins" that the text assures that "we have an Advocate." Those who accept the command to "sin not" are precisely those who are promised that when they should sin their Advocate will not abandon them.[62] Ellen White wrote that *"if any man sin, he is not to give himself up to despair, and talk like a man who is lost to Christ. 'If any man sin, we have an advocate with the Father, Jesus Christ the righteous.'"*[63]

Salvation is a gift that *precedes* and *enables* overcoming:

"Some seem to feel that they must be on probation, and must prove to the Lord that they are reformed, before they can claim His blessing. But they may claim the blessing of God even now. *They must have His grace, the Spirit of Christ, to help their infirmities, or they cannot resist evil.* Jesus loves to have us come to Him just as we are, sinful, helpless, dependent. We may come with all our weakness, our folly, our sinfulness, and fall at His feet in penitence. It is His glory to encircle us in the arms of His love and to bind up our wounds, to cleanse us from all impurity."[64]

"Those who are placed in the highest positions may lead astray, especially if they feel that there is no danger. The wisest err; the strongest grow weary. Excess of caution is often attended with as great a danger as excess of confidence. To go forward without stumbling, we *must have the assurance* that *a hand all-powerful will hold us up,* and *an infinite pity be exercised toward us if we fall.* God alone can at all times hear our cry for help."[65]

It is abundantly evident that the believers' goal must be to sin not. Put more positively, their goal is to do only that which is pleasing in the sight of their Savior. But while the latter is the only true goal, Christ does not cast off sincere but failing children of God when they fall into sin (1 John 2:1). And therefore it should not come as any surprise that Ellen White would write the following:

"There are those who have known the pardoning love of Christ and who really desire to be children of God, yet *they realize that their character is imperfect, their life faulty, and they are ready to doubt whether their hearts have been renewed by the Holy Spirit.* To such I would say, Do not draw back in despair. We shall often have to bow down and weep at the feet of Jesus because of our shortcomings and mistakes, but we are not to be discouraged. *Even if we are overcome by the enemy, we are not cast off, not forsaken and rejected of God.* No; Christ is at the right hand of God, who also maketh intercession for us. Said the beloved John, 'These things write I unto you, that ye sin not. And if any man sin, we have an advocate with the Father, Jesus Christ the righteous.' 1 John 2:1, KJV."[66]

"We shall fail often in our efforts to copy the divine pattern. We shall often have to bow down to weep at the feet of Jesus, because of our shortcomings and mistakes; but we are not to be discouraged; we are to pray more fervently, believe more fully, and try again with more steadfastness to grow into the likeness of our Lord. As we distrust our own power, we shall trust the power of our Redeemer, and render praise to God, who is the health of our countenance, and our God."[67]

God is not unmindful of our honest striving, even though it is not immediately or fully successful. "For He knows our frame; He remembers that we are dust" (Ps. 103:14). "You may not obtain the entire victory at once; but persevere, keep trying."[68]

"You have one Mediator, Jesus Christ, the righteous. In contrition of soul go to him and tell all your sins. The promise is sure, 'If we confess our sins, he is faithful and just to forgive us our sins, and to cleanse us from all unrighteousness.' John says: 'My little children, these things write I unto you, that ye sin not. And if any man sin, we have an advocate with the Father, Jesus Christ the righteous.' *'That ye sin not'*—here is where you bring yourself into condemnation when you continue to sin. But in the strength of Christ cease to sin. Every provision has been made that grace should abide with you, and that sin may appear to you the hateful thing it is. But if any man sin, he is not to give himself up to despair, and talk like a man who is lost to Christ. 'If any man sin, we have an advocate with the Father, Jesus Christ the righteous. And he is the propitiation for our sins; and not for ours only; but also for the sins of the whole world.'"[69] . . . "When you fell into sin you walked in darkness. When you yielded to temptation, you must have ceased to look unto Jesus, the Author and Finisher of your faith. But, having confessed your sins, *believe that the Word of God cannot fail, but that He is faithful that hath promised. It is just as much your duty to believe that God will fulfill His word, and forgive your sins, as it is your duty to confess your sins.* You must exercise faith in God as in one who will do exactly as He has promised to do in His Word, and pardon all your transgressions."[70]

"How may we know that the Lord is indeed our sin-pardoning Redeemer, and prove what is the blessedness, the grace, the love there is in Him for us? O, we must believe His Word implicitly, with contrite and submissive spirit. *There is no need to go mourning and ever repenting, and under a cloud of continual condemnation. Believe the word of God, keep looking unto*

Jesus, dwelling upon his virtues and mercies, and there will be created in the heart an utter abhorrence of that which is evil. You will be among those who hunger and thirst after righteousness. But the more closely we discern Jesus, the more clearly we shall see our own defects of character. As we see our failings, let us confess them to Jesus, and, with true contrition of soul, cooperate with the divine power of the Holy Spirit to overcome all evil. *If we confess our sins, we must believe that they are pardoned,* because the promise is positive: 'If we confess our sins, he is faithful and just to forgive us our sins, and to cleanse us from all unrighteousness.' Let us no more dishonor God by doubting His pardoning love."[71]

The one who is striving for an uninterrupted connection with God stands in a different position than the unbelieving sinner:

"If *one who daily communes with God* errs from the path, if he turns a moment from looking steadfastly unto Jesus, it is not because he sins willfully; for when he sees his mistake, he turns again, and fastens his eyes upon Jesus, and the fact that he has erred does not make him less dear to the heart of God. He knows that he has communion with the Savior; and when reproved [by God] for his mistake in some matter of judgment, he does not walk sullenly, and complain of God, but *turns the mistake into a victory.* He *learns a lesson* from the words of the Master, and takes heed that he be not again deceived. Those who truly love God have *internal evidence* [assurance, Rom. 8:16; Gal. 4:6] that they are beloved of God, that they have communion with Christ, that their hearts are warmed with fervent love toward Him."[72]

Conclusion

Ellen White's warnings against the misuse of the claim "I am saved" were directed, not at a true biblical concept of present assurance in Christ, but against the idea of an irreversible guarantee leading to self-confidence, presumption, and casual disobedience. *She was just as forceful about the necessity of true present assurance,* understood in the context of justification by faith, a daily connection with Christ, and obedience to the known will of God. Those who come to God daily, trusting in His love, feeding on His Word, and submitting themselves to His loving discipline, are "right with God today," and "ready if Christ should come today."[73] And every day that we live by faith makes it easier and more likely that we will make that choice again tomorrow (Rom. 5:10).

We would like to close this chapter with the following prayers Ellen White composed to encourage the search for a genuine experience of Christian assurance of salvation:

Sinners' prayer: "The perishing sinner may say: 'I am a lost sinner; but Christ came to seek and to save that which was lost. He says, "I came not to call the righteous, but sinners to repentance" (Mark 2:17, KJV). I am a sinner, and He died upon Calvary's cross to save me. I need not remain a moment longer unsaved. He died and rose again for my justification, and *He will save me now*. I accept the forgiveness He has promised.' "[74]

Believer's prayer: "Lord, take my heart; for I cannot give it. It is Thy property. Keep it pure, for I cannot keep it for Thee. Save me in spite of myself, my weak, unchristlike self. Mold me, fashion me, raise me into a pure and holy atmosphere, where the rich current of Thy love can flow through my soul."[75]

Daily prayer: "Consecrate yourself to God in the morning; make this your very first work. Let your prayer be, 'Take me, O Lord, as wholly Thine. I lay all my plans at Thy feet. Use me today in Thy service. Abide with me, and let all my work be wrought in Thee.' This is a daily matter. Each morning consecrate yourself to God for that day. Surrender all your plans to Him, to be carried out or given up as His providence shall indicate. Thus day by day you may be giving your life into the hands of God, and your life will be molded more and more after the life of Christ."[76]

[1] "Three Strategic Issues: A World Survey" (Institute of World Mission, Andrews University, 2002). Cited in Nathan Brown, "Liberalism as a Form of Legalism," *Adventist Review*, June 19, 2003, p. 27.

[2] Ellen G. White, *The Ellen G. White 1888 Materials* (Washington, D.C.: Ellen G. White Estate, 1987), p. 547.

[3] This chapter was originally developed as a seminary class lecture by Jerry Moon and has been modified and adapted by Woodrow Whidden.

[4] Cf. E. G. White, *The Desire of Ages,* p. 638.

[5] Ellen G. White, *Testimonies for the Church* (Mountain View, Calif.: Pacific Press Pub. Assn., 1948), vol. 1, pp. 133, 134, 158, 163, 242, 243.

[6] *Ibid.*, p. 243; E. G. White, *Selected Messages*, book 1, p. 373.

[7] Ellen G. White, *Manuscript Releases* (Silver Spring, Md.: Ellen G. White Estate, 1990), vol. 4, p. 356.

[8] Norman Geisler, evangelical theologian and self-described "moderate Calvinist," in *Chosen but Free: A Balanced View of Divine Election* (Minneapolis: Bethany House, 1999) explains: "Of course, there are some significant differences between moderate Calvinists and moderate Arminians, but they do not negate the similarities. One of those differences was discussed above, namely, whether 'once saved, always saved' is accurate. But even here, in actual practice, the similarities are greater than many think. The vast majority of proponents of both views hold that if a professing Christian turns away from Christ and lives in continual sin that this is evidence that he is not saved. The difference is that the moderate Calvinists claim that he was never saved to begin with, and the moderate Arminians believe that he was. And both believe that the unrepentant who continue in sin are not true believers" (p. 130). Thus the doctrine of "once

saved, always saved" is a theoretical guarantee of eternal security, but not an actual guarantee, since in that theological system one cannot infallibly know that one was "once saved."

[9] Ellen G. White, *Thoughts From the Mount of Blessing* (Mountain View, Calif.: Pacific Press Pub. Assn., 1896), pp. 103, 104; E. G. White, *The Desire of Ages*, p. 175; E. G. White, *Testimonies for the Church,* vol. 5, p. 632.

[10] E. G. White, *Steps to Christ*, pp. 26, 27, 68.

[11] E. G. White, *Thoughts From the Mount of Blessing,* pp. 103, 104. (Italics supplied.)

[12] E. G. White, *The Great Controversy,* p. 256; cf. Ellen G. White, *The Acts of the Apostles* (Mountain View, Calif.: Pacific Press Pub. Assn., 1911), p. 563.

[13] Ellen G. White, *Faith I Live By* (Washington, D.C.: Review and Herald Pub. Assn., 1958), p. 157.

[14] *The Seventh-day Adventist Bible Commentary*, ed. Francis D. Nichol, rev. ed. (Washington, D.C.: Review and Herald Pub. Assn., 1978), Ellen White Comments, vol. 7, pp. 930, 931.

[15] *Ibid.,* p. 931.

[16] E. G. White, *The Desire of Ages*, p. 175. (Italics supplied.)

[17] Ellen G. White, *Gospel Workers* (Washington, D.C.: Review and Herald Pub. Assn., 1915), p. 161.

[18] E. G. White, *The Desire of Ages,* p. 347.

[19] E. G. White, *Selected Messages,* book 3, pp. 191, 192.

[20] Ellen G. White, "Faith and Good Works," *Signs of the Times,* May 19, 1898, p. 476.

[21] Ellen G. White, "Abiding in Christ," *Signs of the Times,* June 8, 1891, p. 437. (Italics supplied.)

[22] E. G. White, *The Desire of Ages,* pp. 176, 331.

[23] E. G. White, *Manuscript Releases,* vol. 6, p. 32. (Italics supplied.)

[24] E. G. White, *The Desire of Ages,* pp. 176, 805.

[25] E. G. White, *Testimonies to Ministers and Gospel Workers,* p. 366.

[26] Ellen G. White, *The Ministry of Healing* (Mountain View, Calif.: Pacific Press Pub. Assn., 1905), p. 99; E. G. White, *Manuscript Releases,* vol. 6, p. 31; Ellen G. White, "The Christian's Refuge," *Review and Herald,* Apr. 15, 1884.

[27] Ellen G. White, "Effectual Prayer," *Review and Herald,* Apr. 22, 1884.

[28] Ellen G. White, *Life Sketches of Ellen G. White* (Mountain View, Calif.: Pacific Press Pub. Assn., 1915), p. 39.

[29] *The Seventh-day Adventist Bible Commentary*, Ellen G. White Comments, vol. 5, pp. 1143, 1144. (Italics supplied.)

[30] Ellen G. White, *Messages to Young People* (Nashville: Southern Pub. Assn., 1930), pp. 127, 128.

[31] Ellen G. White, *Christ's Object Lessons* (Washington, D.C.: Review and Herald Pub. Assn., 1923), p. 159.

[32] Ellen G. White, "Ye Must Be Born Again," *Youth's Instructor,* Sept. 9, 1897, p. 294. (Italics supplied.)

[33] E. G. White, *In Heavenly Places,* p. 22. (Italics supplied.)

[34] E. G. White, *The Desire of Ages,* p. 191.

[35] E. G. White, *Thoughts From the Mount of Blessing,* p. 41.

[36] E. G. White, *The Ministry of Healing,* p. 182.

[37] E. G. White, *Testimonies to Ministers,* p. 367. (Italics supplied.)

[38] Cf. Ellen G. White, "What Was Secured by the Death of Christ," *Signs of the Times,* Dec. 30, 1889, pp. 344, 345.

[39] Ellen G. White, *Prophets and Kings* (Mountain View, Calif.: Pacific Press Pub. Assn., 1917), p. 587. (Italics supplied.)

[40] Cf. E. G. White, *Thoughts From the Mount of Blessing,* p. 71.

[41] Ellen G. White letter 17, 1862, to Susan G. Russell, excerpted in *In Heavenly Places,* p. 119.

[42] Ellen G. White, "Doubt Not God's Pardoning Love," *Signs of the Times,* Jan. 3, 1895, p. 176.

[43] E. G. White, "The Christian's Refuge," *Review and Herald,* Apr. 15, 1884, p. 414.

[44] E. G. White, *The Desire of Ages,* p. 429.

[45] E. G. White, *Manuscript Releases,* vol. 10, p. 175. (Italics supplied.)

[46] E. G. White, *In Heavenly Places,* p. 227.

[47] E. G. White, "Effectual Prayer," *Review and Herald,* Apr. 22, 1884, p. 416. (Italics supplied.)

[48] E. G. White, "The Christian a Guardian of Sacred Trusts," *Signs of the Times,* Apr. 4, 1892. (Italics supplied.)

[49] E. G. White, *General Conference Bulletin,* Apr. 10, 1901. (Italics supplied.)

[50] E. G. White, *Selected Messages,* book 1, p. 392. (Italics supplied.)

[51] E. G. White, *Steps to Christ,* pp. 47, 48.

[52] E. G. White, *Selected Messages,* book 1, p. 314. Cf. E. G. White, *Selected Messages,* book 3, pp. 355, 356.

[53] E. G. White, *Selected Messages,* book 3, p. 356. (Italics supplied.)

[54] E. G. White, *Christ's Object Lessons,* p. 155. (Italics supplied.)

[55] E. G. White, *The Great Controversy,* p. 477 (Italics supplied.)

[56] Ellen G. White, "The Necessity of Cooperation With God," *Review and Herald,* Nov. 1, 1892, p. 607. (Italics supplied.)

[57] Ellen G. White, "Spiritual Advancement the Object of Camp-Meetings. No. 4," *Review and Herald,* July 14, 1891, p. 504. (Italics supplied.)

[58] E. G. White, *Selected Messages,* book 1, p. 392.

[59] *Ibid.,* book 3, p. 150.

[60] Ellen G. White, in *General Conference Bulletin,* Apr. 10, 1901.

[61] E. G. White, *Manuscript Releases,* vol. 10, p. 175.

[62] See E. G. White, *In Heavenly Places,* p. 119.

[63] E. G. White, "Doubt Not God's Pardoning Love," *Signs of the Times,* Jan. 3, 1895, p. 176. (Italics supplied.)

[64] E. G. White, *Steps to Christ,* p. 52. (Italics supplied.)

[65] Ellen G. White, "One Wrong Step," *Signs of the Times,* July 28, 1881, p. 242. (Italics supplied.)

[66] E. G. White, *Steps to Christ,* p. 64. (Italics supplied.)

[67] E. G. White, *Selected Messages,* book 1, p. 337.

[68] E. G. White letter 26, 1859, to Henry and J. Edson White, in *An Appeal to Youth,* pp. 53-56.

[69] E. G. White, "Doubt Not God's Pardoning Love," *Signs of the Times,* Jan. 3, 1895, p. 176.

[70] *Ibid.* (Italics supplied.)

[71] *Ibid.* (Italics supplied.)

[72] Ellen G. White, "Operation of the Holy Spirit Made Manifest in the Life," *Review and Herald,* May 12, 1896, p. 358. (Italics supplied.)

[73] E. G. White, *In Heavenly Places,* p. 227.

[74] E. G. White, *Selected Messages,* book 1, p. 392. (Italics supplied.)

[75] E. G. White, *Christ's Object Lessons,* p. 159.

[76] E. G. White, *Steps to Christ,* pp. 70, 71.

Chapter 12

The Observant Life—Spiritual Growth and the Gifts of the Spirit in the Life of the Assured Christian

Introduction

As a teenager I had been sensitized to the need for an interactive experience in matters related to spiritual development. Moreover, the factor that received the most emphasis was the study of God's Word. My brother had led the way for me by clearly grasping and expressing the principle that by "beholding Christ" our characters will be transformed into the likeness of His image. Such transformation would especially transpire through the study of and reflection on the Scriptures.

Later on, as a young minister, I came under the strong influence of the preaching and writing ministry of Elder Morris Venden. Venden was the most influential revival force in Adventism during that era and had strongly accentuated the importance of spiritual growth. Venden's program centered in his advocacy of a consistent study of the Bible and the writings of Ellen White, prayer, reflection on the person and work of Christ, and some form of active Christian witness and service.

I still fondly recall the mellow voice and wonderful illustrations of the low-key but compelling Venden as he sought to initiate late twentieth-century Adventism into the joys and delights of a consistent devotional life. He was fond of pointing out that the manner in which any normal child matures illustrates the development of Christian character. For instance, a young boy does not become taller by stretching out his body on the back-yard clothesline—genuine growth is the normal result of eating a good diet (partaking of the "bread of life," the Word), breathing fresh air ("prayer is the breath of the soul"), and engaging in plenty of vigorous exercise (Christian witness and service). Thus growth into the likeness of the attitudes and character of Jesus will surely result from the wise, intentional implementation of spiritual discipline in the believer's personal experience.

While my generation has been indebted to Pastor Venden for seeking to raise our awareness on such issues, the nagging question still lurks as to whether we really owned, in a practical way, what he was seeking to help us discover. A strange thing, however, has happened in the meantime. Since the 1970s a number of evangelical Protestant writers have also taken up essentially the same themes that Venden had earlier explored with Adventism.[1] Later on, we will explore the specific roles that some of the key spiritual disciplines play in the personal and corporate life of church members. Before then, however, we need to examine the theological background of the practice of spiritual disciplines, the workings of the spiritual gifts, and their relationship to the Christian's personal assurance of salvation. We fully realize the need to approach these subjects with some caution and with carefully nuanced theological analysis.[2]

Thinking Theologically About the Practice of Cooperative Grace

For our current purposes we will label the following reflections as a "theology of Christian cooperation with the work of the Holy Spirit." In addition, closely related is the question of how the ongoing life of cooperative grace informs and affirms the believer's growing confidence in God's power to redeem.

Quite obviously, all personal relationships, both human and divine, thrive in a context of continual communication and the confidence in one another that emerges out of working cooperatively in all sorts of social settings. It is certainly true of the closest or more intense relationships, including friendship and marriage (and possibly professional collaboration). Most married couples instinctively sense that the success of their relationship requires dedicated time in which both partners can comfortably communicate intimate feelings and practical concerns. And that includes simply taking time (and usually dedicated space) to enjoy one another's companionship just for the sheer joy of being together in love.

I personally can look back on decades of professional interaction with colleagues (including lay members in my pastoral experience) during my 40 years of both local pastoral leadership and teaching in higher education. Even as I write this chapter, the institution at which I teach is going through some turbulent waters as we are seeking to clarify, even renew, the reasons for our existence and the mission that we envision God is leading us to carry out. Not surprisingly, through all of this I have been amazed at how various persons on our faculty and staff have so uniquely and richly contributed to the whole process of renewal.

Furthermore, if we had not built up trust in and commitment to one another in working together during the previous months and years, I do not think that we would be making the rewarding progress that we are currently enjoying. To put it quite simply, when we collaborate we learn to trust one another, and assured confidence among the working partners noticeably grows and deepens.

When we translate such dynamics into the realm of intentional spiritual growth, it spotlights two basic facets to these relationships. Maybe we can call them (1) the deeply personal, intimate spiritual pursuits and (2) the more corporate or public experiences that further help to cement our relationships with God and with one another. And it is in these two senses (or realms) that we will explore.

The powerful loving and redemptive bonds that exist within the workings of the holy Trinity can be replicated by those who relate directly to God and with one another in worship and service. But wonderful as such realities and prospects are, a few have raised some interesting theological objections to the intentional practice of the spiritual disciplines, including serving God with our particular spiritual gift(s).

The Disciplines of Spiritual Growth and the Threat of Legalism

One interesting aspect involves whether the exercise of and exposure to spiritual gifts and spiritual disciplines could represent some sort of veiled or subtle attempt to lure Christians into a works righteousness. I know that for me it has been a somewhat sensitive issue. Such concerns have really challenged some of my deeply held personal preferences (maybe even prejudices). To be quite honest, I simply find some spiritual disciplines hard to practice, and the sheer doing of them feels quite unnatural—like paying dues or taxes or fulfilling other aggravating legal obligations.

For instance, the spiritual discipline of study comes easy to me. I just love reading about theology, Christian biography, history, and related matters. But it has proved to be a challenge for me to learn to sit still and prayerfully, reflectively listen to the Word and to engage in consistent seasons of private communion with God. And when it comes to intentional fasting, except for the felt need to practice dining temperance I am terribly lacking, even somewhat turned off, as I contemplate the seeming deprivations of that stern discipline.

Furthermore, even though I am highly sociable and greatly enjoy public worship, fellowship with my Sabbath school class, attending camp meetings and other forms of spiritual retreat, many Wednesday evenings, Friday nights, and Sabbath mornings I would rather be home by myself reading a good book on one of my favorite spiritual or doctrinal themes. So what is the proper motive and perspective I need in the area of personal and corporate spiritual growth?

What I am suggesting is that the key to this whole issue of justifying our personal and corporate experiences (especially the various spiritual disciplines, and the exercise of our Spirit-endowed spiritual gifts) has largely to do with the core Protestant/Arminian concept of cooperative grace. And once more, we are back to the heart of the issue that centers on our understanding of how people get saved.

As discussed in earlier chapters that addressed the dynamics of calling, conviction, regeneration, conversion, forgiveness, sanctification, perseverance (how to stay saved), and the witness of the Spirit, we have tried to demonstrate that God always takes the initiative in redemption. He, however, never ultimately saves any sinner without the responsive cooperation of the will of the spiritually awakened believer.

Therefore, as with how God directly saves us from sin, so it is in actually living the Christian life and growing in grace: we must cooperate with the properly instituted means of spiritual development (including the spiritual disciplines and exercises) that God has ordained and which the Holy Spirit is inviting us to enjoy. But how do such disciplines fit into the larger context of salvation by faith alone?

Recently one of my students has shared with me a most trenchant analysis of evangelical Protestantism's perceived reluctance to embrace the practice of the spiritual disciplines. As already intimated, it seems to reflect a fear that such practices will inevitably degenerate into some sort of works-oriented legalism. Furthermore, as my perceptive student has been quick to point out, evangelical resistance appears to emanate from Reformed Christianity's truncated view of what full salvation truly consists of. Consider the following analysis:[3]

"So what are we to make of the 'faith-works' impasse? The spiritual discipline activities are 'works' that are considered essential to being a Christian. The practitioners of and advocates for the spiritual disciplines have had no reservations in asserting that being a Christian is more than just mentally believing or giving assent to a set of doctrines. Believing correct doctrines is considered to be absolutely necessary, but not all sufficient.[4] Christianity either encompasses the actual way one lives, or it should no longer be considered Christianity, or at least not *real* Christianity.

"Concerning the life of obedience to Christ, A. W. Tozer held the firm conviction that a 'notable heresy [has] come into being throughout evangelical Christian circles—the widely accepted concept that we humans can choose to accept Christ only because we need him as Savior and that we have the right to postpone our obedience to him as Lord as long as we want to!' He then went on to declare that 'salvation apart from obedience is unknown in the sacred scriptures.'[5]

"Since evangelical Christianity has drilled into the heads of the laity the idea that 'salvation = faith + nothing,'[6] an unfortunate dichotomy has formed between faith and works of obedience. This dichotomy has become part of the psyche of evangelicalism, even to the point that it has virtually paralyzed its members from putting forth any serious *efforts* to take cooperative action in changing their lives after the similitude of Christ. It is this mistaken association of 'works' with merit that has caused a knee-jerk attack on any action-oriented or behavioral emphasis within the gospel message. This in turn has forced spiritual discipline or holy living programs to perennially defend themselves as truly being in harmony with the biblical gospel.

"In a nutshell, evangelical theology (at its worst),[7] at the practical/lay level, has incurred the casualties of three essential biblical terms: 'faith' becomes truncated to mental assent; 'works' are rejected because of the suspicion of merit; and 'salvation' has been pigeonholed as a solution for clearing the guilt of sin for admission to heaven at death or the second coming. All three of these understandings tend to either undermine the theological basis for spiritual growth (especially its associated disciplines), or worse, lead to a direct rejection of them as fostering legalism.

"As a result, it has been said that a generation of 'vampire Christians' is being born which functionally say to Jesus, 'I'd like a little of Your blood, please. But I don't care to be Your student or have Your character. In fact, won't You just excuse me while I get on with my life, and I'll see You in heaven.'[8] The spiritual discipline movement firmly rejects any such notions that strongly suggest that a passive posture will effectually bring about Christlikeness. Thus the participants in this movement consider the various Christian disciplines to be the individual, cooperative occasions that give God opportunities to spiritually renovate believers. Believers must *act* if they seriously intend to achieve results."

To sum up the foregoing considerations, the core theological issue at stake in the varied practices of spiritual development has mainly to do with an attitude of growing responsiveness to the convicting power of the Holy Spirit, including the providential leading of God in the lives of believers. Thus there is simply nothing sinister in any genuine motivation to do and be what it takes to be more like Christ.

Furthermore, we are convicted that all believers need to have a rich experience in the key personal and public disciplines and devotional exercises that the Spirit is seeking to incorporate into our walk with God. To do otherwise is to continue to produce at least one more generation of spiritually vapid, even emaciated followers, of Christ.

And finally, all such truly transformative experiences represent a welcoming of God's saving grace, not misguided attempts to save ourselves by building up some record of merit as a reward for our stewardship of time and money, observances, service, and Christian witness. Thus, while some evangelicals have often construed such activities as ways to generate saving merit, the real truth is that no person will be saved without a deep experience in these varied and invigorating Christian exercises.

In the light of the previous considerations, it thus seems fair to suggest the strong possibility that a sizable number of Protestants, including many Seventh-day Adventist Christians, are not floundering in their Christian experience because of rank legalistic attitudes. Rather, it is more likely because of their lack of responsiveness to the leading of the Spirit and a manifest neglect of practical experiences in the things of God.

Just as we must become explicitly intentional in nurturing our personal friendships and close professional and business relationships, so we must apologize to no one for getting very practical and intentional in growing our spiritual relationship with God and our fellow believers. Additionally, these pursuits include a deep experience of a good array of devotional exercises, active Christian witness to non-Christians and the discouraged, and service to others through a life lived by the empowering presence of the Holy Spirit. Therefore it seems that on a personal level the Spirit more normally works through prayer, Bible study, prayer-filled reflection, and retreats (personal and group). And in the public disciplines the Spirit employs the various spiritual gifts that He specifically bestows on the visible, corporate body of Christ, the church.

With these considerations in mind, we must now turn to some pressing practical considerations of the most essential aspects of spiritual growth: the personal spiritual disciplines.

Assurance and the Personal and More Public Disciplines[9]

As already hinted at by Morris Venden, the key personal disciplines associated with spiritual growth are the study of the Word of God and related literature, personal prayer, and time for Holy Spirit-guided reflection on what we have discovered through study and prayer. Closely related to these core pursuits are fasting, simplicity, solitude, submission, confession, personal guidance, and frugality/stewardship. They stand in contrast with the more social disciplines, such as public worship, fellowship, and service.

Since this is not a definitive study of all devotional methods, we will concentrate on those that are most essential to a fruitful life in the Spirit. But before considering selected, specific disciplines, we need to make an important distinction, one involving the issue that John Ortberg calls "training vs. trying."[10]

"Trying" is directly seeking to do specific acts, while "training" involves a whole life of discipline that prepares any person for actual practice. While "training" does require some graced, disciplined efforts, it comprises a whole set of responsive attitudes that prepare a person to know how to think and act in ways appropriate for any given situation. For instance, as a baseball player I can "try" all day to duplicate major league pitching. But the real truth is that it simply will not happen if I have not given myself to the "training" steps that could lead to the baseball big leagues. And so it is with the role of the spiritual disciplines in the life of the Christian: without training, there will be no spiritual big leagues!

Maybe we could further illustrate it this way. Spiritual training is not an end in itself, but a means to a larger end. We could grit our teeth and spend dedicated time praying, studying the Bible, and so forth, and create robotic habits. But the habits are not the real goal. Rather, it is the development of Christlike attitudes, character, and actions. Devotional exercises are a training means to a higher life goal.

Instituting the Priority of the Training Disciplines

While all of the spiritual disciplines have their just importance, certain ones are especially foundational, absolute musts if we are to become mature believers. The study of and prayerful reflection on the Word of God is absolutely essential to any rewarding spiritual experience. If Bible-believing Christians could just integrate the foundational spiritual disciplines (Bible study, reflection, and prayer) into their daily experience, what a marked difference it would make in their lives!

To be more precise, when we speak of the discipline of study we primarily mean the careful and analytical reading of the Bible, the written word of God. We seek to understand what a given passage is truly saying in its original literary and historical context. This phase of biblical interpretation goes by the technical term of *exegesis* (literally "getting the sense out of" the text).

The second phase of interpretation is called application. Focusing on transferring the original meaning into our time and circumstances, it can actually become an exciting search and discovery process as the Word of God begins to open up to our understanding in ways that bring greater theological, spiritual, practical, and ethical clarity into our walk with God.

Reflection takes the truths that we have uncovered from the pages of Scripture and sees how they can apply to our attitudes and actions, as well as the way in which one area of Scripture helps to explain other parts. When we do this in a constant attitude of prayer, we will have many rewarding discoveries, both theological and practical.

While we could say a whole lot more about the actual analytical and reflective study of the Bible, the main practical issue concerns how to get started. We need to approach it in a way so that our habits of study and meditational reflection will become an integral, sustained part of our daily encounter with God. Furthermore, I want to speak to two special groups: new Christians and those who have begun but have not been able to sustain the experience. I offer the following practical suggestions that have proved helpful for many more experienced Christians.

As admitted earlier, I have not had much of a problem with study, especially when it comes to spiritual issues and key theological questions. But where I have really found myself tested has to do with simply sitting still and seeking to allow the voice of God to speak to me more devotionally through the written Word. Yet despite that, through the grace of God and the persistent convicting witness of the Spirit I have been able to develop a consistent habit of quiet time alone with God and His Word.

The first thing to do is to figure out when you are most alert and the least harried by life. For most of us that would be in the morning (though I recognize that not all of us are at our best then). Perhaps we could apply the analogy of breakfast. If the Word of God is spiritual food, then it only makes sense to begin the day with a good hearty meal. But what is true of literal meal habits also applies to spiritual eating and drinking: just as the most neglected or superficially treated meal of the day is breakfast, thus it is with one of the most overlooked aspects of our spiritual life—our failure to begin the day with God.

Therefore, the most important factor in getting started is intentionally and consistently to set aside dedicated time to spend with God through quietly praying and reflecting on the Word. Start in a modest way, especially if your attention span is rather short. I would suggest that you begin with no less than 10 minutes (15 if possible), but be very disciplined, consistent, and above all persistent in the use of your dedicated time with God. And the good news is that if by God's grace you persevere, you will begin to feel the need for more such dedicated, quality time in giving attention to spiritual things.

The next question in getting started (or restarted) is to have a simple plan of what you are going to do with the time. You should select a quiet, dedicated space where you will be least likely to be disturbed. It might be an empty bedroom, a vacated living room, or your home study. But it needs to be a spot in which you are physically comfortable and the atmosphere is conducive to quietness and reflection. With dedicated time and a place set sacredly apart, one then simply needs to begin. And what follows deals with some simple and time-tested practices and reading materials that will aid spiritual maturation.

Now that you are comfortably settled, what should you actually do? Here experience teaches that it is best to begin with a good devotional book featuring a daily selection from Scripture. Normally a page of reflective devotions, based on the Bible passage, follows the key text. This category of devotional literature has a number of good books available. As to possible choices, seek counsel from those in your church or fellowship group already recognized for their devotional habits. Such persons could be your pastor or some other mature spiritual brother or sister in Christ.

To be more specific about personal practice, last year I used George Knight's wonderful devotional book entitled *Lest We Forget: A Daily Devotional.*[11] It contains daily readings that deal with many aspects of how God has led in the history of the Seventh-day Adventist Church and the spiritual lessons that we can learn from His past guidance. This year I am using the devotional book of the year selected for the Philippine Adventist Church—Jon Paulien's *Gospel From Patmos: Everyday Insights for Living From the Last Book of the Bible.*[12] I have found both books extremely rewarding, and I truly wake up each morning looking forward to an interesting, Bible-based inspirational thought from these two Word-saturated, informed, and compelling writers.

Through the years I have also been greatly blessed by many other devotional books produced by Adventist publishing houses. Many of them feature selections from the writings of Ellen White. Some of the best titles are *In Heavenly Places*,[13] *That I May Know Him*,[14] *Our High Calling*,[15] *My Life Today*,[16] and *The Faith I Live By*.[17] While these compilations are the ones that have been my favorites, you will find many others. During your next visit to the Adventist Book Center or a camp meeting book exhibit (or go shopping online) you can leisurely browse in the section displaying these and other outstanding devotional books.

When you have finished the reading for the day, try to read a chapter or major portion of a chapter from the Bible. Begin with the Gospels. Most likely you will find that the easiest Bible book to read is the Gospel of Mark. Then go from there to Luke, Matthew, and John. And finally, spend a few moments with the *Adult Bible Sabbath School Study Guide* portion for that day as laid out in the weekly topic of the current quarterly.

If a chapter a day from the Bible is too daunting at the beginning, at least faithfully read the scripture and the devotional reflection in your chosen devotional book and then just a few verses from the pure word of God in your favorite version of the Bible. But whatever you do, faithfully employ the allotted time that you have dedicated to God and reflective exposure to His Word.

A further word of practical suggestion is in order for those who find the discipline of daily Bible study a bit difficult. Publishers have released a number of fine commentaries especially for new or young Christians. Perhaps the most well known is William Barclay's *Daily Study Bible*,[18] which covers at least all of the books of the New Testament. For Seventh-day Adventists, George Knight has produced two series of lay Bible commentaries. The first series is his Walking With studies, and here I would suggest that you begin with his *Walking With Paul Through the Book of Romans*. But probably his best devotional commentary series is the more recent Exploring set. Thus far he has done volumes on Ecclesiastes, Song of Solomon, Mark, Romans, Galatians, Ephesians, Hebrews, and the letters of John and Jude (he has additional ones in the works). Both the Walking With and the Exploring series are available at Adventist Book Centers or online at AdventistBookCenter.com. They have personally been a great boon to me and many others who have been looking for a boost in our attempts to make our study and devotional experiences more spiritually rich and informed.

As you seek to make the best use of your time, do not forget the simple principle that "a few concentrated minutes of sustained attention is worth far more than a dreamy day." Thus it is not so much the amount of time you initially spend with God in prayer and with His Word, but its quality and faithful consistency.

I have a longtime friend who has been a busy physician, but one who has always taken time to spend with God. When, however, I asked him how he managed such devotional time, he shared with me the principle that a concentrated 10 minutes could propel him into his busy rounds. But the real secret of his success emerged from his practice of trying to extract a key thought or issue from those few minutes with the Word. He would then turn his mind to these thoughts throughout the day whenever he had a spare moment.

After you have established a habit of sacred time devoted to the study of and reflection on God's Word, begin to follow up with a more extended period of prayer and praise to God for the blessings you received in the reading for that morning as well as other blessings in your life. Next, engage in a few moments of intentional intercession with God for special and particular blessings for others and ask Him for grace to meet whatever challenges that you know you will have to face that day.

Such praise and thanksgiving to God for His goodness as well as the special appeals for help for others and your own perceived needs do not have to be in any special language or any certain length of time. Just be open and honest to God about any particular gifts He has bestowed on you.

You might know of still other approaches to a renewal of your devotional life, but I would strongly urge that you give these simple methods a good try. And normally what you will discover is that the time you spend will begin to expand and the quality of your time with God will improve. Your hunger for a deeper and more expansive knowledge of the Word will increase, and the power of God in your life will be yours for the receiving.

Harking back to the breakfast analogy for daily spiritual nourishment: the main thing is to begin modestly, but keep at it consistently. Many persons who have a tough time learning to stomach breakfast should begin with a simple piece of toast (with a tasty spread) and a little glass of their favorite fruit juice. But when they do so persistently and consistently, their tolerance for more food will increase. The same will happen with your spiritual appetites and capacities. In time you will find a desire for more advanced tools and methods of Bible study and devotions.

As you progress in your practice of devotional exercises, do not hesitate to draw upon the wisdom and insights of other more mature

Christians. You will find persons in your circle of fellowship or personal acquaintance who are sources for further counsel, encouragement, and direction. They can serve as your personal coaches as you seek a more advanced experience through the use of various Bible study books and materials. Through their insights and your exposure to good publications and time-tested practices, your ability to pray, praise, and reflect more effectively and intelligently on the persons of the Godhead will continue to grow. Abundant blessings await those who mature in their life with God in the Spirit.

Furthermore, Christian experience suggests that we should supplement our personal devotions with consistent habits of fellowship, such as a good Sabbath school class or some sort of other weekly Bible study and prayer fellowship. It should include regular attendance at the appointed worship services of your local church. Doing so will involve you in public praise, corporate fellowship, the celebration of the ordinances of the Lord (foot washing and the Lord's Supper), and the consistent proclamation of the Word of God from the pulpit.

Public gatherings enable us to experience the more corporate spiritual exercises. Moreover, all of these, in a wonderful combination, will help us to begin to appreciate better the great blessings of the Sabbath as sacred time dedicated to spiritual rest, renewal, selected forms of Christian service, and fellowship with God and His people.

But all of this will not ultimately prove to be lasting unless we incorporate one other aspect of life in the Spirit—the personal exercise of your special gift(s) in the context of the life of the visible church. They will include service, witness, and mutual edification, all bestowed by the Holy Spirit. And it is to these considerations that we now turn.

The Corporate Discipline of Spiritual Gifting

I must confess that it has been only recently that I have begun to realize the close relationship between Christian assurance and spiritual gifting. Great blessings will come to active believers who regularly employ their particular spiritual gifts in the life of the visible, corporate body of Christ. We gain increasing confidence in Christ as we work with Him and the other members of the body.

During my childhood and teen years our father ran his own business. He was a beekeeper, and my brothers and I provided him with a ready source of what we thought was "free, hard labor." Laboring in the bee business in central Florida was not the easiest and most comfortable of working circumstances. The hot steamy weather, compounded by the heavy clothing and protective gear required to ward off the constant threat of beestings, and the heavy lifting involved in moving beehives and harvesting and processing honey, all seemed to smack of chattel slavery to my brothers and me. It was not, however, until my brother Ivan and I went away to boarding academy that we were better able to see our perceived burdens as blessings.

What finally got through to us was the fact that many of our fellow students were always complaining about how they really did not know their dads. For us it was a strange revelation of an alienation that we had never experienced. Finally it began to dawn on us that we had really gotten to know and love our human father through working with him. And as we subsequently reflected a bit further, we concluded that life with our father had not really been all that slavishly bad.

Thus what had earlier appeared to be sheer drudgery ultimately turned out to be one of the most rewarding channels of blessing in our lives. The facts were that we had gained confidence in the integrity and faithfulness of our earthly father because we had daily worked with him in the family business. And so it is with those who, in their lives in the body of Christ, have come to know the loving, redemptive ways of their heavenly Father through working with and for Him in His celestial "family business."

When we carefully study the key New Testament chapters dealing with spiritual gifts (1 Cor. 12, Rom. 12, and Eph. 4), we discover the following:

First of all, spiritual gifts, while exercised by individual believers, really belong not so much to them as they do to the corporate body. This leads to the second major fact: all three passages invoke the analogy of the human body as the key metaphor for the church and the way the spiritual gifts function within the body of Christ. While the eyes, ears, hands, arms, and so forth are all important, they really do not operate independently of one another. In fact, it is downright grisly to think of walking into a room and see body parts floating about aimlessly all over the place!

Thus the metaphor of the body strongly suggests corporate solidarity for all of the various bodily parts and their distinctive, yet highly integrated functions: "There are differences of ministries [gifts], but the same Lord. And there are diversities of activities, but it is the same God who works all in all. But the manifestation of the Spirit [especially in spiritual gifts] is given to each one for the profit of all" (1 Cor. 12:5-7). Please note that what all of this imagery suggests is a strong union with and integration of

187

each member into the collective or corporate functioning of the body, especially when it comes to our Christian experience. So while individual experience is important (especially in the exercise of the spiritual disciplines), each member must also consciously institute a strong collective or corporate element into his or her personal experience.

Furthermore, Paul also makes it clear that no one person has the full complement of the gifts of the Spirit. And thus we conclude that all individuals are dependent on others who will bring the additional gifts to the rest of the members of Christ's body.

What this suggests is that all members need one another, and in being there for each other we are not only personally blessed, but receive a great blessing in our service for and witness to others through the exercise of our individual gifts. And in the process we gain a deeper knowledge of the loving care and workings of our heavenly Father. So while we cooperate with God in blessing others, we at the same time find ourselves blessed by the gifts of others who also work with God. As a result, all of us gain a deeper personal knowledge of His love and power.

What Paul teaches seems to go against a lot of the unhealthy individualism that has created a negative attitude toward the visible, organized, or corporate body of Christ. But when we recognize that we are all in this together and that the church is one of the key ways that we can get more intimately acquainted with our heavenly Father, the blessings of church fellowship and membership become much more practical and rewarding.

Therefore, it simply makes good sense that the spiritual gifts spoken of by Paul appear to be the key staging area for the functioning of the more public spiritual disciplines: worship, service, witness that leads people to Christ, and so forth. As Paul makes it abundantly clear, God has given the spiritual gifts to bless the body through "the equipping of the saints for the work of ministry, for the edifying of the body of Christ, till we all come to the unity of the faith and of the knowledge of the Son of God, to a perfect man, to the measure of the stature of the fullness of Christ; that we should no longer be children, tossed to and fro and carried about with every wind of doctrine, by the trickery of men, in the cunning craftiness of deceitful plotting, but, speaking the truth in love, may grow up in all things into Him who is the head—Christ—from whom the whole body, joined and knit together by what every joint supplies, according to the effective working by which every part does its share, causes growth of the body for the edifying of itself in love" (Eph. 4:12-16). Romans 12:4, 5 sums it up more succinctly: "For as we have many members in one body, but all the members do not have the same function, so we, being many, are one body in Christ, and individually members of one another." I would simply suggest that Paul's final words, "individually members of one another," probably say it about as pithily as it can be stated!

In the light of this wonderful corporate vision that arises out of the metaphor of the body of Christ and the way the body parts (the spiritual gifts of particular persons) work to edify both the body and its individual members, can we continue to hold ourselves aloof from such a glorious organism?

Furthermore, such involvement with the body of Christ enables us to take the focus off of ourselves and put it on others and what we can do to bless them. And here we discover a simple but much-neglected principle of personal Christian assurance—that of "positive displacement." A somewhat clumsy expression, it refers to a wonderful preoccupation that is the privilege of all Christians. As we become occupied with service and witness to others, we will not have much time to worry about our own salvation. And ironically, in doing this we become much more assured Christians.

Of course, it is possible to go to the other extreme, so that "we become so busy with the work of the Lord that we lose sight of the Lord of the work."[19] But practiced with due balance and wisdom, such work for others enables believers to recognize their own blessings and sense the affirming way that God is making their lives useful and meaningful. Through working with God we draw closer to Him and become more assured of His power to save. As we see that He is using us to redeem others, it only makes sense that our confidence in His constantly available power and presence to save us will also increase.

Some Practical Cautions and Guidelines

As already intimated, some have raised serious objections to certain spiritual disciplines. The average Adventist will have little or no objection to the devotional exercises of Bible reading, prayer, and simple forms of personal reflection. But it seems that the area of special meditation techniques have triggered warnings and cautions.

Most likely such Adventist caution results from the popularity of various forms of meditation associated with certain contemplative techniques developed by the Roman Catholic Jesuits and the numerous varieties of meditation inspired by the various Eastern religions and their preoccupation with mysticism. And such caution is very much needed.

But once more we need to remind ourselves of the "abuse, use" principle: just because there are false forms of mystical spirituality, it does not mean that we need to allow them to keep us from the legitimate forms of reflection and spiritual union with Christ through the internal workings of the Holy Spirit in the life of the soul. Therefore, I do urge the reader to contemplate carefully some of the following procedural cautions or guidelines when it comes to any experimentation with the more subjective disciplines related to growth in grace:

1. Is the technique focused on the person, work, and teachings of Christ? 2. Are there any practical or theological implications that might compromise the great "eternal verities" (doctrines) of the Christianity (such as the full inspiration and canonical authority of Scripture, the full deity of Christ, the Trinity, and salvation by grace through faith alone)? 3. Does any practice threaten to downgrade the more distinctive doctrines of the Seventh-day Adventist Church? 4. Would a particular observance or practice tend to uphold and inspire obedience by grace to all of the commandments of God? Or would it tend to moral compromise in the name of grace and tolerance? 5. What about the manifestation of the fruit of the Spirit in the lives of the practitioners of any spiritual discipline? Does a controversial discipline produce a fruitful crop of Christlike virtue? 6. Are believers drawn to participation in and loyalty to the body of Christ (the visible church)? In other words, does any particular spiritual exercise nurture and edify the church of the Lord Jesus of Christ? 7. Does the use of any discipline or gift create a hunger for the Word of God (the messages of the holy Bible) and a life of Christian witness and service? 8. Is there any hint that such a practice would open the door, however subtle, to the deceptions of spiritualism, occult practices, or other communications with the alleged spirits and souls of the dead?

Those who follow such cautions and consistently employ the tried and true personal and corporate disciplines can be assured that spiritual growth will result. And finally, there will be an abundance of spiritual fruit manifested in the lives of the professed followers of Christ.

The Disciplines and Personal Christian Assurance

So what is the theological and practical relationship between spiritual disciplines, spiritual gifts, and Christian assurance? The key point to keep in mind is that by employing various Christian observances we come to know more intimately the assuring, personal love of God for us and for those with whom we share fellowship. As the old fifties popular song said, "To know, know, know him is to love, love, love him," and through these practical devotional exercises we can all go on to testify personally that we do love Him who is the assuring Savior of our soul. Moreover, as we perceive the varied ways in which He works through us to bless others with the exercise of our divinely bestowed spiritual gifts, we will discover a growing confidence in God's power to keep us as His very own redeemed children.

Faith practiced through such time-tested "training" exercises enables the voice of the Spirit to witness more clearly, even more directly, to and with our spirits that we are the beloved children of God. Without the spiritual growth produced through such gifts and disciplines, life in the Spirit would be extinguished and Christian identity would fade.

Furthermore, the disciplined exercise of such intentional practices will inevitably produce spiritual fruit in our lives and our characters that will exemplify the active virtues of Christlike attitudes, words, and acts. Once more we must emphasize that the most basic concept that undergirds all devotional exercises is that a well-connected branch (the believer living by faith in Christ), firmly attached to a healthy vine (Christ who spiritually nurtures our productivity), will produce "much" spiritual fruit. Jesus taught this not only by the famous illustration of the vine and the branches (John 15:1-10), but also in His immortal lines from the Sermon on the Mount:

"For a good tree does not bear bad fruit, nor does a bad tree bear good fruit. For every tree is known by its own fruit. For men do not gather figs from thorns, nor do they gather grapes from a bramble bush. A good man out of the good treasure of his heart brings forth good; and an evil man out of the evil treasure of his heart brings forth evil. For out of the abundance of the heart his mouth speaks" (Luke 6:43-45). In the Matthew 7 version Jesus concludes with the familiar truism that "therefore by their fruits you will know them" (verse 20).

To put it as plainly as I know how to express it: when Christians are able to sense the deep manifestations of the Spirit of God through the direct and fruit-bearing witness of the Holy Spirit in their individual and corporate Christian experiences, they will just supernaturally become more assured of their salvation experience in Christ! Such believers will be more abundantly aware that God is loving them and working through them. This is truly one of the key facets of life in the Spirit.

---

[1] What we are referring to are the writings of the key leaders of what has come to be known as the spiritual formation or spiritual disciplines movement. Its three leading proponents are Richard J. Foster, with his classic book *Celebration of Discipline: The Path to Spiritual Growth* (New York: HarperCollins, 1978, 1988, 1998, 2003); Dallas Willard, especially his

books *The Divine Conspiracy: Rediscovering Our Hidden Life in God* (New York: HarperCollins Publishers, 1997); and *Renovation of the Heart: Putting on the Character of Christ* (Colorado Springs, Colo.: NavPress, 2002); and John Ortberg. For those familiar with this movement, Ortberg has served the role of Willard's popularizer. Ortberg's best-known book is *The Life You Have Always Wanted* (Manila: Christian Literature Crusade, 2002). In fact, some have described Ortberg as the person who has made the rather deep and profound Willard (who is a scholarly philosopher) more accessible to laypersons. When the interested Seventh-day Adventist reader ventures into these works, one is ultimately impressed with how closely their portrayals of the sanctified life resemble those of Ellen G. White (especially Willard's teachings).

[2] The reader should be aware that some considerable controversy and criticism has arisen regarding the works of Richard J. Foster and others active in the movement. While we should never summarily sweep such criticisms aside, we still need to engage with the larger positive directions of such writers as Foster, Willard, and Jon Dybdahl. We will later offer some simple principles by which any spiritually hungry and sensitive Seventh-day Adventist can distinguish the wheat from the chaff in their pursuit of a fruitful life with God.

[3] What follows is a slightly adapted extract from a paper written by Joseph Olstad entitled "The Spiritual Disciplines Movement and John Wesley" (paper presented in fulfillment of the course "Seminar in Christian Theology," taught at the Asian Adventist Seminary of the Adventist International Institute of Advanced Studies, Silang, Philippines, November 2009).

[4] Belief could be considered sufficient as well, as long as it was *necessarily* understood to entail a radical change in lifestyle, the adopting of a completely new set of spirit-inspired devotional practices, obedience to God's moral requirements, and so forth. But since faith is traditionally couched in this setting as the means of justification "without works" (so as not to taint justification with human merit), perhaps it is best to explain it as a vital component of Christianity, but not the only exclusive practice sufficient for a full-orbed Christian experience.

[5] A. W. Tozer, *I Call It Heresy* (Harrisburg, Pa.: Christian Publications, 1974), p. 5.

[6] Theologically this formula is misleading because it assumes that the word "salvation" is concerned only with a legal, justified standing, which of course is accomplished by "faith + nothing." Limiting "salvation" in this way is an unbiblical, even reductionistic, interpretation of the rich and variegated range of meaning inherent in the theological term.

[7] Of course, many evangelical churches are now eager to incorporate the spiritual disciplines into their teaching, but they are usually only those that have a doctrine of salvation that will permit it.

[8] Dallas Willard, *The Great Omission* (New York: HarperOne, 2006), p. 14.

[9] For a good Adventist introduction to the rationale and practice of the spiritual disciplines, I recommend Jon Dybdahl's *Hunger: Satisfying the Longing of Your Soul* (Hagerstown, Md.: Autumn House Pub., 2008). Dybdahl has been an acknowledged leader in the Seventh-day Adventist spirituality awakening and a dedicated, consistent personal practitioner of the spiritual disciplines. Additionally, he has taught on the subject and worked as a personal spiritual mentor to many individuals longing for a deeper walk with God.

[10] See the chapter "Training Versus Trying: The Truth About Spiritual Disciplines" in Ortberg's, *The Life You Have Always Wanted*, pp. 41-58.

[11] George Knight, *Lest We Forget* (Hagerstown, Md.: Review and Herald Pub. Assn., 2008.

[12] Jon Paulien, *The Gospel From Patmos* (Hagerstown, Md.: Review and Herald Pub. Assn., originally published in 2007; reprinted in the Philippines by the Philippine

Publishing House under a special agreement with the Review and Herald Publishing Association).

[13] E. G. White, *In Heavenly Places.*

[14] Ellen G. White, *That I May Know Him* (Washington, D.C.: Review and Herald Pub. Assn., 1964).

[15] E. G. White, *Our High Calling.*

[16] Ellen G. White, *My Life Today* (Washington, D.C: Review and Herald Pub. Assn., 1952).

[17] E. G. White, *The Faith I Live By.*

[18] William Barclay's *Daily Study Bible* commentaries were originally published by Saint Andrews Press, Edinburgh, U.K. The reader may go online and see what is available from either publishers or used book dealers. You should be able to procure as many volumes as you want at reasonable prices.

[19] Once again, while the ultimate source of this epigrammatic truism is unknown, I have recalled it from the presentations of Morris Venden.

Chapter 13

What to Do With Failure, Backsliding, and Fear of the Judgment— Can Sin Arise a Second Time?

One of the sobering realities that all believers must face (especially new ones) is the prospect of failure and disappointment in their Christian growth. For Arminians (including the Adventist ones) there is also the possibility of backsliding and apostasy. Such things can happen, at least in part, because of the simple fact that in the process of conversion, especially during its early stages, God has not chosen to perfect believers instantaneously. Furthermore, even mature Christians have all experienced failings in words, attitudes, and behavior. Normally, for the more mature believer, such setbacks will be the exception, not the rule. But another reality also applies: there will be humbling mistakes and deficits and no instantaneous perfection this side of the Second Coming. Sanctification is "not the work of a moment," but truly the "work of a lifetime."

As already acknowledged and addressed in earlier chapters, misunderstandings of the investigative judgment teaching have created a sense of condemnation. Such fears can certainly arise as maturing believers become more conscious that they have, in some way or other, "fall short of the glory of God" (Rom. 3:23). In fact, we also need to recall the subtle truth that the closer we come to Christ, the more sinful we will appear in our own eyes. So what is the growing but still imperfect Christian to do when a sense of failure and resulting fear of the impending judgment begin to envelop or even threaten his or her personal assurance of salvation?

First of all, we should not become discouraged and think that the Lord has cast us aside and left us to wallow in despair. In fact, the conviction of sin and failure is a very good sign! It reminds us that God is not through dealing with us.

Now, some newer believers might think that such a statement is just an attempt to delude ourselves. But the reason for such optimism arises out of the fact that the conviction of sin by the Spirit is a necessary evidence that God has not taken us and our spiritual growth for granted. In fact, the ongoing conviction of sin is one of the key means by which He seeks to get our attention so that we can regroup and move on to greater spiritual and ethical development and usefulness in His service. Conviction of sin is good evidence that the Spirit of God is in hot pursuit of us to seek to save us not only from sin but from our still sin-infected selves!

Furthermore, we should always keep in mind that legitimate guilt does not have to lead to despair or indifference. If persistently neglected, however, such dangers do become real possibilities. But the main purpose for the Spirit's conviction of sin is so that we can be progressively healed from the sins that so easily afflict us. And it is then that we can go on to new victories over the remnants of our inherited and cultivated tendencies to sin. Moreover, it is through such experiences that we will discover a greater sense of confidence in God's power to deliver from the clutches of evil as well as open to us new vistas of growth and service.

Before we focus on a few key suggestions as to what our appropriate response should be to the Spirit's ongoing work of conviction, we need to deal with the following question: What is the alternative to the Spirit's convicting of sin and failure? Quite frankly, it is something not at all pleasant to contemplate. And it has to do with the possibility of God leaving us to our own deadly devices. But for Him to do that, perhaps in the name of some sort of merciful love, would ultimately block genuine spiritual healing.

For instance, how would you feel if you visited your doctor, and, in the name of mercy, he failed to mention to you that you had a deadly disease that needed immediate medical attention? It would be an especially cruel twist if the disease was also easily curable. If sin is truly a deadly spiritual disease (often carrying with it terminal spiritual, moral, and physical implications), it seems much more sensible for God to give and we to receive His troubling diagnosis. In this situation we can be both realistic and effectively restored when we reach out for the healing grace that He offers. And His healing is truly the only effective antidote for our spiritually terminal condition. Thankfully, the Great Physician of the soul has not chosen to leave us to our devices, but has firmly determined to pursue us to the ends of our sinful tethers and the depths of our vices.

Most likely, what we have been considering is but practical aspects of the grace that we earlier referred to as prevenient. Therefore, just as God persistently came seeking us while we were "dead in trespasses and sins" in order to convict us of our sinful state and to awaken us to the fact that He loves us (in spite of our sinful and sinning natures), so this same grace is constantly communicating His ongoing conviction of sin and His great redemptive power to free us from sin's dominion. God's redemptive initiatives do not cease at the moment of conversion. His loving, merciful, and proactive pursuit of us continues all the way to glory.

What to Do With Failure and the Conviction of Sin

When clear conviction of sin rests on your soul, the first thing to do is to thank God for staying on the trail of your case. Therefore, whenever He confronts us with a sense of our sin, the encouraging truth is that His healing, forgiving, and restoring graces cannot be too far behind. And it is the time when the practical aspects of the spiritual and theological dynamics discussed in chapters 3 to 6 must kick in. Therefore, it is at these critical junctures that the responsive, growing believers must become skilled in knowing and using the resources that God has made available to deliver them from Satan's persistent assaults (see Zech. 3:1-5).

Initially we suggest that any conviction of sin should drive us to (1) the promises and imagery set forth in 1 John 1:9-2:1 and (2) the powerful images of the parables of the lost sheep and the lost son (Luke 15:1-7 and 11-32).

The Good Shepherd, through the ministry of the Holy Spirit, is constantly on the lookout for lost sheep snared in the briers of sin on the lonely hillsides of the dark night of the soul. Furthermore, the Good Shepherd is also teamed up with the "waiting father," who longingly, even hopefully, waits at His front gate, holding out fresh robes, and a new signet ring, and announcing plans for a great festive party during which reconciling grace will be richly bestowed and wildly celebrated.

As we noted in a previous chapter that addressed the manner in which Ellen White related to assurance in the face of the failures and discouragement of struggling Christians, she instinctively pointed any discouraged believer to the reassuring verses in 1 John. Surely, "if anyone sins, we have an Advocate with the Father, Jesus Christ the righteous" (1 John 2:1), who, as "the propitiation for our sins" (verse 2), is "faithful and just to forgive us our sins and to cleanse us from all unrighteousness" (1 John 1:9). When convicted believers feel the sober effects of the gift of penitence in their life, they should instinctively turn their minds to these wonderful promises and immediately picture themselves as being robed with the justifying, forgiving righteousness of Christ and bedecked with adornments befitting the "pearl of great price."* And they should follow it up with thoughts of being personally ushered by Christ into the banqueting hall of the merciful King of the universe.

As Adventists, we can greatly augment such imagery with our emphasis on the work of Jesus in the heavenly sanctuary. Both the Old and New Testaments reveal the central concept of Christ as our high-priestly intercessor. Our Redeemer is at one and the same time both our advocate *with* the Father and the compassionate judge who presides *in the presence* of the waiting Father in the Most Holy Place of the heavenly sanctuary. Can we really begin to fathom the full richness of such comforting and inviting imagery, especially that of "an Advocate with the Father, Jesus Christ the righteous" (1 John 2:1)?

We cannot emphasize too much that the life of faith includes a growing disposition to seek the will of God when it comes to the sin problem and our deliverance from its guilt, power, and presence. It involves a dynamic of give and take between the believer and God, especially because He never works without the cooperative response of the subjects of His kingdom of grace.

Moreover, such a responsive, cooperative outlook will instinctively reject anything that seeks to excuse sin or presume on divine mercy. We do not need God's indulgence toward our sins and sinfulness. What we truly need is His calling, convicting, forgiving, and transforming grace that He constantly offers from the very throne room of the universe. The alluring, persistent appeal from this great nerve center of redemption is "Let us therefore come boldly to the throne of grace, that we may obtain mercy and find grace to help in time of need" (Heb. 4:16).

Fear of the Investigative Judgment

Now, having said all of these wonderfully reassuring things, we face the next issue: the fact that the heavenly throne is not only a location of grace but also the venue for the great pre-Advent judgment of investigation. A day is coming when the cases of all professed believers are going to be judged.

Probably the best way to relate to it is to remind ourselves about the biblical purposes for the pre-Advent investigative judgment. Here we will briefly review and augment some points made in chapter 2. In short, why is it that God needs a judgment, or celestial audit, in which the records of the thoughts and works of believers come under solemn review?

Perhaps the first reason is to alert all human beings that in God's universe every moment, attitude, and action of the lives of all intelligent, freewill, relational, and morally responsible beings has eternal consequences. Loving relationships without moral and ethical implications are simply unthinkable. Thus there can be no renewed relationship with God unless the consequences of these records are justly processed and disposed of. Moreover, a renewed relationship is the goal of every facet of God's varied judgments. And it brings us to the second key reason God has a judgment process.

The judgment review highlights the good news that God is far more intent on our salvation than He is on our condemnation. In fact, He longingly yearns for our valued and renewed relationship with Him. The great reality about God is that He is a redeemer at the very core of His being. The doctrine of the judgment reveals His persistent attempts to assure us that Christ and the other members of the Godhead are for us, not out to get us! And this means that we do have an Advocate with the Father, Jesus Christ the righteous and just judge.

But beyond the issue of our own salvation, the judgment also reminds us that God has an entire universe of unfallen beings that He must deal with, a reality that Paul recognized when he cited Psalm 51:4: "For what if some did not believe? Will their unbelief make the faithfulness of God without effect? Certainly not! Indeed, let God be true but every man a liar. As it is written: 'That You [God] may be justified in Your words, and may overcome when You are judged'" (Rom. 3:3, 4).

God will reveal His utter fairness when He presides over the investigative judgment. The whole universe will be able to evaluate His dealings with fallen humanity. Thus a further reason for God's record keeping of our lives is for His vindication, not for our condemnation.

As already pointed out in chapter 2, the revelation of His perfect administration of justice and mercy will also include some unpleasant revelations about the failures of the redeemed. But as Wesley has reminded us, God brings up such embarrassing flips and flops, not to condemn us, but to demonstrate His wisdom in saving us from them and working through it all to restore the harmony and happiness of the universe. Even beyond all of this, the judgment has further goals. And one of them has to do with the reasons as to why sin will never arise a second time.

No Second Chance for Sin and Sinners to Ever Arise Again

Nahum 1:9 says that "affliction will not rise up a second time," a thought echoed in other biblical passages. The psalmist promised that "the righteous shall inherit the land, and dwell therein forever" (Ps. 37:29), and Daniel saw that the "saints of the Most High shall receive the kingdom, and possess the kingdom forever, even forever and ever" (Dan. 7:18) and that "His kingdom is an everlasting kingdom" (verse 27; compare Isa. 66:22, 23; 65:17; and Rev. 21:4). How is it that God will maintain such an endless condition of sinlessness?

Scripture strongly suggests that it will not be the result of some divine fiat. God will not just forcibly keep the redeemed from reigniting sin and rebellion. On the contrary, the saints' eternal security will be the result of the same sort of patient and winsome appeals that have been so typical of God's steady battle against sin and all of its baleful results since the Fall. But in heaven, such ongoing harmony will be retained in a setting of sinlessness, not the present earthly chaos resulting from the presence of sin and all of its evil effects.

Therefore, it seems reasonable to conclude that the major reason sin will never again rear its ugly head has more to do with how God's love will keep "sealing" and settling the redeemed into a deepening relationship with Him. Such a thought seems to be much more in tune with His character than any arbitrary, forcible restraint. Therefore, a continual "sealing" and settling us in concept reflects not only the metaphors of inoculation against sin but also (more positively) the bonds of freely chosen and finally unshakable love.

My first-grade public school teacher, the late Ruth Bailey, told of how as a little girl she just loved to eat the crispy, fatty glaze that formed on the traditional roast pork shoulder that her mother cooked for family celebrations. But the mother stipulated that Ruth could have the glaze only as part of the main meal.

One day, however, as Ruthie ventured into the empty dining room, she discovered a freshly baked pork roast resting on the table. And sure enough, it was covered with the usual complement of the crispy fat. Conveniently, her mother had left the house for a few moments to go pick up some other groceries at a nearby store. The situation presented an overpowering temptation for the ravenous child. And before she realized it, she had devoured most of the alluring glaze.

While the glutted girl had to deal with the wrath of her chagrinned mother, the worst part of the whole affair for Ruthie was that she had such a bad stomachache from her indulgence that she was never again able to eat the crispy roast pork fat. It effectively inoculated her against that temptation. Roast pork fat had become associated with painful revulsion, not joyous feasting—a negative inoculation.

But we see a more positive aspect of the inoculation explanation as to why sin will never rise again in the experiences of lovers who finally discover the love of their life. When the right one comes along, all of the other possible pretenders to his or her affections effectively fade from what becomes a quickly receding horizon of possible choices. God's love will have become so satisfying that the redeemed will simply never again be deceived into thinking that they could find any joy or pleasure that could ever compare with the delights of divine love! This is both affectively and effectively what it means to be lovingly "sealed" to God for all of eternity.

Therefore, not only is the Bible silent in regard to any second-chance opportunities for salvation after death and the Second Coming, but it also knows nothing about a second chance for sin to arise in God's everlasting kingdom. Here is truly the gist of the biblical doctrine of eternal security.

Furthermore, what seems to ensure such eternal security in heaven is also the same basic guarantee that will play out here on earth in the last moments of time available to the people of God. Sin's rule and Satan's grip over the redeemed need never again hold the ascendancy in the lives of the redeemed, either in earthly time or in glory. Therefore, while it is philosophically possible for sin to take down the redeemed in probationary time and rear its ugly head again in eternity, it is neither necessary nor probable that it will do so for those who have learned by grace to stay focused on Christ and His loving benefits.

Conclusion

So what is "the conclusion of the whole matter" (Eccl. 12:13)? We simply and joyously acknowledge that by faith in Jesus, blessed assurance can be the believers' ongoing privilege for the rest of their earthly sojourn in time and in the heavenly light of God's love for all eternity. No Fall need ever happen again! May God be glorified forever and ever! "Amen. Even so, come, Lord Jesus!" (Rev. 22:20).

★ Possibly this is the true Adventist form of "adornment."

Index of Biblical References

Index of Names and Topics